Lecture Notes in Computer Science 6116

Commenced Publication in 1973
Founding and Former Series Editors:
Gerhard Goos, Juris Hartmanis, and Jan van Leeuwen

Dave Clarke Gul Agha (Eds.)

Coordination Models and Languages

12th International Conference, COORDINATION 2010
Amsterdam, The Netherlands, June 7-9, 2010
Proceedings

Volume Editors

Dave Clarke
K.U.Leuven, Department of Computer Science
Celestijnenlaan 200A, 3001 Heverlee, Belgium
E-mail: dave.clarke@cs.kuleuven.be

Gul Agha
University of Illinois, Computer Science Department
201 N. Goodwin Avenue, MC 258, Urbana, IL 61801, USA
E-mail: agha@cs.uiuc.edu

Library of Congress Control Number: 2010927442

CR Subject Classification (1998): D.2, C.2, C.2.4, F.1.2, I.2.8, I.2.11, C.3

LNCS Sublibrary: SL 2 – Programming and Software Engineering

ISSN 0302-9743
ISBN-10 3-642-13413-0 Springer Berlin Heidelberg New York
ISBN-13 978-3-642-13413-5 Springer Berlin Heidelberg New York

springer.com

Printed in Germany

Typesetting: Camera-ready by author, data conversion by Scientific Publishing Services, Chennai, India
Printed on acid-free paper 06/3180

Foreword

In 2010 the international federated conferences on Distributed Computing Techniques (DisCoTec) took place in Amsterdam, during June 7–9. It was hosted and organized by the Centrum voor Wiskunde en Informatica.

DisCoTec conferences jointly cover the complete spectrum of distributed computing subjects ranging from theoretical foundations to formal specification techniques to practical considerations. The 12th International Conference on Coordination Models and Languages (Coordination) focused on the design and implementation of models that allow compositional construction of large-scale concurrent and distributed systems, including both practical and foundational models, run-time systems, and related verification and analysis techniques. The 10th IFIP International Conference on Distributed Applications and Interoperable Systems in particular elicited contributions on architectures, models, technologies and platforms for large-scale and complex distributed applications and services that are related to the latest trends for bridging the physical/virtual worlds based on flexible and versatile service architectures and platforms. The 12th Formal Methods for Open Object-Based Distributed Systems and the 30th Formal Techniques for Networked and Distributed Systems together emphasized distributed computing models and formal specification, testing and verification methods.

Each of the three days of the federated event began with a plenary speaker nominated by one of the conferences. The first day Joe Armstrong (Ericsson Telecom AB) gave a keynote speech on Erlang-style concurrency, the second day Gerard Holzmann (Jet Propulsion Laboratory, USA) discussed the question "Formal Software Verification: How Close Are We?" The third and last day Joost Roelands (Director of Development Netlog) presented the problem area of distributed social data. In addition, there was a joint technical session consisting of one paper from each of the conferences and an industrial session with presentations by A. Stam (Almende B.V., Information Communication Technologies) and M. Verhoef (CHESS, Computer Hardware & System Software) followed by a panel discussion.

There were four satellite events: the Third DisCoTec Workshop on Context-aware Adaptation Mechanisms for Pervasive and Ubiquitous Services (CAMPUS), the First International Workshop on Interactions Between Computer Science and Biology (CS2BIO) with keynote lectures by Luca Cardelli (Microsoft Research, Cambridge, UK) and Jérôme Feret (INRIA and École Normale Suprieure, Paris, France), the First Workshop on Decentralized Coordination of Distributed Processes (DCDP) with a keynote lecture by Tyler Close (Google), and the Third Interaction and Concurrency Experience Workshop with keynote lectures by T. Henzinger (IST, Austria) and J.-P. Katoen (RWTH Aachen University, Germany).

I hope this rich program offered every participant interesting and stimulating events. It was only possible thanks to the dedicated work of the Publicity Chair Gianluigi Zavattaro (University of Bologna, Italy), the Workshop Chair Marcello Bonsangue (University of Leiden, The Netherlands) and the members of the Organizing Committee—Susanne van Dam, Immo Grabe, Stephanie Kemper and Alexandra Silva. To conclude I want to thank the sponsorship of the International Federation for Information processing (IFIP), the Centrum voor Wiskunde & Informatica and The Netherlands Organization for Scientific research (NWO).

June 2010 Frank S. de Boer

Preface

The 12th International Conference on Coordination Models and Languages, part of the IFIP federated event on Distributed Computing Techniques, took place in Amsterdam, The Netherlands, June 7–10, 2010. In this age of multicore platforms, service-oriented computing and the Internet of Things, COORDINATION remains a relevant forum for the discussion of new techniques and models for programming and reasoning about distributed and concurrent software systems.

The Program Committee received 28 submissions covering a range of topics including the application of coordination in wireless systems, multicore scheduling, sensor networks, event processing, data flow networks and railway interlocking. Each submission was reviewed by at least three Program Committee members. Papers submitted by Program Committee members received additional scrutiny. The review process included a shepherding phase whereby half of the papers received detailed attention in order to produce higher-quality final submissions.

After a careful and thorough review process, the Program Committee selected 12 papers for publication, based on their significance, originality and technical soundness. The program was topped off by a captivating invited talk by Joe Armstrong of Ericsson Telecom AB on Erlang-style concurrency.

The success of COORDINATION 2010 was due to the dedication of many people. We thank the authors for submitting high-quality papers, and the Program Committee and external reviewers for their careful reviews and thorough and balanced deliberations during the selection process. We thank the providers of the EasyChair conference management system, which was used to run the review process and to facilitate the preparations of these proceedings. Finally, we thank the Distributed Computing Techniques Organizing Committee.

June 2010

Dave Clarke
Gul Agha

Organization

Conference Committee

Program Committee Chairs

Dave Clarke	Katholieke Universiteit Leuven, Belgium
Gul Agha	University of Illinois at Urbana-Champaign, USA

Program Committee

Mirko Viroli	Università di Bologna, Italy
Shangping Ren	Illinois Institute of Technology, USA
Marjan Sirjani	Reykjavik University, Iceland
Patrick Eugster	Purdue University, USA
Carolyn Talcott	SRI, USA
Jean-Marie Jacquet	University of Namur, Belgium
Wolfgang de Meuter	Vrije Universiteit Brussel, Belgium
Carlos Canal	Universidad de Málaga, Spain
Vasco T. Vasconcelos	University of Lisbon, Portugal
Rocco De Nicola	University of Florence, Italy
Susan Eisenbach	Imperial College London, UK
Roberto Bruni	University of Pisa, Italy
Amy L. Murphy	ITC-IRST, Italy and University of Lugano, Switzerland
John Field	IBM Research, USA
MohammadReza Mousavi	Eindhoven University of Technology, The Netherlands

Additional Reviewers

Salvador Abreu
Lucia Acciai
Tristan Allwood
Francesco Calzolai
Marco Carbone
Matteo Casadei
Vincenzo Ciancia
Ferruccio Damiani
Joeri De Koster
Erik de Vink
Fatemeh Ghassemi
Elisa Gonzalez Boix
Helle Hvid Hansen
Hossein Hojjat
K. R. Jayaram
Niels Joncheere
Jeroen J. A. Keiren
Narges Khakpour
Ramtin Khosravi
Nicholas Kidd
Ivan Lanese
Michele Loreti
Dimitris Mostrous
Elena Nardini
José Proença
Rosario Pugliese
Usman Raza
Christophe Scholliers
Ilya Sergey
Francesco Tiezzi
Yves Vandriessche

Coordination Steering Committee

Rocco De Nicola (Chair)	University of Florence, Italy
Farhad Arbab	Centrum Wiskunde & Informatica (CWI), The Netherlands
Jan Vitek	Purdue University, USA
Carolyn Talcott	SRI, USA
Herbert Wiklicky	Imperial College London, UK
Chris Hankin	Imperial College London, UK
Doug Lea	State University of New York at Oswego, USA
Gruia-Catalin Roman	Washington University in Saint Louis, USA
Gianluigi Zavattaro	University of Bologna, Italy
Jean-Marie Jacquet	University of Namur, Belgium
Vasco T. Vasconcelos	University of Lisbon, Portugal
Amy L. Murphy	ITC-IRST, Italy and University of Lugano, Switzerland
John Field	IBM Research, USA

Distributed Computing Techniques Federated Event Committee

General Chair

Frank S. de Boer	Centrum Wiskunde & Informatica (CWI), The Netherlands

Publicity Chair

Gianluigi Zavattaro	University of Bologna, Italy

Workshops Chair

Marcello M. Bonsangue	University of Leiden, The Netherlands

Organizing Committee

Susanne van Dam	Centrum Wiskunde & Informatica (CWI), The Netherlands
Immo Grabe	Centrum Wiskunde & Informatica (CWI), The Netherlands
Stephanie Kemper	Centrum Wiskunde & Informatica (CWI), The Netherlands
Alexandra Silva	Centrum Wiskunde & Informatica (CWI), The Netherlands

Table of Contents

Observables for Mobile and Wireless Broadcasting Systems

Jens Chr. Godskesen*

IT University of Copenhagen

Abstract. We discuss the presence of localities in observables for process calculi for mobile and wireless broadcasting systems in the context of weak barbed congruences and demonstrate that observability of the locality of a broadcasting node may be unsuitable when abstracting from node mobility, a natural abstraction current calculi agree upon. The discussion is carried out through a calculus $bA\pi$, a conservative extension of the Applied π-calculus and a contribution of its own. Through examples we demonstrate the applicability of $bA\pi$ and its weak reduction congruence, where the locality of a broadcasting node is not observable, and we prove our bisimulation equivalence to be a *sound* and *complete* co-inductive characterization of the weak reduction congruence.

1 Introduction

Recently we have seen a large interest in the development of calculi for mobile and wireless broadcasting systems, e.g. CBS# [13], CMN [7], the ω-calculus [16], and CMAN [5].[1] The calculi are defined with the purpose of being able to model and reason about a variety of types of systems spanning from ambient intelligence over mobile ad-hoc, sensor, and mesh networks, to cellular networks for mobile telephony. Because broadcasted messages will only reach the nodes within the communication range of the emitting node all the calculi have in common that the broadcast communication primitive is local (synchronous) broadcast. Also the calculi agree on letting nodes autonomously and arbitrarily change their neighbor relationship and thereby change the network topology. The calculi on the other hand differ on their neighborhood representations, in particular only in CMN the neighborhood relation is taken care of by a metric function that tells if two physical locations are close enough to communicate. The other calculi operate with logical locations without knowing physical distances but just the neighborhood relationships.

Related Work. Often, as put forward in the seminal work on *barbed bisimulation* [12,10], process calculi are equipped with a reduction semantics and a reduction congruence where the latter is based on some kind of observables

* Supported by the VKR Centre of Excellence MT-LAB.

[1] CWS [9] and TWCS [8] also consider wireless broadcasting systems but they do not cater for node mobility.

D. Clarke and G. Agha (Eds.): COORDINATION 2010, LNCS 6116, pp. 1–15, 2010.

(barbs). The idea is to strive for a simple reduction semantics and to allow an external observer to observe the system through a limited set of *barbs*. Indistinguishability under these observations gives rise to a natural equivalence which in turn induces a natural congruence, i.e. the equivalence in all contexts closed under structural congruence.

In non-broadcasting calculi for mobility, like e.g. the π-calculus [15,11], an observable is a (channel) *name* on which a message is transmitted (or received), or as for the Ambient-calculus [2] a barb is a name indicating the presence of an (unrestricted) top-level ambient. For non-broadcasting calculi for mobile and distributed computing with localities, like Dπ [14], the barbs are related to specific locations, say sending out a message on a channel at a specific node. For tKlaim [3] it is shown that the observables for Ambients and Dπ have the same discriminating power.

However, as also addressed in [9], it seems to be not obvious to decide what an adequate observable for mobile and local wireless broadcasting calculi should be. One of the problems being that in a network of mobile wireless broadcasting devices each has a location and a transmission range and it is not immediate how to take location and range into account when defining the observables. In CBS# for instance the observables for a network N are pairs consisting of a data term t and a locality (node) name l. Intuitively the observable here means that N is capable of storing t at location l (and hence later l may broadcast t). In CMN an observable for a network N is a pair, an output channel n and a set of node locations L. Intuitively a barb means that any location in L is within metric distance of the transmitting range of the emitting node and hence can receive a message on input channel n. In CMAN an observable is the name of the location of the broadcasting node, and also in TWCS [8] a node locality is always part of a barb.[2] Hence, to our knowledge all contemporary process calculi for mobile and wireless broadcasting systems, which do not employ a metric to measure the physical distance between nodes but operates with logical locations, adopt the legacy from non-broadcasting calculi for localized and distributed computing, like $D\pi$ and tKlaim, and let the locality of the broadcasting node be part of their barbs.

Motivation. In this paper we discuss observables for local synchronous broadcast mobile systems, and in particular we demonstrate that observability of the (logical) locality of a broadcasting node may be unsuitable for a semantics that abstracts from node mobility, a natural abstraction all the calculi mentioned above agree upon. The source of our discussion is a broadcast calculus, $bA\pi$, inspired by and a conservative extension of the Applied π-calculus [1]. We consider $bA\pi$ a contribution of its own since to our knowledge it is the first calculus for mobile and wireless local broadcasting systems that allows for reasoning about an unbounded number of nodes. The calculus is briefly outlined below.

[2] The ω-calculus [16] does not offer an explicit definition of observables, but since it is a conservative extension of the π-calculus we would expect that the set of observables for the ω-calculus at least contains the observables of the π-calculus.

A *node*, $\lfloor p \rfloor_l$, in $bA\pi$ is a *process* p located at some (logical) *location* l. Nodes composed in parallel constitute a *network*, say $\lfloor p \rfloor_k \parallel \lfloor q \rfloor_l \parallel \lfloor r \rfloor_m$. Processes at the same location l may communicate on a name n, for example

$$\lfloor \overline{n}\langle t\rangle.p \rfloor_l \parallel \lfloor n(x).q \rfloor_l \longrightarrow \lfloor p \rfloor_l \parallel \lfloor q\{t/x\} \rfloor_l \tag{1}$$

where $q\{t/x\}$ is q with all free occurrences of x replaced by t. Connectivity between nodes is represented by an annotation, for instance

$$\lfloor p \rfloor_l \parallel \lfloor q \rfloor_m \parallel \{l \mapsto m\} \ , \tag{2}$$

where l is connected to m but not vice versa. We enforce unidirectional instead of bidirectional links between nodes which seems to be more natural for wireless systems. Following the ideas in [13,7,16,5][3] mobility is defined by a simple reduction, say that the node at location m in (2) autonomously moves and becomes *connected* to the node at location l,

$$\lfloor p \rfloor_l \parallel \lfloor q \rfloor_m \parallel \{l \mapsto m\} \longrightarrow \lfloor p \rfloor_l \parallel \lfloor q \rfloor_m \parallel \{l \mapsto m\} \parallel \{m \mapsto l\} \ .$$

Dually, nodes may arbitrarily *disconnect*, for instance l disconnects from m in

$$\lfloor p \rfloor_l \parallel \lfloor q \rfloor_m \parallel \{l \mapsto m\} \parallel \{m \mapsto l\} \longrightarrow \lfloor p \rfloor_l \parallel \lfloor q \rfloor_m \parallel \{m \mapsto l\} \ .$$

A process $\langle t\rangle.p$ can broadcast t and in so doing become p, and a process $(x).q$ can receive a broadcasted message t becoming $q\{t/x\}$. *Local synchronous broadcast* is defined by a *broadcast reduction*, say

$$\begin{aligned}&\lfloor \langle t\rangle.p \rfloor_l \parallel \{m \mapsto l\} \parallel \{n \mapsto l\} \parallel \lfloor (x).q \rfloor_m \parallel \lfloor (x).r \rfloor_n \\ &\quad\longrightarrow \lfloor p \rfloor_l \parallel \{m \mapsto l\} \parallel \{n \mapsto l\} \parallel \lfloor q\{t/x\} \rfloor_m \parallel \lfloor r\{t/x\} \rfloor_n \ ,\end{aligned}$$

where $\langle t\rangle.p$ broadcasts to nodes connected to l, but messages may be lost.

Names may be restricted and in particular we may let a location be unique as in $\nu l.\lfloor p \rfloor_l$. Also, we allow for an unbounded number of nodes, as in $!\nu l.\lfloor p \rfloor_l$, which is a novelty compared to the current calculi for mobility and local broadcast where one is only allowed to reason about a finite number of network nodes.

Due to the reduction (1) where processes at the same location communicate the context $\lfloor n(x).\overline{m}\langle x\rangle \rfloor_l$ can distinguish $\lfloor n\langle t\rangle \rfloor_l$ from $\nu l.\lfloor \overline{n}\langle t\rangle \rfloor_l$ and from $\lfloor \overline{n}\langle t\rangle \rfloor_k$ if $l \neq k$, so it seems natural that $\lfloor \overline{n}\langle t\rangle \rfloor_l$, $\lfloor \overline{n}\langle t\rangle \rfloor_k$, and $\nu l.\lfloor \overline{n}\langle t\rangle \rfloor_l$ must be considered pairwise inequivalent even in a weak setting where mobility is ignored. But what about $\lfloor \langle t\rangle \rfloor_l$, $\lfloor \langle t\rangle \rfloor_k$, and $\nu l.\lfloor \langle t\rangle \rfloor_l$? As it will turn out the three nodes are pairwise inequivalent when mobility is taken into account, but when mobility is abstracted one may argue that they should be considered indistinguishable, intuitively because any node can move and connect to any (even a new) locality and receive the broadcasted message. For instance we have

$$\lfloor \langle t\rangle \rfloor_l \parallel \lfloor (x).\overline{m}\langle x\rangle \rfloor_k \parallel \{k \mapsto l\} \longrightarrow \lfloor 0 \rfloor_l \parallel \lfloor \overline{m}\langle t\rangle \rfloor_k \parallel \{k \mapsto l\}$$

[3] Arbitrary mobility is an over approximation and more realistic mobility models are considered in [6].

and in a weak setting we can obtain a similar computation for $\nu l.\lfloor\langle t\rangle\rfloor_l$ in the same context by letting:

$$\begin{aligned}\nu l.\lfloor\langle t\rangle\rfloor_l \parallel \lfloor(x).\overline{m}\langle x\rangle\rfloor_k \parallel \{k\mapsto l\} &\equiv \nu l'.(\lfloor\langle t\rangle\rfloor_{l'} \parallel \lfloor(x).\overline{m}\langle x\rangle\rfloor_k \parallel \{k\mapsto l\})\\ &\longrightarrow \nu l'.(\lfloor\langle t\rangle\rfloor_{l'} \parallel \lfloor(x).\overline{m}\langle x\rangle\rfloor_k \parallel \{k\mapsto l\} \parallel \{k\mapsto l'\})\\ &\longrightarrow \nu l'.(\lfloor 0\rfloor_{l'} \parallel \lfloor\overline{m}\langle t\rangle\rfloor_k \parallel \{k\mapsto l\} \parallel \{k\mapsto l'\})\\ &\longrightarrow \nu l'.(\lfloor 0\rfloor_{l'} \parallel \lfloor\overline{m}\langle t\rangle\rfloor_k \parallel \{k\mapsto l\}) \equiv \nu l.\lfloor 0\rfloor_l \parallel \lfloor\overline{m}\langle t\rangle\rfloor_k \parallel \{k\mapsto l\}\end{aligned}$$

Notice that an observable identifying the locality of the broadcasting entity clearly will distinguish the three nodes $\lfloor\langle t\rangle\rfloor_l$, $\lfloor\langle t\rangle\rfloor_k$, and $\nu l.\lfloor\langle t\rangle\rfloor_l$, so it may be too strict a barb.

Below we discuss and compare three kinds of barbs: the observability of *i)* output on a name at a given location, *ii)* broadcast of a name at some location, and *iii)* the broadcasting location respectively. For the three congruences induced by each of these barbs we show that the two former coincide and strictly contain the latter in a weak setting where one reduction may be matched by zero or more reductions, and for the corresponding strong congruences where a reduction must be matched by precisely one reduction all three congruences coincide. To illustrate the suitability of $bA\pi$ we provide a labelled operational semantics and give a sound and complete co-inductive characterization of the largest weak congruences mentioned above. Also we give a larger example of a route-request protocol that could not have been modelled in the calculi presented in [13,7,16,5] because it contains an unbounded number of nodes.

The paper is organized as follows: $bA\pi$ is presented in Section 2. The barbs, the reduction semantics, and the barbed congruences are defined and compared in Section 3. The sound and complete co-inductive labelled operational semantics is provided in Section 4. Finally we close by a conclusion.

2 The Calculus

The syntax of our calculus $bA\pi$ is outlined below defining first terms, then processes, and finally networks and extended networks.

We assume a *signature* Σ with a finite set of function symbols f each with an arity. Also we assume an infinite set of *names* $\mathcal{N}$ ranged over by n, an infinite set of *variables* $\mathcal{X}$ ranged over by x. Then the set of *terms* ranged over by s and t is defined by the grammar below where f is a function symbol with arity k.

$$t ::= n \mid x \mid f(t_1, \ldots, t_k)$$

We let $s\{t/x\}$ denote s where x is substituted by t. We let $\mathcal{T}$ denote the set of all terms and let $\hat{t}$ range over *ground* terms with no variables.[4]

The set of *processes* ranged over by p, q, and r is defined by the grammar:

$$p ::= 0 \mid \langle t\rangle.p \mid \overline{u}\langle t\rangle.p \mid (x).p \mid u(x).p \mid \textit{if } (t = s) \textit{ then } p \textit{ else } p \mid \nu n.p \mid p \parallel p \mid !p$$

[4] For a discussion about associating sorts with terms we refer the reader to [1].

where u ranges over variables and names. The processes 0, $\nu n.p$, $p \parallel q$, $!p$ (replication), and *if* $(t = s)$ *then* p *else* q, are standard. The process $\langle t \rangle.p$ may broadcast t and in so doing become p, $\overline{n}\langle t \rangle.p$ may send t on channel n (unicast), $(x).p$ binds x in p and may receive a broadcasted term t and replace all free occurrences of x in p by t, likewise $n(x).p$ binds x in p and may receive a term t sent on channel n. As usual we often leave out a trailing 0.

We let $p\{t/x\}$ denote p where x is substituted by t, taking care to avoid clash of variables and names using α-conversion if needed. The set of *free names* in p is denoted by $fn(p)$, and its *free variables* are denoted by $fv(p)$.

The set of *networks* ranged over by P and Q is defined by the grammar:

$$P ::= 0 \mid \lfloor p \rfloor_l \mid \{l \mapsto m\} \mid \nu n.P \mid P \parallel P \mid !P$$

The network 0 denotes the empty network. $\lfloor p \rfloor_l$ is a node at location l containing the process p. $\{l \mapsto m\}$ tells that the node at location l is connected to node m. $\nu n.P$ is the network P with a new name bound by n, $P \parallel Q$ is the parallel composition of the two networks P and Q, and $!P$ denotes an unbounded number of parallel compositions of the network P.

We extend networks with *variable restrictions* and *active substitutions*, $\{t/x\}$, and we let a *frame*, ϕ, be the static part of a process. Frames, extended processes, and extended networks are defined by the following grammar:

$$\begin{aligned}
\phi &::= 0 \mid \{t/x\} \mid \nu u.\phi \mid \phi \parallel \phi \\
e &::= p \mid \{t/x\} \mid \nu u.e \mid e \parallel e \\
E &::= P \mid \lfloor e \rfloor_n \mid \nu u.E \mid E \parallel E
\end{aligned}$$

We let the new name (variable) operator have higher precedence than the left associative parallel composition.

Intuitively an active substitution $\{t/x\}$ is like an ordinary substitution that floats and may be applied to any process that comes into contact with it. If we control the floating of an active substitution by restricting its variable it may be interpreted as: $\lfloor \textit{let } x = t \textit{ in } p \rfloor_l \stackrel{\text{def}}{=} \lfloor \nu x.(\{t/x\} \parallel p) \rfloor_l$.

The sets of free names and variables in E, denoted by $fn(E)$ and $fv(E)$ respectively, are defined as expected. In particular $fn(\{t/x\}) = fn(t)$ and $fv(\{t/x\}) = \{x\} \cup fv(t)$. We let $E\{t/x\}$ denote E where all free occurrences of x in E are substituted by t. The *domain* at a free location l of E, denoted by $dom_l(E)$, is the set of variables for which E contains a substitution $\{t/x\}$ at location l not under νx. The domain of E, denoted by $dom(E)$ is the union of $dom_l(E)$ for all free locations l in E. We say that $dom(E) = dom(F)$ if $dom_l(E) = dom_l(F)$ for all l. E is *closed* when $fv(E) \subseteq dom(E)$.

For a finite index set I we let $\Pi_{i \in I} E_i$ denote the parallel composition of E_i for all $i \in I$, if $I = \emptyset$ then $\Pi_{i \in I} E_i$ is 0. We shall write $\tilde{u}$ for a disjoint sequence of either names or variables and $u \in \tilde{u}$ if u occurs in the sequence $\tilde{u}$. We let $\tilde{u}\tilde{v}$ denote the concatenation of disjoint sequences. Sometimes we write $(u_k)_{k \in \tilde{v}}$ to denote a disjoint sequence indexed by the elements in $\tilde{v}$. Whenever $\tilde{t} = (t_x)_{x \in \tilde{x}}$

Table 1. Structural congruence

$$\lfloor \nu u.p \rfloor_l \equiv \nu u.\lfloor p \rfloor_l \ , \text{ if } u \neq l \qquad \lfloor !p \rfloor_l \equiv !\lfloor p \rfloor_l \qquad \lfloor p \parallel q \rfloor_l \equiv \lfloor p \rfloor_l \parallel \lfloor q \rfloor_l$$

$$\lfloor p \parallel 0 \rfloor_l \equiv \lfloor p \rfloor_l \qquad \lfloor \{t/x\} \rfloor_l \equiv \lfloor \{s/x\} \rfloor_l \ , \text{ if } s = t$$

$$\lfloor \nu x.\{t/x\} \rfloor_l \equiv \lfloor 0 \rfloor_l \qquad \lfloor \{t/x\} \parallel e \rfloor_l \equiv \lfloor \{t/x\} \parallel e\{t/x\} \rfloor_l$$

$$\{l \mapsto k\} \equiv \{l \mapsto k\} \parallel \{l \mapsto k\} \qquad \lfloor (x).p \parallel (x).q \rfloor_l \equiv \lfloor (x).(p \parallel q) \rfloor_l$$

$$E \parallel 0 \equiv E \qquad E \parallel E' \equiv E' \parallel E \qquad (E \parallel E') \parallel E'' \equiv E \parallel (E' \parallel E'')$$

$$\nu u.\nu v.E \equiv \nu v.\nu u.E \qquad \nu u.E \parallel E' \equiv \nu u.(E \parallel E') \ , \text{ if } u \notin fn(E') \cup fv(E')$$

we write $\{\tilde{t}/\tilde{x}\}$ for $\Pi_{x \in \tilde{x}}\{t_x/x\}$. We write $\{\tilde{n} \mapsto l\}$ and $\{l \mapsto \tilde{n}\}$ for $\Pi_{n \in \tilde{n}}\{n \mapsto l\}$ and $\Pi_{n \in \tilde{n}}\{l \mapsto n\}$ respectively.

We say that a E is *well-formed* if E contains at most one substitution for each variable and exactly one when the variable is restricted. Also, for a well-formed E we assume substitutions are cycle-free and we presuppose that a free variable at a location l is contained in $dom_l(E)$. In the sequel we consider only networks in the set of well-formed extended networks $\mathbf{N}$ and we identify networks up to α-equivalence. The set of well-formed and closed networks is denoted by $\mathbf{N}_c$.

3 Reduction Semantics

In this section we provide our calculus with a natural reduction semantics.

Given a signature we equip it with an equational theory and we write $\Sigma \vdash s = t$ when the equation is in the theory associated with Σ. Often Σ is left implicit writing $s = t$ for $\Sigma \vdash s = t$. Here we refrain from explicitly treating a sort system for terms, implicitly assume terms are well-sorted, and refer the reader to [1].

We write $C(E)$ for the insertion of E in the hole of a variable closing network context C and say that relation $\mathcal{R}$ on $\mathbf{N}$ is a *congruence* if $E \ \mathcal{R} \ E'$ implies $C(E) \ \mathcal{R} \ C(E')$ for any C. Structural congruence on $\mathbf{N}$, $\equiv$, is the least congruence and equivalence relation that is closed under α-conversion and the rules in Table 1. Almost all the rules in Table 1 are standard, but notice that the axiom $\lfloor (x).p \parallel (x).q \rfloor_l \equiv \lfloor (x).(p \parallel q) \rfloor_l$ captures that a broadcasted message may have multiple simultaneous receivers within the same location. Also we allow to collapse multiple occurrences of the same connectivity information. From [1] we adopt the rule $\lfloor \{t/x\} \parallel e \rfloor_l \equiv \lfloor \{t/x\} \parallel e\{t/x\} \rfloor_l$, capturing the essence of active substitutions, and we are always allowed to introduce arbitrary new substitutions at a location as introduced by $\lfloor \nu x.\{t/x\} \rfloor_l \equiv \lfloor 0 \rfloor_l$.

Example 1. Similar to [1] we have $\lfloor \langle t \rangle.p \rfloor_l \equiv \nu x.\lfloor \{t/x\} \parallel \langle x \rangle.p \rfloor_l$, assuming $x \notin fv(\langle t \rangle.p)$, because:

$$\lfloor \langle t \rangle.p \rfloor_l \equiv \lfloor \langle t \rangle.p) \parallel 0 \rfloor_l \equiv \lfloor \langle t \rangle.p \parallel \nu x.\{t/x\} \rfloor_l \equiv \nu x.\lfloor \{t/x\} \parallel \langle t \rangle.p \rfloor_l$$

$$\equiv \nu x.\lfloor \{t/x\} \parallel (\langle x \rangle.p)\{t/x\} \rfloor_l \equiv \nu x.\lfloor \{t/x\} \parallel \langle x \rangle.p \rfloor_l$$

Table 2. Reduction rules, networks

$$(rep)\ \frac{}{!E \longrightarrow E \parallel !E} \qquad (if)\ \frac{}{\lfloor if\ (t = t)\ then\ p\ else\ q\rfloor_l \longrightarrow \lfloor p\rfloor_l}$$

$$(else)\ \frac{}{\lfloor if\ (\hat{t} = \hat{s})\ then\ p\ else\ q\rfloor_l \longrightarrow \lfloor q\rfloor_l}\ \hat{t} \neq \hat{s}$$

$$(com)\ \frac{}{\lfloor \overline{n}\langle\hat{t}\rangle.p \parallel n(x).q\rfloor_l \longrightarrow \lfloor p \parallel q\{\hat{t}/x\}\rfloor_l}$$

$$(brd)\ \frac{}{\lfloor\langle\hat{t}\rangle.p\rfloor_l \parallel \Pi_{k\in\tilde{n}}\lfloor(x).q_k\rfloor_k \parallel \{\tilde{n} \mapsto l\} \longrightarrow \lfloor p\rfloor_l \parallel \Pi_{k\in\tilde{n}}\lfloor q_k\{\hat{t}/x\}\rfloor_k \parallel \{\tilde{n} \mapsto l\}}$$

$$(con)\ \frac{}{0 \longrightarrow \{l \mapsto k\}} \qquad (dis)\ \frac{}{\{l \mapsto k\} \longrightarrow 0}$$

We define the reduction relation, $\longrightarrow$, as the least relation on $\mathbf{N}$ closed under $\equiv$, new names, variables, and parallel composition, and satisfying the rules in Table 2. The rules (*rep*), (*if*), (*else*), and (*com*) are standard. The rule (*brd*) says that a process at a node may broadcast to (some of the) nodes right now connected to that node. The rules (*con*) and (*dis*) allows connection and disconnection between nodes respectively. Notice that nodes connected to an emitter may receive a broadcasted message (but the message may also be lost) whereas disconnected nodes do not have the possibility of reception.

Strong Barbed Congruence. Next we introduce natural strong observational equivalence and congruence relations.

As motivated in the Introduction we are able to observe that a process at a (free) location is capable of sending on a (free) channel, hence the two nodes $\lfloor\overline{n}\langle t\rangle\rfloor_l$ and $\lfloor\overline{n}\langle t\rangle\rfloor_k$ should not be considered equivalent if $k \neq l$ because the process $n(x).\overline{m}\langle x\rangle$ when put at the physical location l can distinguish the two. Similar to Dπ we may therefore introduce a *barb* writing $E \downarrow l_n$ when $E \equiv \nu\tilde{u}.(\lfloor\overline{n}\langle t\rangle.p\rfloor_l \parallel F)$ for some $\tilde{u}$, t, p, and F where l and n do not belong to $\tilde{u}$.

Definition 1. *A symmetric relation $\mathcal{R}$ on $\mathbf{N}_c$ is a* strong barbed congruence *if it is a congruence and if $E\ \mathcal{R}\ F$ implies $dom(E) = dom(F)$, and*

$$E \longrightarrow E' \textit{ implies } \exists F'.\ F \longrightarrow F' \textit{ and } E'\ \mathcal{R}\ F'$$

$$E \downarrow l_n \textit{ implies } F \downarrow l_n$$

$\simeq$ is the largest strong barbed congruence.

It is immediate that $\simeq$ is an equivalence relation containing $\equiv$.

Example 2. Clearly $0 \simeq \nu u.0 \simeq \lfloor 0 \rfloor_l$, but also $0 \simeq \nu n.\lfloor \overline{n}\langle t \rangle.p \rfloor_l \simeq \nu l.\lfloor \overline{n}\langle t \rangle.p \rfloor_l$. Observe $0 \simeq \nu l.\lfloor \phi \rfloor_l$ because $dom(\nu l.\lfloor \phi \rfloor_l) = \emptyset$.

Similar to [1] let f and g be two unary functions occurring in no equations. Further let, where n and m are distinct from l,

$$E = \lfloor \nu n.\{n/x\} \parallel \nu m.\{m/y\} \rfloor_l$$
$$E' = \nu n.\lfloor \{g(n)/x\} \parallel \{f(n)/y\} \rfloor_l$$
$$F = \nu n.\lfloor \{n/x\} \parallel \{f(n)/y\} \rfloor_l$$

then $E \simeq E'$ because in both E and E' the two variables x and y are mapped to two unrelated values that are different from any value any context can build. But, $E \not\simeq F$ because the two may be distinguished by the node

$$\lfloor \mathit{if}\ (y = f(x))\ \mathit{then}\ \overline{n}\langle x \rangle \rfloor_l$$

Example 3. It turns out that $\nu l.\lfloor \langle n \rangle \rfloor_l \not\simeq \lfloor \langle n \rangle \rfloor_l$ because for

$$C = (-) \parallel \lfloor (x).\overline{m}\langle x \rangle \rfloor_k \parallel \{k \mapsto l\}$$

we have $C(\lfloor \langle n \rangle \rfloor_l) \longrightarrow \lfloor 0 \rfloor_l \parallel \lfloor \overline{m}\langle n \rangle \rfloor_k \parallel \{k \mapsto l\} = E$ where $E \downarrow k_m$ which cannot be matched by $C(\nu l.\lfloor \langle n \rangle \rfloor_l)$.

The observation in Example 3 gives rise to alternatively letting a barb be the observation of a broadcasting location, i.e. $E \downarrow l$ when $E \equiv \nu \tilde{u}.(\lfloor \langle t \rangle.p \rfloor_l \parallel F)$ for some t, p, $\tilde{u}$, and F where $l \notin \tilde{u}$. Hence an environment $\{k \mapsto l\} \parallel \lfloor (x).q \rfloor_k$ may observe a network with a barb $\downarrow l$.

Definition 2. *A symmetric relation $\mathcal{R}$ on $\mathbf{N}_c$ is a* strong location barbed congruence *if it is a congruence and if $E\ \mathcal{R}\ F$ implies $dom(E) = dom(F)$, and*

$$E \longrightarrow E' \textit{ implies } \exists F'.\ F \longrightarrow F' \textit{ and } E'\ \mathcal{R}\ F'$$
$$E \downarrow l \textit{ implies } F \downarrow k \textit{ for some } k$$

$\simeq_{loc}$ is the largest strong location barbed congruence.

Example 4. Clearly $\nu l.\lfloor \langle n \rangle \rfloor_l \not\simeq_{loc} \lfloor \langle n \rangle \rfloor_l$. Observe that $\lfloor \langle n \rangle \rfloor_l \not\simeq_{loc} \lfloor \langle n \rangle \rfloor_k$ if $k \neq l$. The reason why is that if it was the case that $\lfloor \langle n \rangle \rfloor_l \simeq_{loc} \lfloor \langle n \rangle \rfloor_k$ then also, since $\simeq_{loc}$ is a congruence (assuming without loss of generality that $n \neq l$), $\nu l.\lfloor \langle n \rangle \rfloor_l \simeq_{loc} \nu l.\lfloor \langle n \rangle \rfloor_k \equiv \lfloor \langle n \rangle \rfloor_k$ which as stated just before is not true.[5]

Finally, we may let a barb be the observation of a broadcast message but without saying the broadcasting location. For simplicity we just use names as barbs and define $E \downarrow \langle n \rangle$ when $E \equiv \nu \tilde{u}.(\lfloor \langle n \rangle.p \rfloor_l \parallel F)$ for some p, l, $\tilde{u}$, and F where $n \notin \tilde{u}$ (but it may be that $l \in \tilde{u}$). Hence, by first connecting to the (unknown) node broadcasting n, a context $\lfloor (x).\mathit{if}\ (x = n)\ \mathit{then}\ p \rfloor_k$ may observe a network with a barb $\downarrow \langle n \rangle$.

[5] Observe then that the second clause in Definition 2 can, without changing the meaning of the definition, be replaced by "$E \downarrow l$ *implies* $F \downarrow l$".

Definition 3. *A symmetric relation $\mathcal{R}$ on $\mathbf{N}_c$ is a* strong message barbed congruence *if it is a congruence and if $E \mathcal{R} F$ implies $dom(E) = dom(F)$, and*

$$E \longrightarrow E' \text{ implies } \exists F'.\, F \longrightarrow F' \text{ and } E' \mathcal{R} F'$$
$$E \downarrow \langle n \rangle \text{ implies } F \downarrow \langle n \rangle$$

$\simeq_{msg}$ is the largest strong message barbed congruence.

Example 5. Recall that $\lfloor\langle n\rangle\rfloor_l \not\simeq_{loc} \lfloor\langle n\rangle\rfloor_k$ if $k \neq l$, and interestingly, although the two nodes may broadcast the same message n, also $\lfloor\langle n\rangle\rfloor_l \not\simeq_{msg} \lfloor\langle n\rangle\rfloor_k$, because letting for some fresh n'

$$C = (-) \parallel \{m \mapsto l\} \parallel \lfloor (x).\langle n'\rangle \rfloor_m$$

then $C(\lfloor\langle n\rangle\rfloor_l) \longrightarrow \lfloor 0 \rfloor_l \parallel \{m \mapsto l\} \parallel \lfloor\langle n'\rangle\rfloor_m = E$ where $E \downarrow \langle n'\rangle$ which cannot be matched by $C(\lfloor\langle n\rangle\rfloor_k)$.

The three notions of strong barbed congruences turn out to be identical demonstrating the robustness of our notion of barbs.

Theorem 1. $\simeq \; = \; \simeq_{loc} \; = \; \simeq_{msg}$

Weak Barbed Congruence. Below we introduce a weak observational equivalence and congruence relation for each of the three kinds of barbs introduced above. The equivalence relations are weak in the standard sense that a reduction may be matched by zero or more reductions, and hence we then abstract from communication within the same location, broadcast communication between localities, and mobility.

Let $\Longrightarrow$ be the reflexive and transitive closure of $\longrightarrow$. We write $E \Downarrow b$ if $E \Longrightarrow E'$ for some E' such that $E' \downarrow b$ where b is one of the three kinds of barbs mentioned above.

Definition 4. *A symmetric relation $\mathcal{R}$ on $\mathbf{N}_c$ is a* weak barbed congruence *if it is a congruence and if $E \mathcal{R} F$ implies $dom(E) = dom(F)$, and*

$$E \longrightarrow E' \text{ implies } \exists F'.\, F \Longrightarrow F' \text{ and } E' \mathcal{R} F'$$
$$E \downarrow l_n \text{ implies } F \Downarrow l_n$$

$\cong$ is the largest weak barbed congruence.

Since changes in connectivity is unobservable for weak barbed congruence it follows that $E \cong E \parallel \{l \mapsto k\}$.

Definition 5. *A symmetric relation $\mathcal{R}$ on $\mathbf{N}_c$ is a* weak location barbed congruence *if it is a congruence and if $E \mathcal{R} F$ implies $dom(E) = dom(F)$, and*

$$E \longrightarrow E' \text{ implies } \exists F'.\, F \Longrightarrow F' \text{ and } E' \mathcal{R} F'$$
$$E \downarrow l \text{ implies } F \Downarrow k \text{ for some } k$$

$\cong_{loc}$ is the largest weak location barbed congruence.

Table 3. Processes in the route-request protocol

$p \stackrel{\text{def}}{=} (x).\mathit{if}\ (\mathit{fst}(x) = \mathit{rep})\ \mathit{then}\ \mathit{if}\ (\mathit{snd}(x) = n)\ \mathit{then}\ \overline{a}\langle \mathit{succ}\rangle\ \mathit{else}\ p\ \mathit{else}\ p$
$q \stackrel{\text{def}}{=} (x).\mathit{if}\ (\mathit{fst}(x) = \mathit{req})\ \mathit{then}\ \langle \mathit{pair}(\mathit{rep}, \mathit{snd}(x))\rangle\ \mathit{else}\ q$
$r \stackrel{\text{def}}{=} (x).\mathit{if}\ (\mathit{fst}(x) = \mathit{req})\ \mathit{then}\ \langle x\rangle.r' \parallel r\ \mathit{else}\ r$
$r' \stackrel{\text{def}}{=} (y).\mathit{if}\ (\mathit{fst}(y) = \mathit{rep})\ \mathit{then}\ \mathit{if}\ (\mathit{snd}(y) = \mathit{snd}(x))\ \mathit{then}\ \langle y\rangle\ \mathit{else}\ r'\ \mathit{else}\ r'$

Definition 6. *A symmetric relation $\mathcal{R}$ on $\mathbf{N}_c$ is a* weak message barbed congruence *if it is a congruence and if $E\ \mathcal{R}\ F$ implies $dom(E) = dom(F)$, and*

$$E \longrightarrow E' \text{ implies } \exists F'.\, F \Longrightarrow F' \text{ and } E'\ \mathcal{R}\ F'$$

$$E \downarrow \langle n\rangle \text{ implies } F \Downarrow \langle n\rangle$$

$\cong_{msg}$ is the largest weak message broadcast barbed congruence.

Example 6. For the same reason as explained in Example 4, $\nu l.\lfloor\langle n\rangle\rfloor_l \not\cong_{loc} \lfloor\langle n\rangle\rfloor_l$ and when $l \neq k$ also $\lfloor\langle n\rangle\rfloor_l \not\cong_{loc} \lfloor\langle n\rangle\rfloor_k$. But interestingly, $\lfloor\langle n\rangle\rfloor_l \cong_{msg} \lfloor\langle n\rangle\rfloor_k$ and when $n \neq l$ then $\nu l.\lfloor\langle n\rangle\rfloor_l \cong_{msg} \lfloor\langle n\rangle\rfloor_l$ as discussed in the Introduction. We show this formally in the next section, confer Example 9 and 10.

The relationship between the strong and weak barbed congruences is illustrated by the following theorem.

Theorem 2. $\simeq\ \subset\ \cong_{loc}\ \subset\ \cong_{msg}\ =\ \cong$.

Example 7. The order of infinite repetitive broadcast sequences may be interchanged. E.g. $\lfloor !\langle n\rangle.\langle m\rangle\rfloor_l \cong_{msg} \lfloor !\langle m\rangle.\langle n\rangle\rfloor_k$ because receivers may disconnect before a message is broadcasted and connect again in order to receive next.

Example 8. Suppose a simple route-request protocol with the purpose of finding out as to whether there exists a route from source to destination in a mobile ad-hoc network. In this simple example we do not cater to find the actual route, just knowledge about its existence is sufficient. We may model the protocol by

$$E_{k,k'} = \lfloor \nu n.\langle \mathit{pair}(\mathit{req}, n)\rangle.p\rfloor_l \parallel \lfloor r\rfloor_k \parallel \lfloor r\rfloor_{k'} \parallel \lfloor q\rfloor_m$$

where (using equations instead of replication) p, q, and r are defined in Table 3 and the equational theory consists of $\mathit{fst}(\mathit{pair}(x, y)) = x$ and $\mathit{snd}(\mathit{pair}(x, y)) = y$. Intuitively, the source at l sends out a request with a unique identifier n. The request is expected to reach its destination at m where a reply containing n is returned. The message may travel in a number of hops through the relay processes at k and k'. As in many realistic routing protocols for mobile ad-hoc networks a relay process forwards a request and maintains a thread waiting for a reply to it while continuing listening to new requests. When a reply with the right identifier appears it is simply forwarded and the waiting thread terminates.

If we can observe which location is about to broadcast then clearly $E_{k,k'} \not\cong_{loc} E_{l,l'}$ if say $k \neq l$ because the process at node k may receive the request after which it is able to forward it. However as discussed in the Introduction it may be too strong to allow for observing the actual locality about to broadcast, often as for the route-request protocol of this example it is more natural to be able to observe only the data broadcasted and not whom did the broadcast. For instance it turns out that $E_{k,k'} \cong E_{l,l'}$ and also that $E_{k,k'} \cong F$, where F is a network with an unbounded number of relay processes at unique locations, i.e.

$$F = \lfloor \nu n.\langle pair(req, n)\rangle.p\rfloor_l \parallel !\nu k.\lfloor r\rfloor_k \parallel \lfloor q\rfloor_m$$

We postpone the proof of our latter propositions to Example 12 in Section 4.

4 Labeled Operational Semantics

In this section we provide a labelled transition system semantics for extended networks based on which we give a sound and complete co-inductive bisimulation characterization of our weak barbed congruence from above.[6]

We define a set of *actions* $\mathcal{A}$, ranged over by α, by:

$$\alpha ::= \nu x.\overline{n}\langle x\rangle @l \mid n(t)@l \mid \nu x_0.\langle x_0\rangle \triangleright n_0, \ldots, \nu x_i.\langle x_i\rangle \triangleright n_i \mid (t) \triangleleft l$$

νx is a variable binder and the free and bound variables of α, denoted by $fv(\alpha)$ and $bv(\alpha)$ respectively, are defined as expected. We write $u \in \alpha$ if u belongs to the names or the free and bound variables of α. Instead of $\nu x_0.\langle x_0\rangle \triangleright n_0, \ldots, \nu x_i.\langle x_i\rangle \triangleright n_i$ we write $\nu\tilde{x}.\langle\tilde{x}\rangle \triangleright \tilde{n}$ whenever $\tilde{x} = x_0, \ldots, x_i$ and $\tilde{n} = n_0, \ldots, n_i$ and we identify $\nu x_0.\langle x_0\rangle \triangleright n_0, \ldots, \nu x_i.\langle x_i\rangle \triangleright n_i$ with any permutation of $\nu x_0.\langle x_0\rangle \triangleright n_0$, $\ldots$, and $\nu x_i.\langle x_i\rangle \triangleright n_i$.

Formally the semantics $(\mathbf{N}, \{\longrightarrow, \xrightarrow{\alpha} \subseteq \mathbf{N} \times \mathbf{N} \mid \alpha \in \mathcal{A}\})$ is defined by extending the rules in Table 2 by the ones in Table 4. The rule (*out*) says that a ground term bound to a new variable x is output at name n at location l and dually (*in*) says that a term is input on name n at location l. Broadcast is taken care of by the rules (*brd*), (*syn*), and (*cls*). In (*brd*) a ground term is broadcasted to a set of locations $\tilde{n}$ that all are connected to and hence within range of the broadcasting node l, the term is bound to a unique fresh variable in each receiving location. The rule (*syn*) allows a process to receive a broadcasted term as part of a broadcasting session if the process belongs to a location l within broadcast range. Rule (*cls*) closes a broadcast to one of the locations. The rule (*rec*) deals with reception of a broadcasted term from a location l in the environment. The remaining rules (*par*), (*new*), and (*str*) are standard.

As in [1] we introduce the notion of two terms s and t being equal in a frame ϕ, denoted by $s =_\phi t$, and defined by:

Definition 7. $s =_\phi t$ *iff* $\phi \equiv \nu\tilde{n}.\{\tilde{t}/\tilde{x}\}$ *and* $s\{\tilde{t}/\tilde{x}\} = t\{\tilde{t}/\tilde{x}\}$ *with* $\tilde{n} \cap (fn(s) \cup fn(t)) = \emptyset$.

[6] The semantics is tailored towards showing that our weak bisimulation is a congruence, a similar result will most likely not hold for a strong bisimulation.

Table 4. Transition Rules

$$(out)\frac{}{\lfloor \overline{n}\langle \hat{t}\rangle.p\rfloor_l \stackrel{\nu x.\overline{n}\langle x\rangle @l}{\longrightarrow} \lfloor p \parallel \{\hat{t}/x\}\rfloor_l}\quad x\notin fv(p) \qquad (in)\frac{}{\lfloor n(x).p\rfloor_l \stackrel{n(t)@l}{\longrightarrow} \lfloor p\{t/x\}\rfloor_l}$$

$$(brd)\frac{}{\lfloor\langle\hat{t}\rangle.p\rfloor_l \parallel \{\tilde{n}\mapsto l\} \stackrel{\nu\tilde{x}.\langle\tilde{x}\rangle\rhd\tilde{n}}{\longrightarrow} \lfloor p\rfloor_l \parallel \Pi_{k\in\tilde{n}}\lfloor\{\hat{t}/x_k\}\rfloor_k \parallel \{\tilde{n}\mapsto l\}}\quad \begin{array}{l}\tilde{x}=(x_k)_{k\in\tilde{n}}\\ \tilde{x}\cap fv(p)=\emptyset\end{array}$$

$$(syn)\frac{E \stackrel{\nu\tilde{x}x.\langle\tilde{x}x\rangle\rhd\tilde{n}l}{\longrightarrow} E'}{E\parallel\lfloor(x).p\rfloor_l \stackrel{\nu\tilde{x}x.\langle\tilde{x}x\rangle\rhd\tilde{n}l}{\longrightarrow} E'\parallel\lfloor p\rfloor_l} \qquad (cls)\frac{E \stackrel{\nu\tilde{x}x.\langle\tilde{x}x\rangle\rhd\tilde{n}l}{\longrightarrow} E'}{E \stackrel{\nu\tilde{x}.\langle\tilde{x}\rangle\rhd\tilde{n}}{\longrightarrow} \nu x.E'}$$

$$(rec)\frac{}{\Pi_{k\in\tilde{n}}\lfloor(x).p_k\rfloor_k \parallel \{\tilde{n}\mapsto l\} \stackrel{(t)\lhd l}{\longrightarrow} \Pi_{k\in\tilde{n}}\lfloor p_k\{t/x\}\rfloor_k \parallel \{\tilde{n}\mapsto l\}}$$

$$(par)\frac{E\stackrel{\alpha}{\longrightarrow}E'}{E\parallel F\stackrel{\alpha}{\longrightarrow}E'\parallel F}\quad bv(\alpha)\cap fv(F)=\emptyset$$

$$(new)\frac{E\stackrel{\alpha}{\longrightarrow}E'}{\nu u.E\stackrel{\alpha}{\longrightarrow}\nu u.E'}\quad u\notin\alpha \qquad (str)\frac{E\equiv F\stackrel{\alpha}{\longrightarrow}F'\equiv E'}{E\stackrel{\alpha}{\longrightarrow}E'}$$

Definition 8. *Two frames ϕ and ψ are* static equivalent, *denoted by $\phi \sim_s \psi$, if $dom(\phi) = dom(\psi)$ and $s =_\phi t$ iff $s =_\psi t$ for all s and t.*

We extend the notion of static equivalence to extended networks. Define the frame, $\{E\}_l$, at the free location l of E inductively by: $\{P\}_l = \{\nu l.E\}_l = 0$, $\{E \parallel F\}_l = \{E\}_l \parallel \{F\}_l$, $\{\nu u.E\}_l = \nu u.\{E\}_l$ if $l \neq u$, $\{\lfloor e\rfloor_k\}_l = 0$ if $l \neq k$, and $\{\lfloor e\rfloor_l\}_l = \{e\}$ where the frame, $\{e\}$, of e is defined inductively by: $\{p\} = 0$, $\{e \parallel f\} = \{e\} \parallel \{f\}$, $\{\nu u.e\} = \nu u.\{e\}$, and $\{\{t/x\}\} = \{t/x\}$. Notice that for $E \in \mathbf{N}_c$ then $\{E\}_l \equiv \nu\tilde{n}.\{\tilde{t}/\tilde{x}\}$ for some $\tilde{t}$ and $\tilde{x}$ where $\tilde{n} \subseteq fn(\tilde{t})$ and $fv(\tilde{t}) = \emptyset$.

Definition 9. *Two closed extended networks E and F are* static equivalent, *denoted by $E \sim_s F$, if $\{E\}_l \sim_s \{F\}_l$ for all l.*

Below we give a co-inductive characterization of $\cong$. We write $E \stackrel{\nu\tilde{x}.\langle\tilde{x}\rangle\rhd\tilde{n}}{\Longrightarrow} E'$ whenever there exists

$$E \Longrightarrow E_1 \stackrel{\nu\tilde{x}_1.\langle\tilde{x}_1\rangle\rhd\tilde{n}_1}{\longrightarrow} \ldots \Longrightarrow E_{i-1} \stackrel{\nu\tilde{x}_i.\langle\tilde{x}_i\rangle\rhd\tilde{n}_i}{\longrightarrow} E_i \Longrightarrow E'$$

where $\tilde{x} = \tilde{x}_1 \ldots \tilde{x}_i$ and $\tilde{n} = \tilde{n}_1 \ldots \tilde{n}_i$, otherwise we write $E \stackrel{\alpha}{\Longrightarrow} E'$ whenever $E \Longrightarrow\stackrel{\alpha}{\longrightarrow}\Longrightarrow E'$. Also, for any $\phi \equiv \nu\tilde{n}.\{\tilde{t}/\tilde{x}\}$ with $fv(\tilde{t}) = \emptyset$ we write $E \circ \phi$ for $\nu\tilde{n}.E\{\tilde{t}/\tilde{x}\}$ assuming $\tilde{n} \cap fn(E) = \emptyset$.

Definition 10. *A symmetric relation* $\mathcal{R}$ *on* $\mathbf{N}_c$ *is a* weak bisimulation *if* $E\ \mathcal{R}\ F$ *implies* $E \sim_s F$ *and*

$$\textit{if } E \longrightarrow E' \textit{ then } \exists F'.\ F \Longrightarrow F' \textit{ and } E'\ \mathcal{R}\ F'$$

$$\textit{if } E \stackrel{\nu x.\overline{n}\langle x\rangle @l}{\longrightarrow} E' \textit{ then } \exists F'.\ F \stackrel{\nu x.\overline{n}\langle x\rangle @l}{\Longrightarrow} F' \textit{ and } E'\ \mathcal{R}\ F'$$

$$\textit{if } E \stackrel{\nu\tilde{x}.\langle\tilde{x}\rangle\rhd\tilde{n}}{\longrightarrow} E' \textit{ then } \exists F'.\ F \stackrel{\nu\tilde{x}.\langle\tilde{x}\rangle\rhd\tilde{n}}{\Longrightarrow} F' \textit{ and } E'\ \mathcal{R}\ F'$$

$$\textit{if } E \stackrel{n(t)@l}{\longrightarrow} E' \textit{ and } fv(t) \subseteq dom_l(E) \textit{ then } \exists F'.\ F \stackrel{n(t)@l}{\Longrightarrow} F' \textit{ and } E'\ \mathcal{R}\ F'$$

$$\textit{if } E \stackrel{(t)\lhd l}{\longrightarrow} E' \textit{ and } fv(t) \subseteq dom_l(E) \textit{ then } \exists F'.\ F \stackrel{(t)\lhd l}{\Longrightarrow} F' \textit{and} E' \circ \{E\}_l\ \mathcal{R}\ F' \circ \{F\}_l$$

The largest weak bisimulation on $\mathbf{N}_c$, $\approx$, is an equivalence relation.

The first three clauses in Definition 10 are standard. As in [1] the clauses for input require that free variables in the received term are already defined by the receiver. In our case this means that free variables received at a name n at l in E must also be defined at l in E. Likewise, free variables received by broadcast from l must be defined at l in E and these variables are substituted by the frame for location l at E preserving well-formedness.

Theorem 3. $\approx$ *is a congruence.*

Weak bisimulation and weak barbed congruence coincides.

Theorem 4. $\approx\ =\ \cong$.

As usual we may define weak bisimulation up to $\equiv$ and show that whenever $\mathcal{R}$ is a weak bisimulation up to $\equiv$ then $\equiv \mathcal{R} \equiv$ is a weak bisimulation.

Example 9. Let $\mathbf{P}_b$ be the set of extended processes with only broadcast prefixes. Then $\lfloor e\rfloor_l \approx \lfloor e\rfloor_k$ for all $e \in \mathbf{P}_b$ because $\mathcal{R}$ is a weak bisimulation up to $\equiv$ where

$$\mathcal{R} = \{(\nu\tilde{u}.(\lfloor e\rfloor_l \parallel E), \nu\tilde{u}.(\lfloor e\rfloor_k \parallel E)) \mid E \in \mathbf{N}_c, l, k \notin \tilde{u},\ \text{and } e \in \mathbf{P}_b\}$$

Example 10. If $l \notin fn(e)$ then $\nu l.\lfloor e\rfloor_l \approx \lfloor e\rfloor_l$ for all $e \in \mathbf{P}_b$ because $\mathcal{R}$ is a weak bisimulation up to $\equiv$ where

$$\begin{aligned}\mathcal{R} = \{\ &(\nu\tilde{u}l.(\lfloor e\rfloor_l \parallel \{\tilde{n} \mapsto l\} \parallel \{l \mapsto \tilde{m}\}) \parallel E, \nu\tilde{u}.(\lfloor e\rfloor_l \parallel E)))\\ &\mid E \in \mathbf{N}_c, e \in \mathbf{P}_b,\ \text{and } l \notin fn(e)\}\end{aligned}$$

Example 11. $\lfloor !\langle n\rangle.\langle m\rangle\rfloor_l \approx \lfloor !\langle m\rangle.\langle n\rangle\rfloor_k$ because $\mathcal{R}$ is a weak bisimulation up to $\equiv$ where

$$\begin{aligned}\mathcal{R} = \{\ &(\lfloor !\langle n\rangle.\langle m\rangle\rfloor_l \parallel \Pi_{i\in I}\lfloor\langle n\rangle.\langle m\rangle\rfloor_l \parallel \Pi_{j\in J}\lfloor\langle m\rangle\rfloor_l \parallel E, \lfloor !\langle m\rangle.\langle n\rangle\rfloor_k \parallel E),\\ &(\lfloor !\langle n\rangle.\langle m\rangle\rfloor_l \parallel E, \lfloor !\langle m\rangle.\langle n\rangle\rfloor_k \parallel \Pi_{i\in I}\lfloor\langle m\rangle.\langle n\rangle\rfloor_k \parallel \Pi_{j\in J}\lfloor\langle n\rangle\rfloor_k \parallel E)\\ &\mid E \in \mathbf{N}_c \text{ and } I \text{ and } J \text{ are finite index sets}\}\end{aligned}$$

Example 12. In order to prove $E_{k,k'} \cong F$ from Example 8 it is sufficient to show

$$!\nu k.\lfloor r\rfloor_k \approx \lfloor r\rfloor_k \parallel \lfloor r\rfloor_{k'} \tag{3}$$

because $\cong = \approx$ and because $\approx$ is a congruence. Further, from Example 9 and 10 we infer that (3) follows from

$$\lfloor r \rfloor_k \parallel !\lfloor r \rfloor_k \approx \lfloor r \rfloor_k \parallel \lfloor r \rfloor_k \tag{4}$$

because $\lfloor r \rfloor_k \parallel !\lfloor r \rfloor_k \approx !\lfloor r \rfloor_k$. The equivalence (4) in turn can be inferred from

$$\lfloor r \rfloor_k \parallel \lfloor r \rfloor_k \approx \lfloor r \rfloor_k \tag{5}$$

because then $\mathcal{R} = \{(E \parallel !\lfloor r \rfloor_k, F \parallel \lfloor r \rfloor_k) \mid E \approx F \parallel \lfloor r \rfloor_k\}$ is a weak bisimulation up to $\equiv$.[7] We leave the formal proof of (5) to the full version of this paper but clearly $\lfloor r \rfloor_k \parallel \lfloor r \rfloor_k$ can do whatever $\lfloor r \rfloor_k$ can, and as long as only one of the relay processes in $\lfloor r \rfloor_k \parallel \lfloor r \rfloor_k$ at a time receives a request then $\lfloor r \rfloor_k$ can do the same. Whenever both relay processes in $\lfloor r \rfloor_k \parallel \lfloor r \rfloor_k$ receive the same request (and hence each may forward it) it may be necessary for $\lfloor r \rfloor_k$ to forward the request also to itself in order to perform multiple forwarding of the same request.

5 Conclusion

In this paper we have discussed the presence of localities in observables for process calculi for mobile and wireless broadcasting systems. We have compared three kinds of barbs: the observability of *i*) output on a name at a given location, *ii*) broadcast of a name at some location, and *iii*) the broadcasting location respectively. For the three strong barbed congruences induced by each of these barbs we showed that they all coincide, however in the weak case the induced barbed congruence by the latter kind of barbs is strictly contained in the barbed congruences induced by the two former that coincide.

Our discussion has been carried out in the setting of a process calculus, $bA\pi$, that is a conservative extension of the Applied π-calculus.[8] We consider $bA\pi$ a contribution of its own and to our knowledge it is the first calculus for mobile and wireless local broadcasting systems that allows for reasoning about an unbounded number of network nodes. Through examples we have demonstrated the applicability of $bA\pi$ and given evidence to the weak reduction congruence, $\cong$, where the locality of a broadcasting node is not observable. Finally, we have proven the bisimulation equivalence, $\approx$, to be a *sound* and *complete* co-inductive characterization of $\cong$.

Several further developments of $bA\pi$ lay forward. For instance it would be obvious to investigate automation of the bisimulation equivalence striving for a symbolic semantics along the lines of [4].

References

1. Abadi, M., Fournet, C.: Mobile vales, new names, and secure communication. In: Symposium on Principles of Programming Languages, pp. 104–115. ACM, New York (2001)

7 Observe that whenever $\lfloor r \rfloor_k \stackrel{(t)\triangleleft l'}{\longrightarrow} \lfloor r_0 \rfloor_k$ for some t, l', and r_0 then $\lfloor r_0 \rfloor_k \approx \equiv \lfloor r_1 \parallel r \rfloor_k$ for some r_1.

8 An Applied π-process p can be translated to $\lfloor p \rfloor_l$ for some fixed l in $bA\pi$.

2. Cardelli, L., Gordon, A.D.: Mobile ambients. In: Nivat, M. (ed.) FOSSACS 1998. LNCS, vol. 1378, p. 140. Springer, Heidelberg (1998)
3. De Nicola, R., Gorla, D., Pugliese, R.: Basic observables for a calculus for global computing. Information and Computation 205(10), 1491–1525 (2007)
4. Delaune, S., Kremer, S., Ryan, M.: Symbolic bisimulation for the applied pi calculus. In: Arvind, V., Prasad, S. (eds.) FSTTCS 2007. LNCS, vol. 4855, pp. 133–145. Springer, Heidelberg (2007)
5. Godskesen, J.C.: A calculus for mobile ad hoc networks. In: Murphy, A.L., Vitek, J. (eds.) COORDINATION 2007. LNCS, vol. 4467, pp. 132–150. Springer, Heidelberg (2007)
6. Godskesen, J.C., Nanz, S.: Mobility models and behavioural equivalence for wireless networks. In: Field, J., Vasconcelos, V.T. (eds.) COORDINATION 2009. LNCS, vol. 5521, pp. 106–122. Springer, Heidelberg (2009)
7. Merro, M.: An observational theory for mobile ad hoc networks. Electron. Notes Theor. Comput. Sci. 173, 275–293 (2007)
8. Merro, M., Sibilio, E.: A timed calculus for wireless systems. In: Sirjani, M. (ed.) FSEN 2009. LNCS, vol. 5961, pp. 228–243. Springer, Heidelberg (2010)
9. Mezzetti, N., Sangiorgi, D.: Towards a calculus for wireless systems. Electr. Notes Theor. Comput. Sci. 158, 331–353 (2006)
10. Milner, R.: Functions as processes. In: Paterson, M. (ed.) ICALP 1990. LNCS, vol. 443, pp. 167–180. Springer, Heidelberg (1990)
11. Milner, R.: Communicating and Mobile Systems: The π-Calculus. Cambridge University Press, Cambridge (May 1999)
12. Milner, R., Sangiorgi, D.: Barbed bisimulation. In: Kuich, W. (ed.) ICALP 1992. LNCS, vol. 623, pp. 685–695. Springer, Heidelberg (1992)
13. Nanz, S., Hankin, C.: A framework for security analysis of mobile wireless networks. Theoretical Computer Science 367(1), 203–227 (2006)
14. Riely, J., Hennessy, M.: A typed language for distributed mobile processes (extended abstract). In: POPL 1998, pp. 378–390 (1998)
15. Sangiorgi, D., Walker, D.: The π-calculus: A Theory of Mobile Processes. Cambridge University Press, Cambridge (2001)
16. Singh, A., Ramakrishnan, C.R., Smolka, S.A.: A process calculus for mobile ad hoc networks. In: Lea, D., Zavattaro, G. (eds.) COORDINATION 2008. LNCS, vol. 5052, pp. 296–314. Springer, Heidelberg (2008)

Behavioural Contracts with Request-Response Operations*

Lucia Acciai[1], Michele Boreale[1], and Gianluigi Zavattaro[2]

[1] Dipartimento di Sistemi e Informatica, Università di Firenze, Italy
[2] Dipartimento di Scienze dell'Informazione, Università di Bologna, Italy

Abstract. In the context of service-oriented computing, behavioural contracts are abstract descriptions of the message-passing behaviour of services. They can be used to check properties of service compositions such as, for instance, client-service compliance. Previous formal models for contracts consider unidirectional *send* and *receive* operations. In this paper, we present two models for contracts with bidirectional *request-response* operations, in the presence of unboundedly many instances of both clients and servers. The first model takes inspiration from the abstract service interface language WSCL, the second one is inspired by Abstract WS-BPEL. We prove that client-service compliance is decidable in the former while it is undecidable in the latter, thus showing an interesting expressiveness gap between the modeling of *request-response* operations in WSCL and in Abstract WS-BPEL.

1 Introduction

One interesting aspect of Service Oriented Computing (SOC) and Web Services technology is the need to describe in rigorous terms not only the format of the messages exchanged among interacting parties, but also their protocol of interaction. This specific aspect is clearly described in the Introduction of the Web Service Conversation Language (WSCL) specification [25], one of the proposals of the World Wide Web Consortium (W3C) for the description of the so-called Web Services *abstract interfaces*:

> Defining which XML documents are expected by a Web service or are sent back as a response is not enough. It is also necessary to define the order in which these documents need to be exchanged; in other words, a business level conversation needs to be specified. By specifying the conversations supported by a Web service —by defining the documents to be exchanged and the order in which they may be exchanged— the external visible behavior of a Web service, its abstract interface, is defined.

The abstract interface of services can be used in several ways. For instance, one could check the *compliance* between a client and a service, that is, a guarantee for the client that the interaction with the service will in any case be completed successfully. One could also check, during the service discovery phase, the *conformance* of a concrete

* The third author is partly supported by the EU integrated projects HATS and is member of the joint INRIA/University of Bologna Research Team FOCUS.

D. Clarke and G. Agha (Eds.): COORDINATION 2010, LNCS 6116, pp. 16–30, 2010.

service to a given abstract interface by verifying whether the service implements at least the expected functionalities and does not require more.

Formal models are called for to devise rigorous forms of reasoning and verification techniques for services and abstract interfaces. To this aim, theories of *behavioural contracts* based on CCS-like process calculi [19] have been thoroughly investigated [3,6,7,8,10,11,12]. However, these models lack of expressiveness in at least one respect: they cannot be employed to describe bidirectional *request-response* interactions, in contexts where several instances of the client and of the service may be running at the same time. This situation, on the other hand, is commonly found in practice-oriented contract languages, like the abstract service interface language WSCL [25] and Abstract WS-BPEL [22].

In this paper, we begin a formal investigation of contract languages of the type described above, that is allowing bidirectional request-response interaction, taking place between instances of services and clients. We present two contract languages that, for simplicity, include only the request-response pattern[1]: the first language is inspired by WSCL while the second one by Abstract WS-BPEL. In both these models, the request-response interaction pattern is decomposed into sequences of more fundamental *send-receive-reply* steps: the client first *sends* its invocation, then the service *receives* such an invocation, and finally the service sends its *reply* message back to the client. The binding between the requesting and the responding sides (instances) of the original operation is maintained by employing naming mechanisms similar to those found in the π-calculus [20]. In both models, we do not put any restriction on the number of client or service instances that can be generated at runtime, so that the resulting systems are in general infinite-state. The difference between the two models is that in the former it is not possible to describe intermediary activities of the service between the receive and the reply steps, while this is possible in the latter. In fact, WSCL models the service behaviour in request-response interactions with a unique *ReceiveSend* primitive indicating the kind of incoming and outgoing messages. On the contrary, in Abstract WS-BPEL there exist two distinct primitives that allows one to model independently the *receive* and the *reply* steps.

We define client-service compliance on the basis of the *must testing* relation of [13]: a client and a service are compliant if any sequence of interactions between them leads the client to a successful state. Our main results show that client-service compliance is decidable in the WSCL-inspired model, while it is undecidable in the Abstract WS-BPEL model: this points to an interesting expressiveness gap between the two approches for the modeling of the request-response interaction pattern. In the former case, the decidability proof is based on a translation of contracts into Petri nets. This translation is not precise, in the sense that intermediate steps of the request-response interaction are not represented in the Petri net. However, the translation is complete, in the sense that it preserves and reflects the existence of unsuccessful computations, which is enough to reduce the original compliance problem to a decidable problem in Petri nets. This yields a practical compliance-checking procedure, obtained by adaptation of the classical Karp-Miller coverability tree construction [18].

---

[1] As discussed in Section 4, the languages that we propose are sufficiently expressive to model also the one-way communication pattern.

The rest of the paper is organized as follows. In Section 2 we present the two formal models and the definition of client-service compliance. Sections 3 contains the Petri nets semantics and the proof of decidability of client-service compliance for the WSCL model. Section 4 reports on undecidability for the Abstract WS-BPEL model. We draw some conclusions and discuss further work in Section 5.

2 Behavioural Contracts with Request-Response

We presuppose a denumerable set of contract variables *Var* ranged over by X, Y, $\cdots$, a denumerable set of names *Names* ranged over by a, b, r, s, $\cdots$. We use I, J, $\cdots$ to denote a sets of indexes.

Definition 1 (WSCL Contracts). *The syntax of* WSCL contracts *is defined by the following grammar*

$$G ::= \mathsf{invoke}(a, \sum_{i\in I} b_i.C_i) \mid \mathsf{recreply}(a, \sum_{i\in I} b_i.C_i) \mid \surd \qquad C ::= \sum_{i\in I} G_i \mid C|C \mid X \mid recX.C$$

where recX._ is a binder for the contract variable X. We assume guarded recursion, *that is, given a contract recX.C all the free occurrences of X in C are inside a guarded contract G.*

A client contract *is a contract C containing at least one occurrence of the guarded* success *contract* $\surd$*, while a* service contract *is a contract not containing* $\surd$.

G is used to denote guarded contracts, ready to perform either an invoke or a receive on a request-response operation a: the selection of the continuation C_i depends on the actual reply message b_i. A set of guarded contracts G_i can be combined into a choice $\sum_{i\in I} G_i$; if the index set I is empty, we denote this term by $\mathbf{0}$. Contracts can be composed in parallel. Note that infinite-state contract systems can be defined using recursion (see example later in the section). In the following, we use $Names(C)$ to denote the set of names occurring in C. Before presenting the semantics of WSCL contracts, we introduce BPEL contracts as well.

Definition 2 (BPEL Contracts). *BPEL contracts are defined like* WSCL *contracts in Definition 1, with the only difference that guarded contracts are as follows*

$$G \;::=\; \mathsf{invoke}(a, \sum_{i\in I} b_i.C_i) \;\mid\; \mathsf{receive}(a).C \;\mid\; \mathsf{reply}(a,b).C \;\mid\; \surd.$$

We now define the operational semantics of both models. We start by observing that the WSCL contract $\mathsf{recreply}(a, \sum_{i\in I} b_i.C_i)$ is the same as the BPEL contract $\mathsf{receive}(a).\sum_{i\in I}(\mathsf{reply}(a,b_i).C_i)$ that receives an invocation on the operation a and then replies with one of the messages b_i. We shall rely on a run-time syntax of contracts, which is obtained from the original one by extending the clause for guarded contract, thus $G \;::=\; \cdots \mid \overline{a}\langle r\rangle \mid r\langle b\rangle.C$. Both terms $\overline{a}\langle r\rangle$ and $r\langle b\rangle.C$ are used to represent an emitted and pending invocation of a request-response operation a: the name r represents a (fresh) channel r that will be used by the invoked operation to send the reply message back to the invoker. From now onwards we will call (WSCL) contract any term that could be obtained from this run-time syntax. In the following, we let $Labels \triangleq \{\tau, \surd\} \cup \{a\langle b\rangle, \overline{a}\langle b\rangle, (a) \mid a, b \in Names\}$.

Definition 3 (Operational semantics). *The operational semantics of a contract is given by the minimal labeled transition system, with labels taken from the set Labels, satisfying the following axiom and rules ($a,b,r \in Names$)*

$$\frac{G_l \stackrel{\alpha}{\longrightarrow} G'_l \quad l \in I}{\sum_{i\in I} G_i \stackrel{\alpha}{\longrightarrow} G'_l} \qquad \frac{r \notin Names(\sum_{i\in I} b_i.C_i)}{\mathsf{invoke}(a, \sum_{i\in I} b_i.C_i) \stackrel{(r)}{\longrightarrow} \sum_{i\in I}(r\langle b_i\rangle.C_i) \mid \overline{a}\langle r\rangle}$$

$$\mathsf{receive}(a).C \stackrel{a\langle r\rangle}{\longrightarrow} C\{^r/_a\} \qquad \mathsf{reply}(r,b).C \stackrel{\tau}{\longrightarrow} C \mid \overline{r}\langle b\rangle \qquad \surd \stackrel{\surd}{\longrightarrow} \mathbf{0}$$

$$\overline{r}\langle b\rangle \stackrel{\overline{r}\langle b\rangle}{\longrightarrow} \mathbf{0} \qquad r\langle b\rangle.C \stackrel{r\langle b\rangle}{\longrightarrow} C \qquad \frac{P \stackrel{\overline{a}\langle b\rangle}{\longrightarrow} P' \quad Q \stackrel{a\langle b\rangle}{\longrightarrow} Q'}{P|Q \stackrel{\tau}{\longrightarrow} P'|Q'}$$

$$\frac{P \stackrel{\alpha}{\longrightarrow} P' \quad \alpha \neq (r)}{P|Q \stackrel{\alpha}{\longrightarrow} P'|Q} \qquad \frac{P \stackrel{(r)}{\longrightarrow} P' \quad r \notin Names(Q)}{P|Q \stackrel{\alpha}{\longrightarrow} P'|Q} \qquad \frac{C\{^{recX.C}/_X\} \stackrel{\alpha}{\longrightarrow} C'}{recX.C \stackrel{\alpha}{\longrightarrow} C'}$$

plus the symmetric version of the three rules for parallel composition. With $C\{^r/_a\}$ we denote the term obtained from C by replacing with r every occurrence of a not inside a receive$(a).D$, *while $C\{^{recX.C}/_X\}$ denotes the usual substitution of free contract variables with the corresponding definition.*

In the following, we use $C \stackrel{\alpha}{\longrightarrow}$ to say that there is some C' such that $C \stackrel{\alpha}{\longrightarrow} C'$. Moreover, we use $C \longrightarrow C'$ to denote reductions, i.e. transitions that C can perform also when it is in isolation. Namely, $C \longrightarrow C'$ if $C \stackrel{\tau}{\longrightarrow} C'$ or $C \stackrel{(r)}{\longrightarrow} C'$ for some r.

We now formalize the notion of client-service compliance resorting to *must-testing* [13]. Intuitively, a client C is *compliant* with a service contract S if all the computations of the system $C|S$ lead to the client's success. Other notions of compliance have been put forward in the literature [6,7,8]; we have chosen this one because of its technical and conceptual simplicity (see e.g. [10]).

Definition 4 (Client-Service compliance). *Given a contract D, a* computation *is a sequence of reduction steps $D_1 \longrightarrow D_2 \longrightarrow \cdots \longrightarrow D_n \longrightarrow \cdots$. It is a* maximal computation *if it is infinite or it ends in a state D_n such that D_n has no outgoing reductions.*

A client contract C is compliant *with a service contract S if for every maximal computation $C|S \longrightarrow D_1 \longrightarrow \cdots \longrightarrow D_l \longrightarrow \cdots$ there exists k such that $D_k \stackrel{\surd}{\longrightarrow}$.*

Example 1 (An impatient client and a latecomer service). This example shows that even very simple WSCL scenarios could result in infinite-state systems. Consider a client C that asks the box office service S for some tickets and then waits for them by listening on *offerTicket*. Our client is impatient: at any time, it can decide to stop waiting and issue a new request. This behaviour can be described in WSCL as follows

$$C \triangleq recX.(\mathsf{invoke}(requireTicket, ok.X) + \mathsf{recreply}(offerTicket, ok.\surd))$$

Consider the box office service S, defined below, that is always ready to receive a *requireTicket* invocation and immediately responds by notifying (performing a call-back) on *offerTicket*.

$$S \triangleq recX.\mathsf{recreply}(requireTicket, ok.(\mathsf{invoke}(offerTicket,ok)|X))$$

It is easy to see that, in case invoke(*offerTicket*, $\cdots$) on the service side and recreply(*offerTicket*, $\cdots$) on the client side never synchronize, $C|S$ generates an infinite-state system where each state is characterized by an arbitrary number of invoke(*offerTicket*, $\cdots$). This infinite computation, moreover, does not traverse states in which the client can perform its $\surd$ action, thus C is not compliant with S according to Definition 4.[2]

3 Decidability of Client-Service Compliance for WSCL Contracts

We translate WSCL contract systems into place/transitions Petri nets [23], an infinite-state model in which several reachability problems are decidable (see, e.g., [15] for a review of decidable problems for finite Petri nets). The translation into Petri nets does not faithfully reproduce the operational semantics of contracts. In particular, in finite Petri nets it is not possible to represent the unbounded number of names dynamically created in contract systems to bind the reply messages to the corresponding invocations. The Petri net semantics that we present models bi-directional request-response interactions as a unique event, thus merging together the four distinct events in the operational semantics of contracts: the emission and the reception of the invocation, and the emission and the reception of the reply. We will prove that this alternative modeling preserves client-service compliance because in WSCL the invoker and the invoked contracts do not interact with other contracts during the request-response.

Another difference is that the Petri net semantics can be easily modified so that when the client contract enters in a successful state, i.e. a state with an outgoing transition $\surd$, the corresponding Petri net enters a particular successful state and blocks its execution. This way, a client contract is compliant with a service contract if and only if in the corresponding Petri net all computations are finite and finish in a *successful* state. As we will show, this last property is verifiable for finite Petri nets using the so-called *coverability* tree [18].

3.1 A Petri Net Semantics for WSCL Contracts

We first recall the definition of Petri nets. For any set S, we let $\mathcal{M}_{fin}(S)$ be the set of the finite multisets (*markings*) over S.

Definition 5 (Petri net). *A Petri net is a pair $N = (S,T)$, where S is the set of* places *and $T \subseteq \mathcal{M}_{fin}(S) \times \mathcal{M}_{fin}(S)$ is the set of* transitions. *A transition (c,p) is written $c \Rightarrow p$. A transition $c \Rightarrow p$ is* enabled *at a marking m if $c \subseteq m$. The* execution *of the transition produces the marking $m' = (m \setminus c) \oplus p$ (where $\setminus$ and $\oplus$ are the multiset difference and union operators). This is written as $m[\rangle m'$. A* dead marking *is a marking in which no transition is enabled. A* marked *Petri net is a triple $N(m_0) = (S,T,m_0)$, where (S,T) is a Petri net and m_0 is the* initial marking. *A computation in $N(m_0)$ leading to the marking m is a sequence $m_0[\rangle m_1[\rangle m_2 \cdots m_n[\rangle m$.*

[2] Other definitions of compliance, see e.g. [6], resort to should-testing [24] instead of must-testing: according to these alternative definitions C and S turn out to be compliant due to the fairness assumption characterizing the should-testing approach.

Note that in $c \Rightarrow p$, the marking c represents the tokens to be "consumed", while the marking p represents the tokens to be "produced". The Petri net semantics that we present for WSCL contracts decomposes contract terms into multisets of terms, that represents sequential contracts at different stages of invocation. We introduce the decomposition function in Definition 7. Instrumental to this definition is the set $\mathrm{Pl}(C)$, for C a WSCL contract, defined below.

Definition 6 ($\mathrm{Pl}(C)$)**.** *For any contract C, let $C^{(k)}$ denote the term obtained by performing k unfolding of recursive definitions in C. Let k be the minimal s.t. in $C^{(k)}$ every $recX.D$ is guarded by one of the following prefixes: invoke$(\cdot,\cdot)$, receive$(\cdot)$, reply$(\cdot,\cdot)$, $a\langle b\rangle$.* $\mathrm{Pl}(C)$ *is defined as follows:*

$$\mathrm{Pl}(C) \triangleq \{\textstyle\sum_{i\in I} G_i,\ a\!\uparrow\!\sum_{i\in I} b_i.C_i,\ c\!\downarrow\!\sum_{i\in I} b_i.C_i \ :\ \sum_{i\in I} G_i,\ \sum_{i\in I} b_i.C_i \textit{ occur in } C^{(k)}, a,c \in Names(C^{(k)})\}.$$

The function $dec(\cdot)$ transforms a WSCL contract C, as given in Definition 1, into a multiset $m \in \mathrm{Pl}(C)$.

Definition 7 (Decomposition). *The* decomposition $dec(C)$ *of a WSCL contract C, as given in Definition 1, is $dec_C(C)$. The auxiliary function $dec_C(D)$ is defined below by lexicographic induction on the pair (n_1,n_2), where n_1 is the number of unguarded (i.e. not under an invoke$(\cdot,\cdot)$, receive$(\cdot)$, reply$(\cdot,\cdot)$, $a\langle b\rangle$) sub-terms of the form $recX.D'$ in D and n_2 is the syntactic size of D.*

$$dec_C\Big(\sum_{i\in I} r\langle b_i\rangle.D_i\Big) = a\!\uparrow\!\sum_{i\in I} b_i.D_i \quad \textit{if } \overline{a}\langle r\rangle \textit{ occurs in } C$$

$$dec_C\Big(\sum_{i\in I} r\langle b_i\rangle.D_i\Big) = c\!\downarrow\!\sum_{i\in I} b_i.D_i \quad \textit{if } \overline{r}\langle c\rangle \textit{ occurs in } C \textit{ and } c \neq b_i \textit{ for every } i \in I$$

$$dec_C(recX.D) = dec_C(D\{^{recX.D}/_X\}) \qquad dec_C(\overline{a}\langle b\rangle) = \emptyset$$

$$dec_C(D_1|D_2) = dec_C(D_1) \oplus dec_C(D_2) \qquad dec_C(D) = D, \textit{ otherwise}$$

There are three kinds of transitions in the Petri net we are going to define: transitions representing the emission of an invocation, transitions representing (atomically) the reception of the invocation and the emission and reception of the reply, and transitions representing (atomically) the reception of the invocation and the emission of a reply that will never be received by the invoker because it is outside the set of admitted replies. These three cases are taken into account in the definition below.

Definition 8 (Petri net semantics). *Let C be a WSCL contract system as in Definition 1. We define $Net(C)$ as the Petri net (S,T) where:*

- $S = \mathrm{Pl}(C)$;
- $T \subseteq \mathcal{M}_{fin}(S) \times \mathcal{M}_{fin}(S)$ *includes all the transitions that are instances of the transitions schemata in Table 1.*

We define the marked net $Net^{\mathrm{m}}(C)$ *as the marked net (S,T,m_0), where the initial marking is $m_0 = dec(C)$.*

Table 1. Transitions schemata for the Petri net semantics of WSCL contracts

$\{\sum_{i\in I} G_i\} \Rightarrow \{a\uparrow \sum_{j\in J} b_j.C_j\}$	if $G_k = \mathsf{invoke}(a, \sum_{j\in J} b_j.C_j)$ for some $k \in I$
$\{a\uparrow \sum_{j\in J} b_j.C_j, \sum_{i\in I} G_i\} \Rightarrow dec(C_y) \oplus dec(D_z)$	if $\begin{cases} G_k = \mathsf{recreply}(a, \sum_{l\in L} c_l.D_l) \text{ for some } k\in I \text{ and} \\ b_y = c_z \text{ for some } y \in J, z \in L \end{cases}$
$\{a\uparrow \sum_{j\in J} b_j.C_j, \sum_{i\in I} G_i\} \Rightarrow \{c_z\downarrow \sum_{j\in J} b_j.C_j\} \oplus dec(D_z)$	if $\begin{cases} G_k = \mathsf{recreply}(a, \sum_{l\in L} c_l.D_l) \text{ for some } k\in I \text{ and} \\ \text{there exists } z \in L \text{ s.t. } c_z \neq b_j \text{ for every } j \in J \end{cases}$

Example 2. Consider the client C and the service S introduced in Example 1 and let

$$C' \triangleq \mathsf{invoke}(requireTicket, ok.C) + \mathsf{recreply}(offerTicket, ok.\surd)$$
$$S' \triangleq \mathsf{recreply}(requireTicket, ok.(\mathsf{invoke}(offerTicket, ok)|S)).$$

The marked net $Net^{\mathrm{m}}(S|C)$ is depicted on the right. A bunch of unreachable places (like $ok\downarrow ok.\surd$, $ok\uparrow ok.\surd, \ldots$) have been omitted for the sake of clarity.

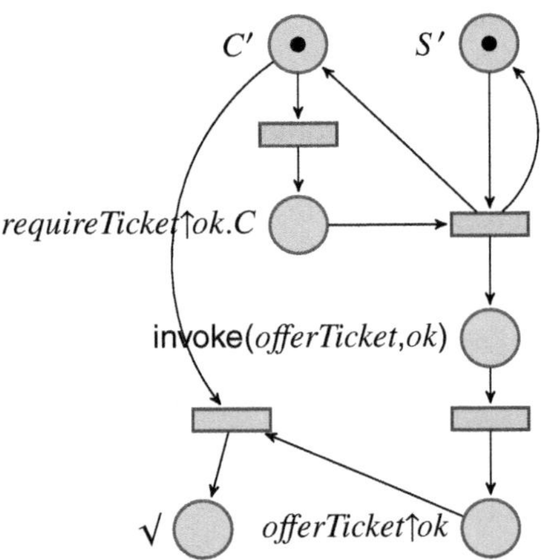

We divide the proof of the correspondence between the operational and the Petri net semantics of WSCL contracts in two parts: we first prove a *soundness* result showing that all Petri net computations reflect computations of contracts, and then a *completeness* result showing that contract computations leading to a state in which there are no uncompleted request-response interactions are reproduced in the Petri net.

In the proof of the soundness result we use the following structural congruence rule to remove empty contracts and in order to rearrange the order of contracts in parallel compositions. Let $\equiv$ be the minimal congruence for contract systems such as

$$C|\mathbf{0} \equiv C \qquad C|D \equiv D|C \qquad C|(D|E) \equiv (C|D)|E \qquad recX.C \equiv C\{^{recX.C}/_X\}$$

As usual, we have that the structural congruence respects the operational semantics.

Proposition 1. *Let C and D be two contract systems such that $C \equiv D$. If $C \xrightarrow{\alpha} C'$, then there exists D' such that $D \xrightarrow{\alpha} D'$ and $C' \equiv D'$.*

The following result establishes a precise relationship between the form of m and the form of C when $dec(C) = m$.

Lemma 1. *Let C be a* WSCL *contract system and suppose dec(C) = m. The following holds:*

1. *if* $m = \{\sum_{i\in I} G_i\} \oplus m'$ *then* $C \equiv \sum_{i\in I} G_i \mid D$*, for some D such that* $dec(D) = m'$*;*
2. *if* $m = \{a\uparrow\sum_{j\in J} b_j.C_j\} \oplus m'$ *then* $C \equiv \sum_{j\in J} r\langle b_j\rangle.C_j \mid \overline{a}\langle r\rangle \mid D$*, for some D and r such that* $r \notin Names(D)$ *and* $dec(D) = m'$*;*
3. *if* $m = \{c\downarrow\sum_{j\in J} b_j.C_j\} \oplus m'$ *then* $c \neq b_j$ *for each* $j \in J$ *and* $C \equiv \sum_{j\in J} r\langle b_j\rangle.C_j \mid \overline{r}\langle c\rangle \mid D$*, for some D and r such that* $r \notin Names(D)$ *and* $dec(D) = m'$*.*

Proposition 2. *Let C be a* WSCL *contract. Consider the Petri net* $Net(C) = (S,T)$ *and a marking m of Net(C). We have that m is dead if and only if D has no outgoing reductions, for every D such that dec(D) = m.*

In order to prove that the Petri net semantics preserves client-service compliance, we need to introduce the notion of *success* marking. A *success* marking m contain at least one token in a place corresponding to a successful client state, formally, $m(\sum_{i\in I} G_i) > 0$ for some contract $\sum_{i\in I} G_i$ such that $G_k = \surd$, for some $k \in I$.

We are now ready to prove the *soundness* result.

Theorem 1 (Soundness). *Let C be a* WSCL *contract. Consider the Petri net* $Net(C) = (S,T)$ *and let m be a marking of Net(C). If* $m[\rangle m'$ *then for each D such that dec(D) = m there exists a computation* $D \triangleq D_0 \longrightarrow D_1 \longrightarrow \cdots \longrightarrow D_l$*, with* $dec(D_l) = m'$*. Moreover, if m is not a success marking then there exists no* $j \in \{0,\cdots,l-1\}$ *such that* $D_j \xrightarrow{\surd}$*.*

Proof: The proof proceeds by case analysis on the three possible kinds of transition.

1. If $m[\rangle m'$ by applying the first kind of transition then $m = \{\sum_{j\in J} G_j\} \oplus m''$, with $G_k = \mathsf{invoke}(a, \sum_{i\in I} b_i.C_i)$ for a $k \in J$. Moreover, $m' = \{a\uparrow\sum_{i\in I} b_i.C_i\} \oplus m''$.
   By Lemma 1, $D \equiv \sum_{j\in J} G_j \mid C' \longrightarrow \overline{a}\langle r\rangle \mid \sum_{i\in I} r\langle b_i\rangle.C_i \mid C' \triangleq D'$ and $dec(D')=m'$.
2. If $m[\rangle m'$ by applying the second kind of transition then $m = \{a\uparrow\sum_{j\in J} b_j.C_j, \sum_{i\in I} G_i\} \oplus m''$, with $G_k = \mathsf{recreply}(a, \sum_{l\in L} c_l.D_l)$, for some $k \in J$, and $b_y = c_z$ for some $y \in J$ and $z \in L$. By Lemma 1, if $dec(D) = m$ then $D \equiv \overline{a}\langle r\rangle \mid \sum_{j\in J} r\langle b_j\rangle.C_j \mid \sum_{i\in I} G_i \mid C'$, for any C' such that $dec(C') = m''$. Therefore, by $G_k = \mathsf{recreply}(a, \sum_{l\in L} c_l.D_l)$:
$$\begin{aligned} D &\longrightarrow \textstyle\sum_{j\in J} r\langle b_j\rangle.C_j \mid \sum_{l\in L} \mathsf{reply}(r,c_l).D_l \mid C' \\ &\longrightarrow \textstyle\sum_{j\in J} r\langle b_j\rangle.C_j \mid \overline{r}\langle c_z\rangle \mid D_z \mid C' \\ &\longrightarrow C_y \mid D_z \mid C' \quad \triangleq D' \end{aligned}$$
   with $dec(D') = dec(C_y) \oplus dec(D_z) \oplus m'' = m'$. Notice that each intermediate state in the reduction sequence from D to D' cannot perform a successful transition.
3. If $m[\rangle m'$ by applying the third kind of transition then $m = \{a\uparrow\sum_{j\in J} b_j.C_j, \sum_{i\in I} G_i\} \oplus m''$, with $G_k = \mathsf{recreply}(a, \sum_{l\in L} c_l.D_l)$, for some $k \in J$, and there is $z \in L$ such that $b_y \neq c_z$ for each $y \in J$. By Lemma 1, if $dec(D) = m$ then $D \equiv \overline{a}\langle r\rangle \mid \sum_{j\in J} r\langle b_j\rangle.C_j \mid \sum_{i\in I} G_i \mid C'$, for any C' such that $dec(C') = m''$. Therefore, by $G_k = \mathsf{recreply}(a, \sum_{l\in L} c_l.D_l)$, we get
$$\begin{aligned} D &\longrightarrow \textstyle\sum_{j\in J} r\langle b_j\rangle.C_j \mid \sum_{l\in L} \mathsf{reply}(r,c_l).D_l \mid C' \\ &\longrightarrow \textstyle\sum_{j\in J} r\langle b_j\rangle.C_j \mid \overline{r}\langle c_z\rangle \mid D_z \mid C' \triangleq D' \end{aligned}$$

with $dec(D') = \{c_z \downarrow \sum_{j \in J} b_j.C_j\} \oplus dec(D_z) \oplus m'' = m'$. Notice that each intermediate state in the reduction sequence from D to D' cannot perform a successful transition. □

Definition 9 (Stable contracts). *A* WSCL *contract C (in the run-time syntax) is said* stable *if it contains neither unguarded* reply(*r*,*b*) *actions nor pairs of matching terms of the form $\overline{r}\langle b \rangle$ and $r\langle b \rangle$.*

Notice that any *initial* WSCL contract (according to the syntax of Definition 1) is stable.

Lemma 2. *Suppose C is stable and that $C \longrightarrow C'$. Then, there exists C'' stable such that $C' \longrightarrow C_1 \longrightarrow \cdots \longrightarrow C_l \longrightarrow C''$ $(l \geq 0)$ and for each $i = 1, \cdots, l$ it holds that $C_i \stackrel{\surd}{\not\longrightarrow}$.*

Proof: If C' is not stable then it may contain both unguarded reply actions and pairs of the form $\overline{r}\langle b \rangle$ and $r\langle b \rangle$. According to the operational semantics of contracts, all unguarded reply actions and $\overline{r}\langle b \rangle$ and $r\langle b \rangle$ can be consumed performing a sequence of reductions. Therefore a stable contract C'' can be reached from C' without traversing any state capable of $\stackrel{\surd}{\longrightarrow}$. □

We now move to the completeness part.

Theorem 2 (Completeness). *Let C be a* WSCL *contract and let D be a contract reachable from C through the computation $C = C_0 \longrightarrow C_1 \longrightarrow \cdots \longrightarrow C_n = D$. If D is stable then there exists a computation $m_0[\rangle m_1[\rangle m_2 \cdots m_{l-1}[\rangle m_l$ of the marked Petri net $Net^{\mathrm{m}}(C)$ such that $dec(D) = m_l$. Moreover, if there exists no $k \in \{0, \cdots, n\}$ such that $C_k \stackrel{\surd}{\longrightarrow}$ then for every $j \in \{0, \cdots, l\}$ we have that m_j is not a success marking.*

Proof: The proof is by induction on the length n of the derivation $C = C_0 \longrightarrow C_1 \longrightarrow \cdots \longrightarrow C_n = D$. The base case ($n = 0$) is trivial. In the inductive case there are two possible cases: C_{n-1} is stable or it is not stable. In the first case the proof is straightforward. In the second case, there are two possible scenarios to be considered: either C_n contains an unguarded action reply(r,b) term, or it contains a pair of matching terms $\overline{r}\langle b \rangle$ and $r\langle b \rangle$. We consider the first of these two cases, the second one can be treated similarly.

Let C_{n-1} be a non stable contract containing an unguarded action reply(r,b). This action cannot appear unguarded in the initial contract C: let C_j, with $j > 0$, be the first contract traversed during the computation of C in which the action reply(r,b) appears unguarded. Hence, we have that $C_{j-1} \longrightarrow C_j$ consists of the execution of a receive action. We now consider a different computation from C to D obtained by rearranging the order of the steps in the considered computation $C = C_0 \longrightarrow C_1 \longrightarrow \cdots \longrightarrow C_n = D$. Namely, let $C = C_0 \longrightarrow C_1 \longrightarrow \cdots \longrightarrow C_{l-1} \longrightarrow C'_l \longrightarrow \cdots \longrightarrow C'_{n-2} \longrightarrow C_{n-1} \longrightarrow C_n = D$ be the computation obtained by delaying as much as possible the execution of the receive action generating the unguarded action reply(r,b). In the new computation, this action appears for the first time in the contract C_{n-1}. Moreover, C'_{n-2} must be a stable contract otherwise C_n is not stable. Hence, we can straightforwardly prove the thesis by applying the inductive hypothesis to the shorter computation $C = C_0 \longrightarrow C_1 \longrightarrow \cdots \longrightarrow C_{l-1} \longrightarrow C'_l \longrightarrow \cdots \longrightarrow C'_{n-2}$ leading to the stable contract C'_{n-2}. □

As a simple corollary of the last two theorems, we have that client-service compliance is preserved by the Petri net semantics.

Corollary 1 (Compliance preservation). *Let C and S be respectively a* WSCL *client and service contract, as in Definition 1. We have that C is compliant with S if and only if in the marked Petri net $Net^{\mathrm{m}}(C|S)$ all the maximal computations traverse at least one success marking.*

Proof: ($\Rightarrow$). Trivial by Theorem 1.

($\Leftarrow$). Suppose that in $Net^{\mathrm{m}}(C|S)$ all the maximal computations traverse at least one success marking and suppose by contradiction that C is not compliant with S. This means that there is a maximal computation from $C|S$ that does not traverse a state D such that $D \xrightarrow{\surd}$. This computation can either end in a state D' with no outgoing reductions or can be infinite.

In the first case we get a contradiction by Theorem 2. Indeed there would be a maximal computation from $Net^{\mathrm{m}}(C|S)$ traversing only non-success markings.

Consider the second case. From the infinite sequence of reductions, we can build an infinite set of maximal computations of arbitrary length, starting from C and ending in a stable state (Lemma 2) without traversing a succes state. By Theorem 2, for each of these maximal computations there exists a corresponding maximal computation in the net $Net^{\mathrm{m}}(S|C)$ that does not traverse a success marking. We can arrange these computations so as to form a tree where m' is a child of m iff $m[\rangle m'$: this is an infinite, but finite-branching, tree. By König's lemma, in $Net^{\mathrm{m}}(S|C)$ there exists then an infinite computation that does not traverse a success marking and we get a contradiction. □

3.2 Verifying Client-Service Compliance Using the Petri Net Semantics

In the light of Corollary 1, checking whether C is compliant with S reduces to verifying if all the maximal computations in $Net^{\mathrm{m}}(C|S)$ traverse at least one success marking. In order to verify this property, we proceed as follows:

- we first modify the net semantics in such a way that the net computations block if they reach a success markings;
- we define a (terminating) algorithm for checking whether in the modified Petri net all the maximal computations are finite and end in a success marking.

The modified Petri net semantics simply adds one place that initially contains one token. All transitions consume such a token, and reproduce it only if they do not introduce tokens in success places, i.e., places $\sum_{i\in I} G_i$ such that $G_k = \surd$ for some $k \in I$

Definition 10 (Modified Petri net semantics). *Let C be a* WSCL *contract and $Net(C) = (S,T)$ the corresponding Petri net as defined in Definition 8. We define $ModNet(C)$ as the Petri net (S',T') where:*

- *$S' = S \cup \{run\}$, where run is an additional place;*
- *for each transition $c \Rightarrow p \in T$, then T' contains a transition that consumes the multiset $c \uplus \{run\}$ and produces either p, if p contains a place $\sum_{i\in I} G_i$ such that $G_k = \surd$ for some $k \in I$, or $p \uplus \{run\}$, otherwise.*

The marked modified net *$ModNet^{\mathrm{m}}(C)$ is defined as the net $ModNet(C)$ with initial marking m_0 where*

$$m_0 = \begin{cases} dec(C) \uplus \{run\} & \text{if } dec(C) \text{ is not a success marking} \\ dec(C) & \text{otherwise.} \end{cases}$$

We now state an important relationship between $Net^{\mathrm{m}}(C)$ and $ModNet^{\mathrm{m}}(C)$. It can be proved by relying on the definition of modified net.

Proposition 3. *Let C be a* WSCL *contract, $Net^{\mathrm{m}}(C)$ (resp. $ModNet^{\mathrm{m}}(C)$) the corresponding Petri net (resp. modified Petri net). We have that all the maximal computations of $Net^{\mathrm{m}}(C)$ traverse at least one success marking if and only if in $ModNet^{\mathrm{m}}(C)$ all the maximal computations are finite and end in a success marking.*

We now present the algorithm for checking whether in a Petri net all the maximal computations are finite and end in a success marking. In the algorithm and in the proof, we utilize the following preorder over multisets on Places(C): $m \leq m'$ iff for each p, $m(p) \leq m'(p)$. It can be shown that this preorder is a *well-quasi-order*, that is, in any infinite sequence of multisets there is a pair of multisets m and m' such that $m \leq m'$ (see e.g. [16]).

Theorem 3. *Let C be a* WSCL *contract as in Definition 1 and let $ModNet^{\mathrm{m}}(C) = (S,T,m_0)$ be the corresponding modified Petri net. The algorithm described in Table 2 always terminates. Moreover, it returns TRUE iff all the maximal computations in $ModNet^{\mathrm{m}}(C)$ are finite and end in a success marking.*

4 Undecidability of Client-Service Compliance for BPEL Contracts

We now move to the proof that client-service compliance is undecidable for BPEL contracts. The proof is by reduction from the termination problem in Random Access Machines (RAMs) [21], a well known Turing powerful formalism based on registers containing nonnegative natural numbers. The registers are used by a program, that is a set of indexed instructions I_i which are of two possible kinds:

- $i : Inc(r_j)$ that increments the register r_j and then moves to the execution of the instruction with index $i+1$ and
- $i : DecJump(r_j, s)$ that attempts to decrement the register r_j; if the register does not hold 0 then the register is actually decremented and the next instruction is the one with index $i+1$, otherwise the next instruction is the one with index s.

Without loss of generality we assume that given a program $I_1, \cdots, I_n$, it starts by executing I_1 with all the registers empty (i.e. all registers contain 0) and terminates trying to perform the first undefined instruction I_{n+1}.

In order to simplify the notation, in this section we introduce a notation corresponding to standard input and output prefixes of CCS [19][3]. Namely, we model simple synchronization as a request-response interaction in which there is only one possible reply message. Assuming that this unique reply message is ok (with $ok \in Names$ not necessarily fresh), we introduce the following notation:

$$\overline{a}.P \;=\; \mathsf{invoke}(a,ok.P) \qquad\qquad a.P \;=\; \mathsf{receive}(a).\mathsf{reply}(a,ok).P$$

[3] The input and output prefixes correspond also to the representation of the one-way interaction pattern in contract languages such as those in [10,6,11].

Table 2. An algorithm for checking the coverability of success markings

1. If the initial marking m_0 is not a success marking then label it as the root and tag it "new".
2. While "new" markings exist do the following:
   (a) Select a "new" marking m.
   (b) If no transitions are enabled at m, return FALSE.
   (c) While there exist enabled transitions at m, do the following for each of them:
      i. Obtain a marking m' that results from firing the transition.
      ii. If on the path from the root to m there exists a marking m'' such that $m'(p) \geq m''(p)$ for each place p then return FALSE.
      iii. If m' is not a success marking introduce m' as a node, draw an arc from m to m', and tag m' "new".
   (d) Remove the tag "new" from the marking m.
3. Return TRUE.

In order to reduce RAM termination to client-service compliance, we define a client contract that simulates the execution of a RAM program, and a service contract that represent the registers, such that the client contract reaches the success $\surd$ if and only if the RAM program terminates.

Given a RAM program $I_1, \cdots, I_n$, we consider the client contract C as follows

$$\prod_{i \in \{1,\cdots,n\}} [\![I_i]\!] \mid inst_{n+1}.\surd$$

$$[\![I_i]\!] = \begin{cases} recX.(inst_i.\overline{inc_j}.ack.(\overline{inst_{i+1}} \mid X)) & \text{if } I_i = (i : Inc(r_j)) \\ recX.(inst_i.\overline{dec_j}.(ack.(\overline{inst_{i+1}} \mid X) + zero.(\overline{inst_s} \mid X))) & \text{if } I_i = (i : DecJump(r_j, s)) \end{cases}$$

An increment instruction $Inc(r_j)$ is modeled by a recursive contract that invokes the operation inc_j, waits for an acknowledgement on ack, and then invokes the service corresponding to the subsequent instruction. On the contrary, a decrement instruction $DecJump(r_j, s)$ invokes the operation dec_j and then waits on two possible operations: ack or $zero$. In the first case the service corresponding to the subsequent instruction with index $i+1$ is invoked, while in the second case the service corresponding to the target of the jump is invoked instead.

We now move to the modeling of the registers. Each register r_j is represented by a contract representing the initially empty register in parallel with a service responsible to model every unit subsequently added to the register

$$\begin{aligned} [\![r_j]\!] = {} & recX.(dec_j.\overline{zero}.X + inc_j.\overline{unit_j}.\mathsf{invoke}(u_j, ok.\overline{ack}.X)) \mid \\ & recX.unit_j.(X \mid \mathsf{receive}(u_j).\overline{ack}.recY.(dec_j.\mathsf{reply}(u_j, ok) + \\ & \qquad inc_j.\overline{unit_j}.\mathsf{invoke}(u_j, ok.\overline{ack}.Y))). \end{aligned}$$

The idea of the encoding is to model numbers with chains of nested request-response interactions. When a register is incremented, a new instance of a contract is spawn invoking the operation $unit_j$, and a request-response interaction is opened between the previous instance and the new one. In this way, the previous instance blocks waiting for the reply. When an active instance receives a request for decrement, it terminates by closing the request-response interaction with its previous instance, which is then reactivated. The contract that is initially active represents the empty register because it replies to decrement requests by performing an invocation on the *zero* operation.

We extend structural congruence $\equiv$, introduced in Section 3, to $\equiv_{ren}$ to admit the injective renaming of the operation name

$$C \equiv_{ren} D \text{ if there exists an injective renaming } \sigma \text{ such that } C\sigma \equiv D$$

Clearly, injective renaming preserves the operational semantics.

Proposition 4. *Let C and D be two contract systems such that $C \equiv_{ren} D$. If $C \xrightarrow{\alpha} C'$, then there exists D' and a label α' obtained by renaming the operation names in α such that $D \xrightarrow{\alpha'} D'$ and $C' \equiv_{ren} D'$.*

Now, we introduce $\{\!\!\{r_j, c\}\!\!\}$ that we use to denote the modeling of the register r_j when it holds the value c. Namely, $\{\!\!\{r_j, 0\}\!\!\} = [\![r_j]\!]$, while if $c > 0$ then

$$\{\!\!\{r_j,c\}\!\!\} = \begin{cases} b_0\langle ok\rangle.\overline{ack}.recX.(dec_j.\overline{zero}.X + inc_j.\overline{unit_j}.\mathsf{invoke}(u_j,ok.\overline{ack}.X)) \mid \\ b_1\langle ok\rangle.\overline{ack}.recY.(dec_j.\overline{b_0}\langle ok\rangle + inc_j.\overline{unit_j}.\mathsf{invoke}(u_j,ok.\overline{ack}.Y)) \mid \\ \cdots \mid \\ recY.(dec_j.\overline{b_{c-1}}\langle ok\rangle + inc_j.\overline{unit_j}.\mathsf{invoke}(u_j,ok.\overline{ack}.Y)) \mid \\ recX.unit_j.(X \mid \mathsf{receive}(u_j).\overline{ack}.recY.(dec_j.\mathsf{reply}(u_j,ok) + \\ \qquad\qquad inc_j.\overline{unit_j}.\mathsf{invoke}(u_j,ok.\overline{ack}.Y))) \end{cases}$$

In the following theorem, stating the correctness of our encoding, we use the following notation: $(i, c_1, \cdots, c_m)$ to denote the state of a RAM in which the next instruction to be executed is I_i and the registers $r_1, \cdots, r_m$ respectively contain the values $c_1, \cdots, c_m$, and $(i, c_1, \cdots, c_m) \rightarrow_R (i', c'_1, \cdots, c'_m)$ to denote the change of the state of the RAM R due to the execution of the instruction I_i.

Theorem 4. *Consider a RAM R with instructions $I_1, \cdots, I_n$ and registers $r_1, \cdots, r_m$. Consider also a state $(i, c_1, \cdots, c_m)$ of the RAM R and a corresponding contract C such that $C \equiv_{ren} \overline{inst_i}|[\![I_1]\!]|\cdots|[\![I_n]\!]|inst_{n+1}.\surd|\{\!\!\{r_1,c_1\}\!\!\}|\cdots|\{\!\!\{r_m,c_m\}\!\!\}$. We have that*

- *either the RAM computation has terminated, thus $i = n+1$*
- *or $(i, c_1, \cdots, c_m) \rightarrow_R (i', c'_1, \cdots, c'_m)$ and there exists $l > 0$ such that $C \longrightarrow C_1 \longrightarrow \cdots \longrightarrow C_l$ and*
  - *$C_l \equiv_{ren} \overline{inst_{i'}}|[\![I_1]\!]|\cdots|[\![I_n]\!]|inst_{n+1}.\surd|\{\!\!\{r_1,c'_1\}\!\!\}|\cdots|\{\!\!\{r_m,c'_m\}\!\!\}$*
  - *for each k $(1 \le k < l)$: $C_k \stackrel{\surd}{\not\longrightarrow}$*

As a corollary we get that client-service compliance is undecidable.

Corollary 2. *Consider a RAM R with instructions $I_1, \cdots, I_n$ and registers $r_1, \cdots, r_m$. Consider the client contract $C = \overline{inst_1}|[\![I_1]\!]|\cdots|[\![I_n]\!]|inst_{n+1}.\surd$ and the service contract $S = \{\!\!\{r_1,0\}\!\!\}|\cdots|\{\!\!\{r_m,0\}\!\!\}$. We have that C is compliant with S if and only if R terminates.*

5 Conclusion

We have presented two models of contracts with bidirectional request-response interaction, studied a notion of compliance based on must testing and established an expressiveness gap between the two models showing that compliance is decidable in the first one while it is undecidable in the second one.

As for future work, we plan to investigate the (un)decidability of other definitions of compliance present in the literature. In fact, the must-testing approach —the one that we consider in this paper— has been adopted in early works about service compliance (see e.g. [10]). More recent papers consider more sophisticated notions. For instance, the should-testing approach [24] adopted, e.g., in [9] admits also infinite computations if in every reached state there is always at least one path leading to a success state. Other approaches require the successful completion of all the services in the system (see e.g. [8,12]) in order to deal with multiparty service compositions in which there is no distinction between a client and a service.

Moreover, it would be interesting to apply the techniques presented in this paper to more sophisticated orchestration languages, like the recently proposed calculi based on the notion of *session* [5,4]. For instance, in [2], a type system is presented ensuring a client progress property – basically, absence of deadlock – in a calculus where interaction between (instances of) the client and the service is tightly controlled via session channels. It would be interesting to check to what extent the decidability techniques presented here apply to this notion of progress. Also connections with *behavioural types* [17,1] deserve attention. In the setting of process calculi, these types are meant to provide behavioural abstractions that are in general more tractable than the original process. In the present paper, the translation function of WSCL contracts into Petri nets can be seen too as a form of behavioural abstraction. In the case of tightly controlled interactions (sessions) [2], BPP processes, a proper subset of Petri nets featuring no synchronization [14], have been seen to be sufficient as abstractions. For general pi-processes, full CCS with restriction is in general needed. One would like to undertake a systematic study of how communication capabilities in the original language (unconstrained interaction vs. sessions vs. request-response vs....) trades off with tractability of the behavioural abstractions (CCS vs. BPP vs. Petri nets vs. ...).

References

1. Acciai, L., Boreale, M.: Spatial and behavioural Types in the pi-calculus. In: van Breugel, F., Chechik, M. (eds.) CONCUR 2008. LNCS, vol. 5201, pp. 372–386. Springer, Heidelberg (2008); Full version to appear in Inf. and Comp.
2. Acciai, L., Boreale, M.: A Type System for Client Progress in a Service-Oriented Calculus. In: Degano, P., De Nicola, R., Meseguer, J. (eds.) Montanari Festschrift. LNCS, vol. 5065, pp. 642–658. Springer, Heidelberg (2008)
3. Boreale, M., Bravetti, M.: Advanced mechanisms for service composition, query and discovery, LNCS. Springer, Heidelberg (to appear 2010)
4. Boreale, M., Bruni, R., De Nicola, R., Loreti, M.: Sessions and Pipelines for Structured Service Programming. In: Barthe, G., de Boer, F.S. (eds.) FMOODS 2008. LNCS, vol. 5051, pp. 19–38. Springer, Heidelberg (2008)

5. Boreale, M., Bruni, R., Caires, L., De Nicola, R., Lanese, I., Loreti, M., Martins, F., Montanari, U., Ravara, A., Sangiorgi, D., Vasconcelos, V.T., Zavattaro, G.: SCC: A Service Centered Calculus. In: Bravetti, M., Núñez, M., Zavattaro, G. (eds.) WS-FM 2006. LNCS, vol. 4184, pp. 38–57. Springer, Heidelberg (2006)
6. Bravetti, M., Zavattaro, G.: Contract based Multi-party Service Composition. In: Arbab, F., Sirjani, M. (eds.) FSEN 2007. LNCS, vol. 4767, pp. 207–222. Springer, Heidelberg (2007)
7. Bravetti, M., Zavattaro, G.: A Theory for Strong Service Compliance. In: Murphy, A.L., Vitek, J. (eds.) COORDINATION 2007. LNCS, vol. 4467, pp. 96–112. Springer, Heidelberg (2007)
8. Bravetti, M., Zavattaro, G.: Towards a Unifying Theory for Choreography Conformance and Contract Compliance. In: Lumpe, M., Vanderperren, W. (eds.) SC 2007. LNCS, vol. 4829, pp. 34–50. Springer, Heidelberg (2007)
9. Bravetti, M., Zavattaro, G.: Contract-Based Discovery and Composition of Web Services. In: Bernardo, M., Padovani, L., Zavattaro, G. (eds.) SFM 2009. LNCS, vol. 5569, pp. 261–295. Springer, Heidelberg (2009)
10. Carpineti, S., Castagna, G., Laneve, C., Padovani, L.: A Formal Account of Contracts for Web Services. In: Bravetti, M., Núñez, M., Zavattaro, G. (eds.) WS-FM 2006. LNCS, vol. 4184, pp. 148–162. Springer, Heidelberg (2006)
11. Castagna, G., Gesbert, N., Padovani, L.: A Theory of Contracts for Web Services. In: Proc. of POPL 2008, pp. 261–272. ACM Press, New York (2008)
12. Castagna, G., Padovani, L.: Contracts for Mobile Processes. In: Bravetti, M., Zavattaro, G. (eds.) CONCUR 2009. LNCS, vol. 5710, pp. 211–228. Springer, Heidelberg (2009)
13. De Nicola, R., Hennessy, M.: Testing equivalences for processes. Theor. Comput. Sci. 34, 83–133 (1984)
14. Esparza, J.: Petri Nets, Commutative Context-Free Grammars, and Basic Parallel Processes. Fundam. Inform. 31(1), 13–25 (1997)
15. Esparza, J., Nielsen, M.: Decidability Issues for Petri Nets - a survey. Bulletin of the EATCS 52, 244–262 (1994)
16. Finkel, A., Schnoebelen, P.: Well-Structured Transition Systems Everywhere! Theor. Comput. Sci. 256(1-2), 63–92 (2001)
17. Igarashi, A., Kobayashi, N.: A generic type system for the Pi-calculus. Theor. Comput. Sci. 311(1-3), 121–163 (2004)
18. Karp, R.M., Miller, R.E.: Parallel Program Schemata. Journal of Computer and System Sciences 3, 147–195 (1969)
19. Milner, R.: Communication and concurrency. Prentice-Hall, Englewood Cliffs (1989)
20. Milner, R., Parrow, J., Walker, D.: A calculus of mobile processes. Information and Computation 100, 1–40 (1992)
21. Minsky, M.L.: Computation: finite and infinite machines. Prentice-Hall, Englewood Cliffs (1967)
22. OASIS: Web Services Business Process Execution Language (WSBPEL) (2007), Standard available at, `www.oasis-open.org/committees/wsbpel`
23. Petri, C.A.: Kommunikation mit Automaten. Ph. D. Thesis. University of Bonn (1962)
24. Rensink, A., Vogler, W.: Fair testing. Inf. Comput. 205(2), 125–198 (2007)
25. W3C: Web Services Conversation Language (WSCL) (2002), Standard proposal, `http://www.w3.org/TR/wscl10`

NOW: A Workflow Language for Orchestration in Nomadic Networks

Eline Philips*, Ragnhild Van Der Straeten, and Viviane Jonckers

Software Languages Lab, Vrije Universiteit Brussel, Belgium
{ephilips,rvdstrae}@vub.ac.be, vejoncke@soft.vub.ac.be

Abstract. Existing workflow languages for nomadic or mobile ad hoc networks do not offer adequate support for dealing with the volatile connections inherent to these environments. Services residing on mobile devices are exposed to (temporary) network failures, which should be considered the rule rather than the exception. This paper proposes a nomadic workflow language built on top of an ambient-oriented programming language which supports dynamic service discovery and communication primitives resilient to network failures. Our proposed language provides high level workflow abstractions for control flow and supports rich network and service failure detection and handling through compensating actions. Moreover, we introduce a powerful variable binding mechanism which enables dynamic data flow between services in a nomadic environment. By adding this extra layer of abstraction on top of an ambient-oriented programming language, the application programmer is offered a flexible way to develop applications for nomadic networks.

1 Introduction

We are surrounded by all kinds of wireless communication facilities which enable mobile devices to be connected in a mobile ad hoc network. Nomadic networks[1] fill the gap between traditional and mobile ad hoc networks as these nomadic environments consist of both a group of mobile devices and a fixed infrastructure [2]. As these kind of networks are omnipresent (for instance in shopping malls, airports, ...), an abundance of interesting applications can be supported. However, the development of such applications is not straightforward as special properties of the communication with mobile devices, such as connection volatility, have to be considered. These complex distributed applications can be developed by using technologies such as service-oriented computing. The composition of services can be achieved by using the principles of workflow languages. In stable networks, workflow languages are used to model and orchestrate complex applications. The workflow engine is typically centralized and the interactions between the different services are synchronous. Although workflow

* Funded by a doctoral scholarship of the "Institute for the Promotion of Innovation through Science and Technology in Flanders" (IWT Vlaanderen).

[1] Not to be confused with the term *nomadic computing*.

D. Clarke and G. Agha (Eds.): COORDINATION 2010, LNCS 6116, pp. 31–45, 2010.

languages such as (WS)BPEL[9] are suited to orchestrate (web)services, they are not suited for nomadic networks where services are not necessarily known a priori. Furthermore, services in a nomadic network must be dynamically discovered at runtime, since they can be hosted by mobile devices. Moreover, services that become unavailable should not block the execution of an entire workflow. Distributed engines for workflows exist and more recently mobile ad hoc networks [5][8] and nomadic networks [3] are also targeted by the workflow community. However, these workflow languages have almost no support for handling the high volatility of these kinds of networks. For instance, there is no support for the reconnections of services which happen frequently.

In this paper, we introduce a nomadic workflow language NOW which features the basic control flow patterns [4] sufficient for most workflows and dynamic service discovery. These patterns and services can be robustly deployed in a nomadic network and support complex (network) failure handling through compensating actions. Moreover, the language enables passing data between services using a dynamic variable binding mechanism.

This paper is organized as follows: we first introduce a motivating example which specifies the requirements a nomadic workflow language must fulfill. Afterwards, we present AmbientTalk, an ambient-oriented programming language which is developed at the Software Languages Lab and upon which we build our language. In section 4 we present the concepts of control flow, dynamic data passing mechanism and compensating actions before describing the implementation of a concrete workflow pattern. Finally we discuss related work and conclude with our contributions and future work.

2 Motivation

In this section we describe an example scenario which emphasizes requirements that must be supported by a nomadic workflow language. We also introduce a graphical representation delineating the workflow description of this application and afterwards highlight the requirements our workflow language must fulfill.

2.1 Example

Peter lives in Brussels and wants to spend his holidays in New York city. His plane leaves Brussels International Airport at 13:50 and makes a transit at the airport of Frankfurt. Ten minutes before boarding he is still stuck in a traffic jam. At the airport, Peter is announced as a missing passenger and a flight assistant is informed to start looking for him. Peter also receives a reminder on his smart phone. After 10 minutes, the boarding responsible closes the gates and informs Avia Partners (the company that takes care of the luggage) to remove Peter's suitcase from the plane. He also ensures that the airport of Frankfurt is notified of the free seat so a last minute offer from Frankfurt to Newark becomes available. Peter gets notified he can return home and catch another flight later.

This example clearly introduces some of the concepts of a nomadic system. First of all, we can identify different kinds of participants in this scenario: mobile

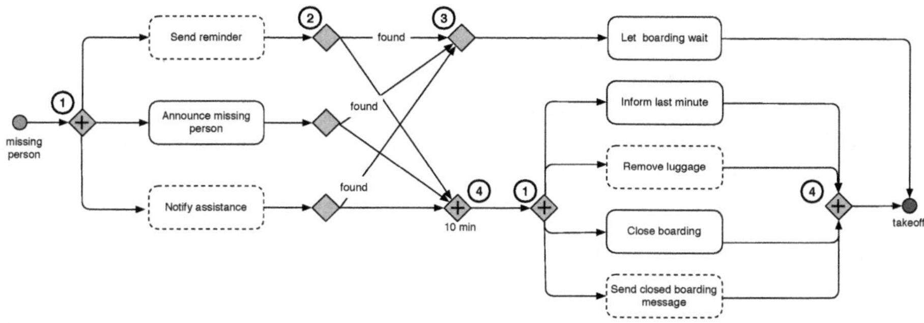

Fig. 1. Workflow description of the motivating example

devices, mobile services and stationary services. Mobile devices represent the visitors and passengers in the airport building whereas mobile services are part of the infrastructure of the airport (for instance flight assistants, guides). The stationary services (like a departure screen or check-in desk) are also part of the infrastructure, but use a more reliable connection.

Figure 1 gives a representation of this example where BPMN notation is used for the patterns involved. The circles in the picture represent *events*: in the beginning of the workflow there's a general event and at the end there's a termination event. Note that the numbered circles are not part of the syntax, they are used later on for pointing to specific elements of the description. Rounded rectangles represent *activities* which are a generic type of work that can be performed by either mobile (dashed line) or stationary services (solid line). The figure also contains several diamonds which depict *gateways* that can merge or split the control flow. There are two different kind of gateways used in this workflow description: the diamond with a + sign represents a logic *and*, whereas the empty one symbolizes a *xor*.

The different control flow patterns [4] which are needed to describe the scenario as a workflow are (labeled in figure 1 with their corresponding numbers):

1. *parallel split*: execution of two or more branches in parallel [4].
2. *exclusive choice*: divergence of a branch into two or more branches, such that the thread of control is passed to one subsequent branch. This branch is chosen based on a selection mechanism [4].
3. *structured discriminator*: convergence of two or more incoming branches into one subsequent branch, such that the thread of control is passed to the subsequent branch the first time an incoming branch is enabled [4].
4. *synchronize*: convergence of two or more branches into one subsequent branch, such that the thread of control is passed to the subsequent branch when all incoming branches have been enabled [4].

2.2 Requirements

As this motivating example shows, a workflow language for nomadic networks must fulfill the following requirements:

1. support two kind of services: stationary and mobile.
2. automatic handling of failures in communication with mobile services (for example transparently rediscover a service of the same type).
3. support basic control flow patterns.
4. detection of failures (such as disconnection and timeout) and ability to specify compensating actions for these detected failures.
5. support data flow such that information can be passed between services.

It is important to note that the description and execution of the workflow resides on the backbone of the nomadic system, whereas the different services are either located on fixed devices or on mobile devices that move around through the environment. By situating the workflow description on the fixed infrastructure, we ensure that the workflow itself cannot disconnect and become unavailable during its execution and thus can serve as a reliable central node for orchestration and failure handling. This is the most important benefit of a nomadic network compared with a mobile ad hoc network.

3 AmbientTalk

In this section, we briefly explain the programming language AmbientTalk [6][7], which we use to build our nomadic workflow language on top of. The *ambient-oriented* programming paradigm [1] is specifically aimed at such applications. We highlight only the important features which we will need for the rest of this paper.

AmbientTalk offers direct support for the different characteristics of the ambient-oriented programming paradigm:

- In a mobile network (mobile ad hoc or nomadic network), objects must be able to discover one another without any infrastructure (such as a shared naming registry). Therefore, AmbientTalk has a *discovery engine* that allows objects to discover one another in a peer-to-peer manner.
- In an mobile network (mobile ad hoc or nomadic network), objects may frequently disconnect and reconnect. Therefore, AmbientTalk provides *fault-tolerant asynchronous message passing* between objects: if a message is sent to a disconnected object, the message is buffered and resent later, when the object reconnects.

3.1 Distributed Programming in AmbientTalk

Listing 1 shows how to create an AmbientTalk object with a method `missingPerson`. This object is exported with the *type tag* `AnnouncementService`, which means that from now on this object can be discovered using this tag.

Listing 1. Implementation of an announcement service in AmbientTalk.

```
deftype AnnouncementService;

def service := object: {
    def missingPerson(person, time) {
        def found := false;
        // Announce missing person
        // If person turns up, change value of "found" variable
        found; // Return the value of found }};
export: service as: AnnouncementService;
```

AmbientTalk uses a classic event-handling style by relying on blocks of code that are triggered by event handlers. Event handlers are (by convention) registered by a call to a function that starts with `when:`. So, when you want to discover an annoucement service and call its method `missingPerson`, you should write the following piece of AmbientTalk code:

```
// When a service classified as AnnouncementService is discovered,
// this object is accessible via "service"
when: AnnouncementService discovered: { |service|
    // Send asynchronous message "missingPerson" to the discovered object
    when: service<-missingPerson("Peter", 10) becomes: { |reply|
        // When a reply is received and it equals true, the person is found
        // and boarding should wait. Otherwise, boarding can be closed
        // and the luggage can be removed }};
```

The syntax `obj<-msg()` denotes an *asynchronous message sent* which immediately returns a *future*, which is a placeholder for the actual return value. Once this return value is computed, the future is said to be *resolved* with this value which "replaces" the future.

As can be seen from the above example, service discovery and replies of remote queries are represented in AmbientTalk as events that trigger the appropriate event handlers. While in this simple example the control flow remains apparent enough to understand, the control flow of large-scale event-driven applications can quickly become puzzling. In the following sections we discuss how to add a layer of abstraction on top of AmbientTalk (which uses messages/events as the level of abstraction) such that the asynchronously executing processes can be orchestrated by means of workflow abstractions.

4 Nomadic Workflow Patterns

This section describes the control flow patterns in our workflow language NOW, the support for data flow and compensating actions.[2] Afterwards, we present the concrete implementation of a pattern, *synchronize*, and show in detail the concepts we introduced.

4.1 Control Flow Patterns

In this section we describe the implementation of workflow patterns of van der Aalst [4] on top of AmbientTalk (requirement 3 in section 2.2). The current

[2] The implementation is available at `http://code.google.com/p/ambienttalk/`

implementation consists of 13 control flow patterns: sequence, parallel split, synchronize, exclusive choice, simple merge, multi choice, structured synchronizing merge, multi merge, structured discriminator, structured partial join, multiple instances without synchronization, static partial join for multiple instances and implicit termination. We first show the syntax of these patterns and afterwards describe how these patterns can be composed.

Syntax of Patterns in NOW. The grammar of control flow patterns in NOW is shown in Backus-Naur form in listing 2.

Listing 2. Abstract grammar of the control flow patterns.

```
<components>          := <component> | <component> "," <components>
<component>           := <activity> | <pattern>
<ATblock>             := "{ |" <parameter list> "|" <body> "}"
<condition action>    := "[" <ATblock> "," <component> "]"
<condition actions>   := <condition action> | <condition action> "," <condition actions>
<syncpattern>         := <synchronize> | <structured synchronizing merge> |
                         <simple merge> | <multi merge> | <structured partial join>
<pattern>             := <syncpattern> | <sequence> | <parallel split> | <multi choice> |
                         <exclusive choice> | <structured discriminator> | <connection> |
                         <multiple instances without synchronization> |
                         <static partial join for multiple instances>
<sequence>            := "Sequence(" <components> ")"
<parallel split >     := " ParallelSplit (" <components> ")"
<synchronize>         := "Synchronize(" <component> ")"
<exclusive choice>    := "ExclusiveChoice(" <condition actions> ")"
<simple merge>        := "SimpleMerge(" component ")"
<multi choice>        := "MultiChoice(" <condition actions> ")"
<multi merge>         := "MultiMerge(" <component> ")"
<connection>          := "Connection(" <syncpattern> ")"
<structured discriminator>          := "StructuredDiscriminator(" <component> ")"
<structured partial join>           := "StructuredPartialJoin (" <component> ")"
<structured synchronizing merge>    := "StructuredSynchronizingMerge(" <component> ")"
<multiple instances without synchronization>   := "MIWithoutSync(" <component> ")"
<static partial join for multiple instances>   := "StPartJoinMI(" <component> ")"
```

Patterns are implemented as AmbientTalk objects which always implement the `init` method (constructor) and `start` method which starts the execution of the workflow.

Composition of Control Flow Patterns. As we can derive from the above syntax, each pattern consists of several components which can be either activities or patterns themselves. Executing an activity results in the invocation of a service which is implemented as a distributed object in AmbientTalk. Recapitulate from section 3.1, this invocation is executed by sending an asynchronous message to the distributed object. The result of this invocation is a future, and the installed event handlers are triggered when this future is resolved. In order to compose patterns in a flexible way, patterns must be oblivious to the difference between their components, which can either be activities or patterns themselves. Hence, the execution of a pattern must also return a future so the necessary event handlers can be installed to wait for its termination. Consider two sequence patterns in the code snippet below. The execution of the first sequence, `seq1.start()`, returns a future which resolves when `seq1` is fully executed. The second line in the code shows a simple example of a composition, namely a sequence `seq1` which is part of a bigger sequence `seq2`.

```
def seq1 := Sequence( serviceB.b(), serviceC.c() );
def seq2 := Sequence( serviceA.a(), seq1, serviceD.d() );
```

However, composition of patterns becomes more complex when patterns like synchronization are involved. In listing 2 we see that some patterns like synchronization or simple merge are considered `syncpatterns`. This distinction is made because patterns with multiple incoming branches need to be composed using `connections`.

Consider such an example in figure 2 where first a parallel split (marked with circle 1) diverges the control flow into three outgoing branches, and afterwards a synchronization (marked with circle 2) converges these branches.

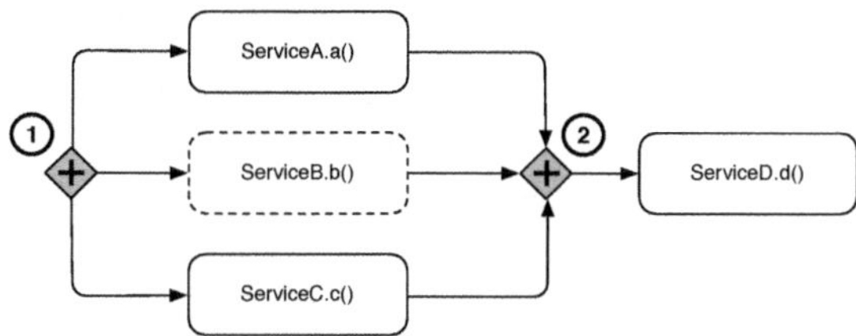

Fig. 2. Control flow patterns: parallel split followed by synchronize

This example can be written in NOW as shown in listing 3. The first line in the code defines a synchronization pattern which must invoke a method `d()` on `ServiceD` after all its incoming branches are enabled.

Listing 3. Parallel split follwed by synchronize.

```
def sync := Synchronize( serviceD.d() );
def parSplit := ParallelSplit( [ serviceA.a(), sync ],
                               [ serviceB.b(), sync ],
                               [ serviceC.c(), sync ] );
```

By introducing a `Connection`, a link is made between the outgoing branches of the parallel split and the incoming ones of the synchronization. This connection pattern informs the synchronize `sync` of how many incoming branches it has. The parallel split which is defined on the second line is initialized with three tables (one for each branch), containing the components of that branch. Recall from figure 1 that it is not required that each outgoing branch of a parallel split is connected to the same synchronization pattern (thus the need to introduce connections). The first branch of the parallel split in the example (on line 2 in the code snippet) is converted into `Sequence.new( serviceA.a(), Connection.new(sync) )`.

4.2 Data Flow in Nomadic Networks

In this section we describe a data flow mechanism which enables us to pass information between (possibly non-consecutive) activities (requirement 5 in section 2.2). We present the mechanism used for parameter bindings when invoking a service (execute an activity). The formal syntax for an activity is given below:

Listing 4. Abstract grammar of activities.

```
<activity>   := <service> “.” <method> “(” <arguments> “)” |
                <service> “.” <method> “(” <arguments> “)@output(” <parameters> “)”
<parameters> := <parameter> | <parameter> “,” <parameters> | <void>
<arguments>  := <expression> | <expression> “,” <arguments> | <void>
<parameter>  := <symbol>
```

When an activity is executed, its formal parameters are bound to their values which are looked up in the *environment* before the method is invoked at the service. The environment is a simple dictionary associating variables with values. The invoked method at the service can return a number of result values which are bound to the correct variables using the `@output` syntax, as shown in the example below. Returning a wrong number of values or parameters which are not found in the current environment results in an error.

```
TemperatureService.getTemp(location)@output(currentTemp)
```

Instead of using a simple global or static environment for our workflow language, we developed a dynamic system where the environment flows through the workflow graph and is dynamically adapted. See figure 3 for an example of how the environment gets updated in each step of a sequence pattern. It is important to note, that each workflow instance has its own environment satisfying the *case data* pattern of Russell [18] where data is specific to a certain process instance.

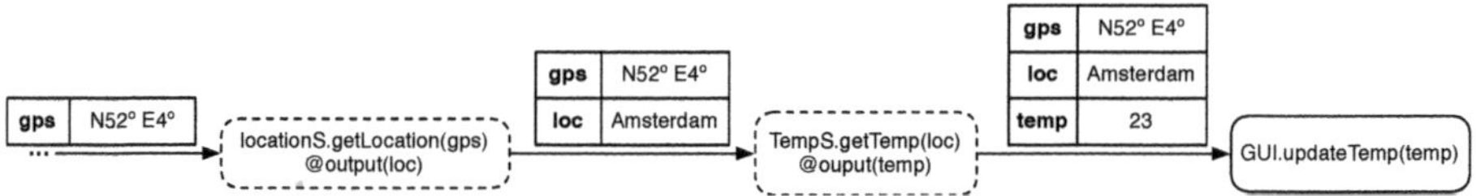

Fig. 3. Passing Environments in a Sequence

By introducing this dynamic data flow by means of passing an environment, we satisfy the key requirements of a data flow mechanism in a workflow model. As Sadiq et al stated [17], a data flow model must have the ability to:

- manage both the input and output data of activities
- ensure that data produced by one activities is available for other activities that need this data
- ensure consistent flow of data between activities

The first requirements is fulfilled, since the formal parameters are looked up in the environment before starting the execution of an activity. After this execution, the output values are associated with their variable name and added to this dictionary. By introducing the notion of an environment which flows through the entire workflow we ensure that the second requirement is also satisfied. The last requirement is also fulfilled because of the same reason.

This mechanism can be thought of as dynamic scoping but with special semantics for patterns such as a synchronization, which merges multiple incoming branches, as is illustrated in figure 4. If a part of a workflow can be reached by more than one single path, it is possible that the environments are completely different.

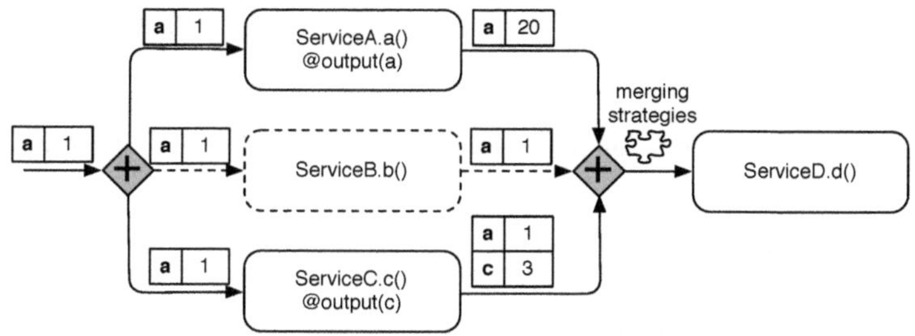

Fig. 4. Environments: Merging Strategies for Synchronization Patterns

As is shown in the example, when a `parallel split` is encountered, the environment is conceptually duplicated for each branch. Further adaptations of the environment are local to each branch. However, when a synchronization point is reached, the environments from all incoming branches need to be merged. We identified several possible merging strategies which might be useful in certain cases:

- Prioritize one of the incoming branches when resolving conflicts.
- Pick the environment of one incoming branch and ignore the others.
- Conflicts are merged into a table containing the different values (with or without duplicates)
- Remember the "scope" from before merging and restore it (not always possible)
- Employ a user provided function to resolve conflicts.

The dynamic approach we propose, provides a much richer and powerful mechanism than a globally shared environment or simple flow of output values (from one activity to the next) could achieve. As in our approach the data flow is attached to the control flow, it is possible that local changes to the environment can occur in different branches. The dynamic mechanism we offer eases the burden of manually arranging static scopes of variables. Our approach combines several advantages of the data patterns that are proposed by Russell et al [18].

4.3 Compensating Actions

In a dynamically changing environment, the challenge is to make the high heterogeneity of services co-operate and deal with their transient and permanent failures. AmbientTalk already has built-in support to handle both disconnections and reconnections with the event handlers `when: disconnected:` and `when: reconnected:`. In NOW, we provide a *Failure* pattern which wraps a part of a workflow and imposes compensating actions and strategies (requirement 4 in section 2.2). Since we want to handle (transient) failures at different levels of granularity the failure pattern can be used on one specific service or wrap an entire subworkflow. Examples of events we capture in a failure pattern are disconnections, reconnection, timeouts and possibly service exceptions/errors. Possible compensating actions include retrying, rediscovery (potentially yielding a different service), skipping, waiting or executing a specific subworkflow to handle the event.

Listing 5. Abstract grammar of the Failure pattern and the possible compensations.

```
<component>          := <activity> | <pattern>
<failure pattern>    := “Failure(” <component> “,” <compensations> “)”
<compensations>      := <failure event> | <failure event> “,” <compensations>
<failure event>      := <disconnection> | <timeout> | <exception> | <service not found>
<timeout>            := “Timeout(” <duration> “,” <compensation> “)”
<disconnection>      := “Disconnect(” <compensation> “)”
<exception>          := “Exception(” <symbol> “,” <compensation> “)”
<service not found>  := “ServiceNotFound(” <compensation> “)”
<compensation>       := <retry> | <rediscover> | <skip> | <restart> | <wait> | <component>
<retry>              := “Retry(” <times> “,” <compensation> “)”
<rediscover>         := “Rediscover(” <times> “,” <compensation> “)”
<skip>               := “Skip()”
<restart>            := “Restart(” <times> “)”
<wait>               := “Wait(” <time> “,” <compensation> “)”
```

Listing 5 shows the abstract grammar of the *failure* pattern and its possible compensating actions. A compensating action is not always successful, hence we provide a way of limiting the amount of times each compensating action is tried. When a compensating action has reached its maximum attempts, another (more drastic) one can be provided. We provide four kind of failures (disconnection, timeout, service not found and exception from a service) for which six different forms of compensating actions (retry, rediscover, skip, restart, wait, or execute a new subworkflow) are possible. The compensating action *retry* tries to invoke the failed activity (not the entire wrapped workflow) a number of times. *Rediscover* will (re)discover a service with the same type tag (which might result in invoking the same service when only one is available). The *skip* compensation just skips the entire wrapped part of the workflow whereas *restart* restarts it. We also provide a *wait* compensating action, which will simply wait for a specified time. Another possible compensating action can be the execution of a subworkflow (activity or a pattern).

Russell [11] already classified workflow exception patterns that are used by workflow systems. The exceptions he discusses are for instance *constraint violation*, *deadline expiracy* and *work item failure*. The failures we support are specific to the (temporary) network failures that can arise, although some basic exception handling can be achieved by using the `exception` failure.

Consider the example of updating a user interface with the current temperature at a user's location. As is depicted in figure 5, the location and weather service or both mobile. The default compensating actions for mobile services are to retry sending the message on a timeout, and to rediscover on a disconnection. By using the failure pattern (drawn as a dashed rectangle wrapping part of a workflow), we can specify other compensating actions and override this default behavior, as is shown for the weather service in figure 5.

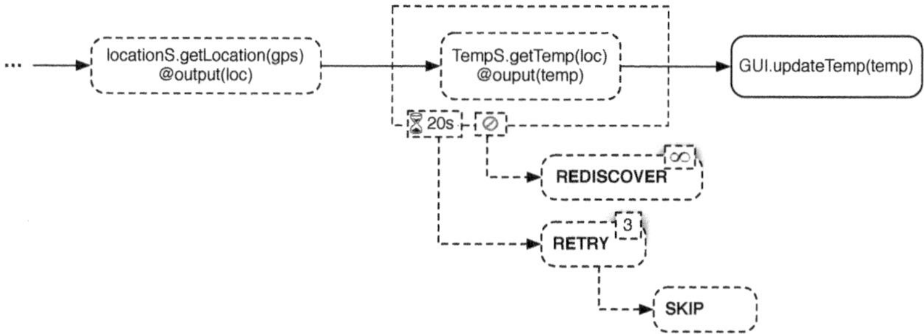

Fig. 5. Compensating actions specified for different kind of failures

When the weather service activity has a timeout (after 20 seconds no reply is returned) we try to resend the message three times. If this is still unsucessfull we move on to the next compensating action which just skips this activity (so no temperature gets displayed on the screen). In case of a disconnection however, a service of the same type must be (re)discovered. The implementation of this workflow can be seen in the following code snippet. Note that since there are no arguments specified, the compensating action of a disconnect event (`Rediscover` on line 4) is tried indefinitely.

```
def seq := Sequence( locationS.getLocation('gps)@output('loc),
                     Failure( TempS.getTemp('loc),
                              [ Timeout(20, Retry(3, Skip())),
                                Disconnect(Rediscover()) ]),
                     GUI.updateTemp('loc, 'temp) );
```

Failure patterns can be nested so different strategies can be formulated on different levels of granularity. A whole workflow can be surrounded by a failure pattern specifying "After a disconnection, wait 20 seconds and try to rediscover" and smaller parts of this workflow can be wrapped with more specific failure patterns, which possibly overrides (shadows) the behavior imposed by the first failure pattern.

As the first requirement in section 2.2 stated, a workflow language targetting nomadic networks must support both stationary and mobile services. Mobile services are wrapped with a `Failure` pattern such that these services are rediscovered in case of a disconnection. Transparently compensating possible disconnections of mobile services is hence also satisfied (requirement 2).

4.4 Implementation of a Concrete Pattern

As van der Aalst defines, synchronization is a pattern that converges two or more incoming branches into a subsequent one when all incoming branches have been enabled [4]. A synchronize can occur after a pattern, for instance a parallel split, that has split the control flow into several outgoing branches.

Just like every control flow pattern we have implemented, a synchronize is an AmbientTalk object which has an `init` and `start` method. A synchronization is instantiated with a component (`cmp`)that must be executed after each branch is enabled.

Besides a start and init method (which are common by all patterns), a synchronize has a specific method `addSync` and data member `syncTable`. The `addSync` method is called by the connection pattern to notify the synchronization that it must wait for one more branch to be enabled. As a synchronization has to wait for each branch to be enabled, it has to wait for each branch to

```
def Synchronize := object: {
    def started := false;              // check if pattern is already started or not
    def result, resolver;              // [result, resolver] is a future
    def nextComponent;                 // the component to be executed after synchronization
    def newEnv := Environment.new();   // the environment that is passed to nextComponent
    def syncTable := [];               // stores [future, env] tables for each incoming branch

    def init(cmp) {
        nextComponent := cmp;
        [result, resolver] := makeFuture(); };

    def addSync(future) {
        syncTable := syncTable + [ [future, []] ]; };

    def start(env) {
        // only start the component once
        if: !started then: {
            started := true;
            execute(); };
        result; };

    def execute() {
       def envs := [];
       syncTable.each: { |branch| envs := envs + branch[2]; };
       if: (envs.length() == syncTable.length()) then: {
           // all incoming branches have been enabled (futures are resolved)
           // merge the environments using the predefined strategy
           if: (is: nextComponent taggedAs: Activity) then: {
                // find the variable bindings in newEnv
                // invoke service (nextComponent.service) with these variable bindings
                // and possibly bind the output variables
                // and afterwards resolve the future with its reply
                 resolver.resolve(reply); // explicitly resolve the future
             } else: { // Start the component and resolve future with its reply
                 when: nextComponent.start(newEnv) becomes: { |reply|
                     resolver.resolve(reply); // explicitly resolve the future
                 }}}
        } else: { // not every future (of incoming branch) is resolved yet }};
} taggedAs: [SyncPattern];
```

resolve its *future* (explained in section 3.1). So, whenever `addSync` is called, the future of that branch is added to a `syncTable` such that when the synchronization pattern is started, it can iterate over this table and wait for each future to be resolved. Besides saving the futures, the `syncTable` also stores the environment with which the future is resolved.

A synchronize pattern must be started with one parameter, `env`, which is an environment that is passed among activities (as is explained in section 4.2). When the pattern is not yet started (line 23), the `execute` method is called which results in looking up the environments of the resolved futures in the `syncTable`. The if-test on line 17 is necessary, since the *start* method is called by each incoming branch. When the environments of all incoming branches have been stored in the table, they are merged using a specified strategy. Thereafter, the component after synchronization is executed. In case of an activity, the formal parameters of the method are looked up in the environment, and the service is invoked. After its invocation, the output variables are bound to the output values of the service invocation. At last, the future of the synchronize pattern is resolved with the reply of this component. Recall that this is needed to allow composition of patterns (as is explained in section 4.1). When the component is a workflow pattern, the pattern is started (with the merged environment) and afterwards the future of the synchronize is resolved with the received result (lines 42–45).

5 Related Work

Workflow languages targetting web services, like Bite [12] and Mobile Business Processes [16], can only operate on services that are known beforehand by means of a fixed URL. There also exist orchestration languages, like Orc [14] [15] which uses a process calculus to express the coordination of different processes. Chromatic Orc [19] extends this calculus with exception handling by introducing throw and try catch expressions that can both run in parallel and hence do not cause terminations. However, this language assumes s stable network interconnecting the services. Another orchestration language is Reo [13], a glue language that allows orchestration of different heterogeneous, distributed and concurrent software components, however one has to manually manage the disconnection of a component. Hence, these orchestration languages do not (completely) cope with the transient disconnections that are inherent to dynamically changing environments, like a nomadic network. CiAN [5] is a workflow language for mobile ad hoc networks. But, since it has a choreographed architecture, the responsibilities are divided a priori by an allocation algorithm. This approach does not hold in a dynamically changing environment, where services can join and disjoin at any moment in time. Another workflow system, Workpad [3], is designed with nomadic networks in mind, but also assumes that devices are connected upon startup. Open Workflows [8] is a system which targets workflow construction, allocation, and execution for mobile devices in mobile ad hoc networks. This system focusses on the dynamic construction of workflows based upon contextual information, something we do not target.

6 Conclusion and Future Work

In this paper, we have presented the design and implementation of a nomadic workflow language on top of a runtime system that does allow the orchestration of distributed services in a nomadic network, thanks to both a peer-to-peer and dynamic service discovery mechanism and communication primitives resilient to the volatile connections inherent to such networks. NOW provides high level patterns for control flow and mechanisms for detecting and handling both service and network failures which are inherent to a nomadic network. The language also supports a dynamic mechanism for variable bindings such that data can be passed between the services of the nomadic workflow.

We identified a number of key items as future work: First of all, we would like to support *group communication* and the notion of an *entity* such as a passenger in the airport who does not execute a certain task like a service. Group communication is opportune for a dynamically changing environment where the number of communication partners (services or entities) can not be known beforehand and can vary over time. It would also be appropriate to enable *intentional descriptions* of communication partners as the changing network topology complicates extensional reasoning over these partners. The idea is to extend our language with CRIME [10], a logic coordination language we have developed, and enable writing constraints for groups of services (and entities). The addition of these intentional descriptions also gives rise to the need for compensating actions when constraints are violated. Furthermore, support for some more advanced synchronization patterns is opportune because complete synchronization will not always be possible in environments where communication partners can go out of range at any point in time. We want to come up with synchronization patterns for group communication which can succeed for instance when only a certain percentage of communication partners has replied.

Acknowledgements. The authors would like to thank Stijn Verhaegen, Andoni Lombide Carreton, Niels Joncheere and the anonymous reviewers for their comments on earlier drafts of this paper. They have signicantly improved the readability and quality of this paper.

References

1. Dedecker, J., Van Cutsem, T., Mostinckx, S., D'Hondt, T., De Meuter, W.: Ambient-Oriented Programming. In: OOPSLA 2005, p. 3. ACM Press, New York (2005)
2. Mascolo, C., Capra, L., Emmerich, W.: Mobile computing middleware. In: Gregori, E., Anastasi, G., Basagni, S. (eds.) NETWORKING 2002. LNCS, vol. 2497, pp. 20–58. Springer, Heidelberg (2002)
3. Mecella, M., Angelaccio, M., Krek, A., Catarci, T., Buttarazzi, B., Dustdar, S.: Workpad: an adaptive peer-to-peer software infrastructure for supporting collaborative work of human operators in emergency/disaster scenarios. In: CTS 2006 (2006)
4. Russell, N., ter Hofstede, A.H.M., van der Aalst, W.M.P., Mulyar, N.: Workflow control-flow patterns: A revised view. Technical report, BPMcenter.org (2006)

5. Sen, R., Roman, G.C., Gill, C.D.: Cian: A workflow engine for manets. In: Lea, D., Zavattaro, G. (eds.) COORDINATION 2008. LNCS, vol. 5052, pp. 280–295. Springer, Heidelberg (2008)
6. Van Cutsem, T., Mostinckx, S., Gonzalez Boix, E., Dedecker, J., De Meuter, W.: Ambienttalk: object-oriented event-driven programming in mobile ad hoc networks. In: Proceedings of SCCC 2007, pp. 3–12. IEEE Computer Society, Los Alamitos (2007)
7. Van Cutsem, T., Mostinckx, S., De Meuter, W.: Linguistic symbiosis between event loop actors and threads. Computer Languages Systems & Structures 35(1) (2008)
8. Thomas, L., Wilson, J., Roman, G.C., Gill, C.D.: Achieving Coordination through Dynamic Construction of Open Workflows. In: Middleware 2009, pp. 268–287 (2009)
9. Andrews, T., Curbera, F., Dholakia, H., Goland, Y., Klein, J., Leymann, F., Liu, K., Roller, D., Smith, D., Thatte, S., Trickovic, I., Weerawarana, S.: Business Process Execution Language for Web Services (2003)
10. Mostinckx, S., Scholliers, C., Philips, E., Herzeel, C., De Meuter, W.: FactSpaces: Coordination in the Face of Disconnections. In: Murphy, A.L., Vitek, J. (eds.) COORDINATION 2007. LNCS, vol. 4467, pp. 268–285. Springer, Heidelberg (2007)
11. Russell, N., van der Aalst, W., ter Hofstede, A.: Workflow Exception Patterns. In: Dubois, E., Pohl, K. (eds.) CAiSE 2006. LNCS, vol. 4001, pp. 288–302. Springer, Heidelberg (2006)
12. Curbera, F., Duftler, M., Khalaf, R., Lovell, D.: Bite: Workflow composition for the web. In: Krämer, B.J., Lin, K.-J., Narasimhan, P. (eds.) ICSOC 2007. LNCS, vol. 4749, pp. 94–106. Springer, Heidelberg (2007)
13. Arbab, F.: Reo: a channel-based coordination model for component composition. Mathematical Structures in Comp. Sci. 14(3), 329–366 (2004)
14. Kitchin, D., Quark, A., Cook, W., Misra, J.: The orc programming language. In: Lee, D., Lopes, A., Poetzsch-Heffter, A. (eds.) FMOODS 2009. LNCS, vol. 5522, pp. 1–25. Springer, Heidelberg (2009)
15. Cook, W., Patwardhan, S., Misra, J.: Workflow patterns in orc. In: Ciancarini, P., Wiklicky, H. (eds.) COORDINATION 2006. LNCS, vol. 4038, pp. 82–96. Springer, Heidelberg (2006)
16. Pajunen, L., Chande, S.: Developing workflow engine for mobile devices. In: EDOC 2007, p. 279 (2007)
17. Sadiq, S., Orlowska, M., Sadiq, W., Foulger, C.: Data Flow and Validation in Workflow Modelling. In: Proceedings of ADC 2004, pp. 207–214 (2004)
18. Russell, N., ter Hofstede, A.H.M., Edmond, D., van der Aalst, W.M.P.: Workflow Data Patterns: Identification, Representation and Tool Support. In: Delcambre, L.M.L., Kop, C., Mayr, H.C., Mylopoulos, J., Pastor, Ó. (eds.) ER 2005. LNCS, vol. 3716, pp. 353–368. Springer, Heidelberg (2005)
19. Matsuoka, A., Kitchin, D.: A semantics for Exception Handling in Orc (2009), `http://orc.csres.utexas.edu/papers/OrcExceptionSemantics.pdf`

A Calculus for Boxes and Traits in a Java-Like Setting

Lorenzo Bettini[1], Ferruccio Damiani[1], Marco De Luca[1], Kathrin Geilmann[2], and Jan Schäfer[2]

[1] Dipartimento di Informatica, Università di Torino
[2] Department of Computer Science, University of Kaiserslautern

Abstract. The box model is a component model for the object-oriented paradigm, that defines components (the boxes) with clear encapsulation boundaries. Having well-defined boundaries is crucial in component-based software development, because it enables to argue about the interference and interaction between a component and its context. In general, boxes contain several objects and inner boxes, of which some are local to the box and cannot be accessed from other boxes and some can be accessible by other boxes. A trait is a set of methods divorced from any class hierarchy. Traits can be composed together to form classes or other traits. We present a calculus for boxes and traits. Traits are units of fine-grained reuse, whereas boxes can be seen as units of coarse-grained reuse. The calculus is equipped with an ownership type system and allows us to combine coarse- and fine-grained reuse of code by maintaining encapsulation of components.

1 Introduction

In the development of software systems the reuse of code is vital. Most mainstream programming languages are object-oriented, based on the concept of classes. The granularity level of classes is often not appropriate for reuse. Since classes play the primary role of generators of instances, they must provide a complete set of features describing an object. Therefore, classes are often too coarse-grained to provide a minimal set of sensible reusable features [11] and too fine-grained to provide a software fragment that can be deployed independently [26].

Component-based software systems are built by linking components together or by building new components from existing ones. A key issue in component-based development is to have clear encapsulation boundaries for components. Knowing the component's boundaries enables modular analysis and the reuse of components in different program contexts without being bothered by unexpected interference between the component and its context. Typical OOLs do not have a language-level component concept other than single objects. In practice, however, objects often rely on other objects to hold additional state and realize additional behavior, forming implicit components at runtime. The box model [20,19,21] is a component model, which makes these components explicit. It defines components both on a syntactic level (by a set of classes) and as a runtime entity (as a set of objects). Components are instantiated and similar to objects: they have an identity and a local state. A component instance is called a *box*.

D. Clarke and G. Agha (Eds.): COORDINATION 2010, LNCS 6116, pp. 46–60, 2010.

In general, a box may contain several objects and can have nested boxes. To guarantee encapsulation of certain objects of a box an ownership type system [8,6,15,9] is used. It defines two ownership domains [1,24,19] for each box, namely a *local* and a *boundary* domain. Each object of a box and each inner box is located in one of these domains. Objects (and inner boxes) in the local domain are considered to be private to the component and are only accessible by objects of the same box and of inner boxes, whereas objects (boxes) in the boundary domain can be accessed by objects of other boxes. This is called the encapsulation property of the type system. Additionally, the box model defines a restriction to casts: it forbids downcasts to types which are subtypes of the type declared in the interface of a box. The cast restriction and the encapsulation property of the type system together give a clear encapsulation boundary to boxes, therefore it is possible to use boxes as a *unit for coarse-grained reuse*.

Traits have been designed to play the role of *units for fine-grained reuse* in order to counter the problems of class-based inheritance with respect to code reuse. A trait is a set of methods, completely independent from any class hierarchy. The common behavior (i.e., the common methods) of a set of classes can be factored into a trait. Traits were introduced and implemented in the dynamically-typed class-based language SQUEAK/SMALLTALK [11][1]. Various formulations of traits in a JAVA-like setting can be found in the literature (see, e.g., [25,17,3,23,4,14]). Also two recent languages, SCALA and FORTRESS, incorporate forms of the trait construct.

In this paper, we present a JAVA-like core calculus for boxes and traits. The calculus supports interface-based polymorphism and uses traits and boxes as units of fine-grained and coarse-grained reuse, respectively. Namely, we consider: *Interfaces*, as object types, defining only method signatures. *Box interfaces*, as box types, defining only method signatures. *Traits*, as units of behavior reuse, defining only methods. *Classes*, as generators of objects, implementing interfaces by using traits. *Box classes*, as generators of boxes, implementing box interfaces by using traits. At the best of our knowledge, this is the first attempt to combine boxes and traits. In order to focus on the interactions between traits and boxes, we do not consider class-based inheritance in our calculus (along the lines and design choices of [3] and of the FORTRESS language).

Controlling the access to specific objects in specific contexts (boxes) is crucial to coordinate the access to sensible data and to keep consistency in an application. Our approach scales to a concurrent and distributed setting, since the synchronization of the access to data is orthogonal to our ownership type system. This type system complements concurrency mechanisms providing guarantees that the access of specific resources is allowed only to the desired components.

The combination of traits and boxes allows us to use a fine-grained reuse mechanism for the implementation of components (that is, coarse-grained units that can be deployed independently). Namely, it allows us to share code among components, without giving up the encapsulation properties. As we will point out at the end of Section 2, due to the ownership type system that usually comes with boxes in order achieve encapsulation, supporting this combination is quite challenging.

[1] A related reuse construct called "trait" was introduced in [27], for the language SELF.

```
interface IObserver { void update(String o); }
interface ISubject {
  void register(IObserver o);
  void unregister(IObserver o);
}
trait TSubject is {
  List<IObserver> obs; // required field
  String getTopic(); // required method
  void register(IObserver o) { obs.add(o); }
  void unregister(IObserver o) { obs.remove(o); }
  void notify() { /* iterate over observers */ }
}
trait TTopicHolder {
  String topic; // required field
  void notify(); // required method
  void setTopic(String t) { topic = t; notify(); }
  String getTopic() { return topic; }
}
```

```
interface ICachedSubject extends ISubject {
  String getPrevTopic();
}
trait TCachedSubject is
  TSubject[notify aliasAs oldNotify]
          [exclude notify] + {
  String prevTopic; // required field
  void oldNotify(); // required method
  String getPrevTopic() { return prevTopic; }
  void notify() {
    prevTopic = getTopic(); oldNotify();
  }
}
class CSubject implements ICachedSubject
   by TCachedSubject, TTopicHolder {
   String topic; String prevTopic;
   List<IObserver> obs;
}
```

Fig. 1. Implementation of a Subject with interfaces and traits

Organization of the Paper. In Section 2, we introduce boxes and traits by an example. Syntax, operational semantics, type system, and properties of the calculus are presented in Section 3. We conclude by discussing some related and further work.

2 Motivating Example

In this section we present our language and its core features from the programmer's point of view. We describe traits, boxes, ownership annotations and their combination.

Programming with Traits. In the language considered in this paper a trait consists of *methods*, of *required methods*, which parametrize the behavior, and of *required fields* that can be directly accessed in the body of the methods, along the lines of [2,4]. Traits are building blocks to compose classes and other, more complex, traits. A suite of trait composition operations allows the programmer to build classes and composite traits. A distinguished characteristic of traits is that the composite unit (class or trait) has complete control over conflicts that may arise during composition and must solve them explicitly. Traits do not specify any state. Therefore a class composed by using traits has to provide the required fields. The trait composition operations considered in our language are as follows: A *basic trait* defines a set of methods and declares the required fields and the required methods. The *symmetric sum* operation, +, merges two traits to form a new trait. It requires that the summed traits must be disjoint (that is, they must not provide identically named methods) and have compatible requirements (two requirements on the same method/field name are compatible if they are identical). The operation `exclude` forms a new trait by removing a method from an existing trait. The operation `aliasAs` forms a new trait by adding a copy of an existing method with a new name. The original method is still available and, when a recursive method is aliased, its recursive invocation refers to the original method. The operation `renameTo` forms a new trait by renaming all the occurrences of a required field name or of a required/provided method name in an existing trait.

In Figure 1 we show an example of the subject part of a subject-observer pattern (this example will be extended with boxes in the rest of the section) in order to explain the main features of our traits and interfaces. Note that the trait `TCachedSubject` reuses `TSubject` by aliasing the method `notify` and provides another version of `notify` (this can be seen as method overriding in standard class-based inheritance). The class `CSubject` implements the derived interface `ICachedSubject` by using the trait `TCachedSubject` and by declaring all the fields which are required by the trait. The trait `TTopicHolder` provides the required method `getTopic`.

Programming with Boxes. Our component model, the box model, extends the object-oriented programming world of interfaces, classes, objects, references, object-local state and methods with components, which we call boxes. Similar to an object, a box is a runtime entity, which is created dynamically, has an identity and a state. In general, it groups several objects together and its state is composed of the contained object states. During runtime each object belongs to exactly one box, thus defining a clear runtime boundary. A more detailed description including the discussion of design decisions and showing the use of the model for modular specification can be found in [20].

On source level, boxes are described by modules. A module is a set of classes and traits. Exactly one class for each module has to be a *box class*, which has to implement a *box interface*. The box class is the only class that is visible outside the module, all other classes and traits are not. When a box class is instantiated, a new box is created together with the object of the box class. The resulting object has the type of the corresponding box interface because classes cannot be used as types outside of their defining module. The box interface exactly defines which types, i.e., interfaces, the box exposes. Only types which transitively appear in the box interface as parameters or return types of methods can be used outside of a module. In particular, this means that downcasting of these types to not-exposed types is forbidden and checked at runtime. Note that a box is a runtime entity, so the downcasting of objects of another box is restricted even if it is of the same module. Boxes form a tree at runtime, with a special global box at the root. A box is nested in the box that created it. The main expression of the program is always evaluated in the global box.

Figure 2 shows the implementation of the subject-observer example with the use of boxes and ownership annotations. The ownership annotations are explained below. The implementation introduces a module with a box class `KSubjectManager`, which manages and uses the `CSubject` class to represent its subject. `CSubject` implements the `ITopicHolder` and the `ICachedSubject` interfaces. These interfaces, however, should not be visible to clients, because they reveal implementation details and allow the modification of the topic of the subject. Instead, clients should only be allowed to use the `ISubject` interface, which is a super type of `ICachedSubject`. In order to guarantee this with boxes, the box interface `BSubjectManager`, which is implemented by the box class, only returns the `ISubject` interface. This ensures that, outside the subject manager box, downcasts to more specific interfaces are not possible and result in runtime errors. Note that, inside a box, casts to owned objects are not restricted and behave like in standard Java. The cast restriction allows the implementation to be changed without breaking compatibility with clients, even in the presence of downcasting. This also

```
interface IObserver<a>{ void update(a String o); }
interface ISubject<a,b> {
  void register(a IObserver<b> o);
  void unregister(a IObserver<b> o);
}
interface ICachedSubject<a,b>
  extends ISubject<a,b> { ... }
interface ITopicHolder<a> {
  void setTopic(a String top);
  a String getTopic();
}
trait TSubject<a,b> is {
  local List<a IObserver<b>> obs;
  b String getTopic();
  ... // similar to Fig. 1
}
trait TCachedSubject<a,b> is
  TSubject<a,b>[notify aliasAs oldNotify]
                [exclude notify] + {
  ... // similar to Fig. 1
}
trait TTopicHolder<a> is ... // similar to Fig. 1
box interface BSubjectManager<a> { void init();
  boundary ISubject<a,global> getSubject(); }
```

```
module {
  box class KSubjectManager<a>
    implements BSubjectManager<a>
    by TSubjectManager<a> {
    boundary CSubject<a,global> subj;
  }
  trait TSubjectManager<a> is {
    boundary CSubject<a,global> subj;
    boundary ISubject<a,boundary> getSubject(){
      return subj; }
    void init() {
      subj = new boundary CSubject<a>(); }
    ... // further code
  }
  class CSubject<a>
    implements ICachedSubject<a,global>,
               ITopicHolder<global>
    by TCachedSubject<a,global> +
       TTopicHolder<global> {
    global String topic;
    global String prevTopic;
    local List<a IObserver<global>> obs;
  }
}
```

Fig. 2. Implementation of a Subject Manager

```
box interface BClient { void init(global BSubjectManager<owner> sm); }
module {
  box class KClient<a> implements BClient, IObserver<global> by TClient { }
  trait TClient is { void update(global String o) { ... }
                     void init(global BSubjectManager<owner> sm) {
                       sm.init(); sm.boundary ISubject<owner> s = sm.getSubject(); s.register(this);
                       ((ICachedSubject) s).getPrevTopic(); /* invalid cast */ }
} }
```

Fig. 3. An example usage of the `SubjectManager`-box

improves the reasoning about the behavior and about properties of a box in a modular way (see [20] for more details).

Figure 3 shows an example client implementation. The subject can be obtained from the subject manager by using the `getSubject` method. This allows the client to register as an observer, because the `ISubject` interface can be used by the client. However, it is not possible for the client to downcast to the `ICachedSubject` interface, for example. This allows the implementation of the `CSubject` class to be changed to use arbitrary other interfaces. In addition, the module can be analyzed in a modular way to guarantee that the topic of the internal subject cannot be changed outside of a box.

Programming with Ownership Annotations. The purpose of the box model is to define a precise boundary of object-oriented runtime components. In addition, the box model conceptually structures the heap into hierarchical components. One important aspect of components is encapsulation. Encapsulation is partly achieved by the cast restriction, which restricts what a client can do with an exposed object of a box, but it does not ensure that certain objects are never exposed by a box. To guarantee this aspect of encapsulation we add an ownership type system to our language. The basic idea is to group the objects of a box into distinct domains – a *local* and a *boundary* domain. Local objects are encapsulated in the box and cannot be referenced from the outside, boundary objects are accessible from the outside. The owner object of a box, i.e., the instance of the box class, is always accessible by the outside. It does not belong to the boundary domain of the box, instead it belongs to some domain of its surrounding box. In general the accessibility between objects follows three rules, called the *accessibility invariant*: (*i*) objects in the same box can access each other, (*ii*) when an object can access a box, it can access the boundary objects of the box, (*iii*) objects can access any object of a surrounding box.

To guarantee the accessibility invariant, we extend the type system of our language with ownership annotations. A type `T` is annotated with a domain annotation `d` by writing `d T`. A domain annotation can be `local`, `boundary`, `owner`, or `global`. In addition, types can have domain parameters to express genericity in domain annotations. A domain annotation is always relative to a certain box. By default, this is the current box, i.e., the box of the `this`-object. For example, the type `local I` means that all instances of that type belong to the local domain of the current box. A box can also be explicitly specified by using a local variable referencing a box owner, i.e., an object of a box class. For example, the domain annotation `x.boundary` refers to the boundary domain of the box of the object referred by `x`. Note that in our language local variables are always `final`. The `owner` domain annotation refers to the domain in which the current `this`-object belongs to, the `global` domain represents the global domain. Types are only assignable if they have compatible domain annotations. Domain annotations are compatible if at runtime they always refer to the same domain. The domain annotations restrict the usage of types to guarantee the encapsulation of objects. In particular, it is guaranteed that all access paths from an object outside of a box to an object of a local domain of a box must go through either the owner of the box, or a boundary object. This is ensured by the type system by the restricting of assignments as described above and the prevention of certain domain annotations like `x.local`, for example.

In the subject manager example (cf. Figure 2) the `CSubject` object should be accessible outside the box. Thus it is put into the boundary domain. The `String` objects, which represent the topics of the subject are put into the global domain, as they should be accessible from everywhere. The `List` object of the subject, which holds the list of observers, however, should not be directly accessible from outside the box. It is thus put into the local domain. Note that the domain of the elements of the list, namely the observer objects, is left open as a parameter and is thus generic. To lower the annotation overhead for such a type system, type inference can be used (see [19]). This allows most annotations of classes and traits to be inferred and mainly requires to annotate interfaces. The client code in Figure 3 shows how the subject manager is used. The `KSubjectManager` instance is stored in a local variable `sm`. The domain of the subject object from the subject manager is then typed as `sm.boundary`. Figure 4 shows the runtime structure of the system after the method `init` is executed and the observer has been notified about some changes on the topic. The `KSubjectManager` object is the owner of its box. The `CSubject` object is in the boundary domain, the `List` object in the local domain of the box. The `KClient` can access the topic `String` objects, which live in the global domain, as well as the `CSubject` object, as it lives in the boundary

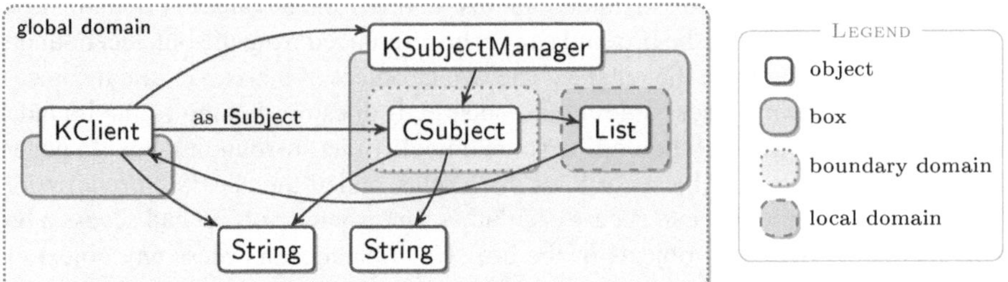

Fig. 4. Runtime view to the subject-observer example

domain of the `KSubjectManager` box. As the client has access to the box owner, it also has access to its boundary domain. The cast restriction of the box only allows the client to use the `ISubject` interface. The ownership type system guarantees that the client can never obtain a reference to the `List` object as it lives in the local domain of the `KSubjectManager` box.

Programming with Traits, Boxes and Ownership Annotations. A desirable feature of a programming language is the ability to support both fine- and coarse-grained reuse. The combination of traits and boxes provides this ability. Consider for instance the code in Figure 2. In order to better support encapsulation and ownership type-checking, classes are only visible inside the module where they are declared. The possibility of declaring traits at the top level (that is, outside of any module), like the traits `TSubject`, `TCatchedSubject` and `TTopicHolder`, makes it possible to reuse code across different modules. Type-checking a trait in isolation from the classes that use it is quite challenging. The problem is due the fact that, while type-checking the body of the method `m`, in order to be able to perform the ownership type-checks it is needed to know both the class `C` that contains the method `m` and the box class associated to the module containing the declaration of `C`. In this paper we address this problem by introducing a minimal core calculus for boxes and traits and by equipping it with a constraint-based ownership type system.

3 A Calculus for Boxes and Traits

Syntax. The syntax of our calculus, WELTERWEIGHT BOX TRAIT JAVA (WBTJ), is presented in Fig. 5. We use similar notations as FJ [12]. For instance: "$\bar{\mathtt{e}}$" denotes the possibly empty sequence "$\mathtt{e}_1, \ldots, \mathtt{e}_n$" and the pair "$\bar{\mathtt{N}}\ \bar{\mathtt{f}};$" stands for "$\mathtt{N}_1\ \mathtt{f}_1; \ldots \mathtt{N}_n\ \mathtt{f}_n;$". The empty sequence is denoted by "$\bullet$" and the length of a sequence $\bar{\mathtt{e}}$ is denoted by $|\bar{\mathtt{e}}|$.

A program consists of interfaces, box interfaces, traits, modules and an expression, which represents the main method of the program. Every module contains one box class implementing a box interface, normal classes implementing normal interfaces and traits. The traits declared inside a module can be used only in the module itself, while the traits defined at the top level (that is, outside of any module) can be used by different modules. For simplicity, we assume that each class (and each box class) has a companion interface

ID	::= [box] interface $\mathtt{I}\langle\overline{\alpha}\rangle$ extends $\overline{\mathtt{I}\langle\bar{\mathtt{d}}\rangle}$ { $\bar{\mathtt{S}}$; }	interfaces
S	::= N m ($\bar{\mathtt{N}}$ $\bar{\mathtt{x}}$)	method headers
N	::= $\mathtt{I}\langle\bar{\mathtt{d}}\rangle$	source types
G	::= N | $\mathtt{C}\langle\bar{\mathtt{d}}\rangle$	types
d	::= α | b.c | global	domain annotations
b	::= box | x | <u>null</u> | <u>?</u>	domain owners
c	::= local | boundary	domain kinds
TD	::= trait $\mathtt{T}\langle\overline{\alpha}\rangle$ is TE	traits
TE	::= { $\bar{\mathtt{F}}$; $\bar{\mathtt{S}}$; $\bar{\mathtt{M}}$ } | $\mathtt{T}\langle\bar{\mathtt{d}}\rangle$ | TE + TE | TE[exclude m] | TE[m aliasAs m] | TE[m renameTo m] | TE[f renameTo f]	trait expressions
F	::= N f	fields
M	::= S { return e; }	methods
e	::= x | null | this.f | this.f = e | e.m($\bar{\mathtt{e}}$) | new $\mathtt{C}\langle\bar{\mathtt{d}}\rangle$ | (N)e | let N x = e in e	expressions
CD	::= [box] class $\mathtt{C}\langle\overline{\alpha}\rangle$ implements $\mathtt{I}\langle\bar{\mathtt{d}}\rangle$ by TE { $\bar{\mathtt{F}}$; }	classes
MODULE	::= module { $\overline{\mathtt{CD}}$ $\overline{\mathtt{TD}}$ }	modules
PROGRAM	::= $\overline{\mathtt{ID}}$ $\overline{\mathtt{TD}}$ $\overline{\mathtt{MODULE}}$ e	programs

Fig. 5. WBTJ: Syntax (I $\in$ interface names, T $\in$ trait names, C $\in$ class names, m $\in$ method names, f $\in$ field names, α, β $\in$ domain parameters)

(resp. box interface) that it implements. Interfaces and box interfaces list the public methods of a class. The language has no constructors; new objects are created by setting all fields to null. Note that constructors can be simulated by ordinary method calls. Each class or box class declares fields and defines methods through a trait expression.

Classes are only visible inside their module, therefore within a module MODULE only objects of classes declared in MODULE can be created. In our simple language, interface names and box interface names are the only source level types. It would be straightforward to extend the language to allow the programmer to use class names as source level types inside their module.

The set of expressions is quite standard. Just observe that, since interface names and box interface names are the only source level types, fields can be selected only on this.

For conciseness of the formalization, we have streamlined the notation of ownership annotations used in Sect. 2. Instead of writing the owning domain in front of the type, we now write it as the first parameter of the type. This also means that there is no owner keyword, because the first domain parameter always represents the owning domain. A domain annotation can either be a domain parameter α, the global domain, or is of the form $b.c$, where the first part defines the owner of the domain, and the second part defines the domain kind, that is, whether it is the boundary or local domain. The keyword box denotes the owner of the current box. The name of a local variable x is used for objects of box classes and denotes the box owned by x. For example, x.local denotes the local domain of the box owned by x. Owners null and ? do not belong to the user syntax (indicated by an underline), but can appear during reduction. ? as owner represents an invalid domain annotation, and null is the owner of the global domain. In fact, all occurrences of global are treated as null.local.

$$
\begin{array}{rcl}
[\![[\mathtt{box}]\ \mathtt{class}\ \mathtt{C}\langle\overline{\alpha}\rangle\ \mathtt{implements} & & \\
\mathtt{I}\langle\bar{\mathtt{d}}\rangle\ \mathtt{by}\ \mathtt{TE}\ \{\ \bar{\mathtt{F}};\ \}]\!] & \stackrel{\mathrm{def}}{=} & [\mathtt{box}]\ \mathtt{class}\ \mathtt{C}\langle\overline{\alpha}\rangle\ \mathtt{implements}\ \mathtt{I}\langle\bar{\mathtt{d}}\rangle\ \mathtt{by}\ \{\bar{\mathtt{F}};\ \bullet;\ [\![\mathtt{TE}]\!]\}\ \ \{\ \bar{\mathtt{F}};\ \} \\
[\![\{\bar{\mathtt{F}};\ \bar{\mathtt{S}};\ \bar{\mathtt{M}}\}]\!] & \stackrel{\mathrm{def}}{=} & \bar{\mathtt{M}} \\
[\![\mathtt{T}\langle\bar{\mathtt{d}}\rangle]\!] & \stackrel{\mathrm{def}}{=} & [\![\mathtt{TE}[^{\bar{\mathtt{d}}}/_{\overline{\alpha}}]]\!] \qquad \textbf{if}\ \mathtt{trait}\ \mathtt{T}\langle\overline{\alpha}\rangle\ \mathtt{is}\ \mathtt{TE} \\
[\![\mathtt{TE}_1 + \mathtt{TE}_2]\!] & \stackrel{\mathrm{def}}{=} & [\![\mathtt{TE}_1]\!] \cdot [\![\mathtt{TE}_2]\!] \\
[\![\mathtt{TE}\ [\mathtt{exclude}\ \mathtt{m}]]\!] & \stackrel{\mathrm{def}}{=} & \bar{\mathtt{M}}' \cdot \bar{\mathtt{M}}'' \qquad \textbf{if}\ [\![\mathtt{TE}]\!] = \bar{\mathtt{M}}' \cdot \mathtt{M} \cdot \bar{\mathtt{M}}''\ \textbf{and}\ \mathtt{M} = \cdots \mathtt{m}(\cdots)\{\cdots\} \\
[\![\mathtt{TE}\ [\mathtt{m}\ \mathtt{aliasAs}\ \mathtt{m}']]\!] & \stackrel{\mathrm{def}}{=} & \bar{\mathtt{M}} \cdot (\mathtt{N}\ \mathtt{m}'(\bar{\mathtt{N}}\ \bar{\mathtt{x}})\{\mathtt{return}\ \mathtt{e};\}) \\
& & \qquad \textbf{if}\ [\![\mathtt{TE}]\!] = \bar{\mathtt{M}}\ \textbf{and}\ \mathtt{N}\ \mathtt{m}(\bar{\mathtt{N}}\ \bar{\mathtt{x}})\{\mathtt{return}\ \mathtt{e};\} \in \bar{\mathtt{M}} \\
[\![\mathtt{TE}[\mathtt{f}\ \mathtt{renameTo}\ \mathtt{f}']]\!] & \stackrel{\mathrm{def}}{=} & [\![\mathtt{TE}]\!][^{\mathtt{f}'}/_{\mathtt{f}}] \\
[\![\mathtt{TE}[\mathtt{m}\ \mathtt{renameTo}\ \mathtt{m}']]\!] & \stackrel{\mathrm{def}}{=} & mR([\![\mathtt{TE}]\!],\mathtt{m},\mathtt{m}') \\
mR(\mathtt{N}\ \mathtt{n}(\bar{\mathtt{N}}\ \bar{\mathtt{x}})\{\mathtt{return}\ \mathtt{e};\},\mathtt{m},\mathtt{m}') & \stackrel{\mathrm{def}}{=} & \mathtt{N}\ \mathtt{n}[^{\mathtt{m}'}/_{\mathtt{m}}](\bar{\mathtt{N}}\ \bar{\mathtt{x}})\{\mathtt{return}\ \mathtt{e}[^{\mathtt{this.m}'}/_{\mathtt{this.m}}];\} \\
mR(\mathtt{M}_1 \cdot \ldots \cdot \mathtt{M}_n,\mathtt{m},\mathtt{m}') & \stackrel{\mathrm{def}}{=} & (mR(\mathtt{M}_1,\mathtt{m},\mathtt{m}')) \cdot \ldots \cdot (mR(\mathtt{M}_n,\mathtt{m},\mathtt{m}'))
\end{array}
$$

Fig. 6. Flattening WBTJ to FWBTJ

Flattening. The *flattening principle* has been introduced in the original formulation of traits in SQUEAK/SMALLTALK [11] in order to provide a canonical semantics to traits. Flattening states that the semantics of a method introduced in a class through a trait should be identical to the semantics of the same method defined directly within a class. This makes it possible to reason about the properties of a language with traits by relying on the semantics of the subset of the language without traits.

In order to formalize flattening for WBTJ we consider a subset of the calculus that we call FWBTJ (FLAT WBTJ), where there are no trait declarations and the syntax of trait expressions is simplified as follows: $\mathtt{TE} ::= \{\bar{\mathtt{F}};\ \bullet;\ \bar{\mathtt{M}}\}$. A FWBTJ class $\mathtt{class}\ \mathtt{C}\langle\overline{\alpha}\rangle\ \mathtt{implements}\ \mathtt{I}\langle\bar{\mathtt{d}}\rangle\ \mathtt{by}\ \{\ \bar{\mathtt{F}};\ \bullet;\ \bar{\mathtt{M}}\ \}\ \{\ \bar{\mathtt{F}};\}$ can be understood (modulo the domain annotations) as the standard JAVA class $\mathtt{class}\ \mathtt{C}\langle\overline{\alpha}\rangle\ \mathtt{implements}\ \mathtt{I}\langle\bar{\mathtt{d}}\rangle\ \{\ \bar{\mathtt{F}};\ \bar{\mathtt{M}}\ \}$. Similarly for box classes. Therefore, the canonical (static and dynamic) semantics for WBTJ can be specified by providing: (*i*) a semantics for FWBTJ, and (*ii*) a flattening translation that maps a WBTJ program into a FWBTJ program.

The flattening translation is specified through the function $[\![\cdot]\!]$, given in Figure 6, that maps each WBTJ class or box class declaration to a FWBTJ class or box class declaration, respectively, and maps a trait expression to a sequence of method declarations. We write $[\![\mathtt{PROGRAM}]\!]$ to denote the program obtained from PROGRAM by dropping all the trait declarations and by translating all the class and box class declarations. The clauses in Figure 6 should be self-explanatory. Note that the flattening clause for field renaming is simpler than the flattening clause for method renaming (which uses the auxiliary function *mR*); this is due to the fact that fields can be accessed only on `this`.

Flattening aims only to provide a canonical semantics to traits, it is not an especially effective implementation technique (see, e.g., [17,13]).

Typing. A desirable property of a formulation of traits within a statically typed programming language is to conform to the *trait type-checking in isolation principle* (that guided, for instance, the design of the pioneering experimental language CHAI_2 [25]). It states that typing must support the type-checking of traits in isolation from the classes or traits that use them. So that it is possible to type-check a method defined in a trait only once (instead of having to reinspect its code whenever that trait is used by a class or by another trait). In order to conform to the above principle a type system must be able to type-check a method definition without knowing the classes that will use it. This can be done by exploiting the constraint-base typing technology.

Ownership Typing for FWBTJ. Before introducing the constraint-based ownership type system for WBTJ, we introduce an ownership type system for FWBTJ. The ownership type system for FWBTJ, which is similar to the ownership type system described in [19], represents the specification for the constraint-based ownership type system for WBTJ. In the following we will use H to range over (box) class and (box) interface names. The ownership type rules are of the form $\Gamma;\mathtt{G};\mathtt{b} \vdash_{\mathrm{o}} \ldots$, where Γ is type environment of local variables, G is the type of the current context class or interface, and b refers to the current box owner.

The subtyping relation of our language is quite standard, it is the transitive, reflexive closure of the `extends`- and `implements`-relation between interfaces and classes, except that box interfaces and box classes are subtypes of box interfaces only (analogous for normal classes and interfaces). This leads to two disjoint type hierarchies, which are needed to define the accessibility between domains (see below).

The typing rules for the ownership type system are mostly standard. The interesting rules are those for classes and for expressions. The rule for classes is:

(T-CLASS)
$$\frac{\emptyset;\mathtt{C}\langle\bar{\alpha}\rangle;\mathtt{box} \vdash_{\mathrm{o}} \bar{\mathtt{N}} \qquad \mathtt{this}:\mathtt{C}\langle\bar{\alpha}\rangle;\mathtt{C}\langle\bar{\alpha}\rangle;\mathtt{box} \vdash_{\mathrm{o}} \bar{\mathtt{M}} \qquad \mathit{isBoxType}(\mathtt{C}) \Leftrightarrow \mathit{isBoxType}(\mathtt{I}) \quad \text{All methods of interface } \mathtt{I} \text{ are implemented in } \bar{\mathtt{M}}}{\vdash_{\mathrm{o}} \mathtt{class}\ \mathtt{C}\langle\overline{\alpha}\rangle\ \mathtt{implements}\ \mathtt{I}\langle\bar{\mathtt{d}}\rangle\ \mathtt{by}\ \{\bar{\mathtt{F}};\ \bullet;\ \bar{\mathtt{M}}\}\ \{\ \bar{\mathtt{N}}\ \bar{\mathtt{f}};\ \}}$$

A class is well-typed if all fields have valid types in the class C and the current box, and all methods are well-typed in the context of the class C. This rule (implicitly parametrized by the module in which C is defined) instantiates the context used in the rules for expressions and to test validity of types and accessibility of domains. For the typecheck on method calls and field selection expressions, the declared types of parameters and fields have to be translated to the domain in which they are used, i.e. the declared domains have to be replaced by actual ones. A domain parameter α is replaced by the actual domain, the box keyword is replaced depending whether the type to translate is a boxtype or not. For normal types, box is replaced by the owner of the type, for boxtypes box is translated to the owner if the expression in which the translation occurs denotes a valid owner. The translation function can introduce domain annotations with ? as owner. These domains signify failed translations and, in the typing rules, the check for validity of types with these annotations will fail. The rule for field access is:

(T-FIELD)
$$\frac{\Gamma;\mathtt{G};\mathtt{b} \vdash_{\mathrm{o}} \mathtt{this}:\mathtt{C}\langle\bar{\mathtt{d}}\rangle \qquad \mathtt{N} = \mathit{trans}(\mathtt{C}\langle\bar{\mathtt{d}}\rangle, \mathtt{this}, \mathit{ftype}(\mathtt{C},\mathtt{f})) \qquad \Gamma;\mathtt{G};\mathtt{b} \vdash_{\mathrm{o}} \mathtt{N}}{\Gamma;\mathtt{G};\mathtt{b} \vdash_{\mathrm{o}} \mathtt{this.f}:\mathtt{N}}$$

To type `this.f`, we have to find the type for `this`, lookup the declared type of the field `f` (done by *ftype*) and then translate the declared type into the current context. Then, the translated type has to be type correct as well. The rule for calls look similar, but translates the declared parameter types.

$$\frac{}{\Gamma;\mathtt{G};\mathtt{b}\vdash_o \mathtt{d}\rightarrow\mathtt{d}}\ \text{(A-REFL)}\qquad \frac{}{\Gamma;\mathtt{G};\mathtt{b}\vdash_o \mathtt{b.c_1}\rightarrow\mathtt{b.c_2}}\ \text{(A-OWNER)}\qquad \frac{}{\Gamma;\mathtt{G};\mathtt{b}\vdash_o \mathtt{d}\rightarrow\mathtt{null.c}}\ \text{(A-NULL)}\qquad \frac{}{\Gamma;\mathtt{H}\langle\bar{\mathtt{d}}\rangle;\mathtt{b}\vdash_o \mathtt{b.c}\rightarrow\bar{\mathtt{d}}}\ \text{(A-PARAM)}$$

$$\frac{}{\Gamma;\mathtt{H}\langle\bar{\mathtt{d}}\rangle;\mathtt{b}\vdash_o \mathtt{d_1}\rightarrow\bar{\mathtt{d}}}\ \text{(A-PARAM-2)}\qquad \frac{\neg isBoxType(\mathtt{H})}{\Gamma;\mathtt{H}\langle\bar{\mathtt{d}}\rangle;\mathtt{b}\vdash_o \mathtt{d_1}\rightarrow\mathtt{b.c}}\ \text{(A-PARAM-3)}\qquad \frac{isBoxType(\mathtt{H})}{\Gamma;\mathtt{H}\langle\bar{\mathtt{d}}\rangle;\mathtt{b}\vdash_o \mathtt{d_1}\rightarrow\mathtt{b.boundary}}\ \text{(A-PARAM-4)}$$

$$\frac{\Gamma;\mathtt{G};\mathtt{b}\vdash_o \mathtt{b}':\mathtt{H}\langle\bar{\mathtt{d}}\rangle \qquad \Gamma;\mathtt{G};\mathtt{b}\vdash_o \mathtt{d}\rightarrow\mathtt{d_1}}{\Gamma;\mathtt{G};\mathtt{b}\vdash_o \mathtt{d}\rightarrow\mathtt{b}'\mathtt{.boundary}}\ \text{(A-BOUNDARY)}\qquad \frac{\Gamma;\mathtt{G};\mathtt{b}\vdash_o \mathtt{b}':\mathtt{H}\langle\bar{\mathtt{d}}\rangle}{\Gamma;\mathtt{G};\mathtt{b}\vdash_o \mathtt{b}'\mathtt{.boundary}\rightarrow\mathtt{d_1}}\ \text{(A-BOUNDARY-2)}$$

Fig. 7. Accessibility relation

The first key element of the type system is the *accessibility relation* on domains presented in Figure 7. Judgments of the form $\Gamma;\mathtt{T_{cb}};\mathtt{b}\vdash_o \mathtt{d_1}\rightarrow\mathtt{d_2}$ tell us that domain $\mathtt{d_1}$ can access domain $\mathtt{d_2}$ in the given context meaning that all objects in $\mathtt{d_1}$ can access all objects in domain $\mathtt{d_2}$. The relation formalizes the accessibility between domains depending on the ownership hierarchy of boxes. A domain has access to itself (A-REFL) and to the global domain (A-NULL). The domains with the same owner, i.e. belonging to the same box, can access each other (A-OWNER). The rules (A-PARAM) to (A-PARAM4) relate the domains of the current context type to the domains of the current box. (A-PARAM) states that the domains of the current box can access the domains of the context type and (A-PARAM2) says that the owning domain, i.e. d_1, has access to all parameter domains. These two rules guarantee that it is impossible to pass domains through other domains without following the box hierarchy. The owning domain of the context type, i.e. the domain of the `this` object, has access to the domains of the current box if it is not a box type (A-PARAM3). If the context type is a boxtype, its owning domain has only access to the boundary domain of the current box (A-PARAM4). This rule applies if the current box is an inner box of the box containing the context type and local domains of inner boxes are protected against the access from surrounding boxes. A domain can always access the boundary domain of a box, which it can access (A-BOUNDARY) and the boundary domain has always access to the owning domain of the box (A-BOUNDARY2).

The second key element of the ownership type system is the definition of *valid domains and types* shown in Figure 8. The notion of validity is strongly related to the accessibility relation. The most important rule is (V-ANNOTATION), which guarantees that

$$\frac{}{\Gamma;\mathtt{G};\mathtt{b}\vdash_o \mathtt{box.c}}\ \text{(V-DOMAIN-BOX)}\qquad \frac{}{\Gamma;\mathtt{G};\mathtt{b}\vdash_o \mathtt{null.c}}\ \text{(V-DOMAIN-BOX)}\qquad \frac{}{\Gamma;\mathtt{H}\langle\bar{\mathtt{d}}\rangle;\mathtt{b}\vdash_o \mathtt{d}_i}\ \text{(V-DOMAIN-BOX)}$$

$$\frac{\Gamma;\mathtt{G};\mathtt{b}\vdash_o \mathtt{x}:\mathtt{H}\langle\bar{\mathtt{d}}\rangle \qquad isBoxType(\mathtt{H})}{\Gamma;\mathtt{G};\mathtt{b}\vdash_o \mathtt{x.boundary}}\ \text{(V-DOMAIN-VAR)}\qquad \frac{\begin{array}{c}\Gamma;\mathtt{G};\mathtt{b}\vdash_o \bar{\mathtt{d}} \qquad \Gamma;\mathtt{G};\mathtt{b}\vdash_o \diamond \qquad \Gamma;\mathtt{G};\mathtt{b}\vdash_o \mathtt{d_1}\rightarrow\bar{\mathtt{d}}\\ \Gamma;\mathtt{G};\mathtt{b}\vdash_o \mathtt{b.c}\rightarrow\bar{\mathtt{d}} \qquad |params(\mathtt{H})| = |\bar{\mathtt{d}}|\end{array}}{\Gamma;\mathtt{G};\mathtt{b}\vdash_o \mathtt{H}\langle\bar{\mathtt{d}}\rangle}\ \text{(V-ANNOTATION)}$$

Fig. 8. Valid domains and types

$$\begin{array}{llr} \psi & ::= \mathit{isValid}(\mathtt{O}) \mid \mathit{isValid}(\mathtt{T}\langle\bar{\mathtt{d}}\rangle) \mid \mathtt{O} <: \mathtt{O}' \mid \mathtt{O} \not<: \mathtt{O}' \mid \mathtt{O} \neq \mathtt{O}' & \text{constraints} \\ & \mid \ \bar{\mathtt{X}} = \mathit{trans}(\mathtt{O}, \mathtt{e}, \mathtt{O}') \mid (\mathtt{O} \neq \chi)\ ?\ (\mathtt{O} <: \mathtt{O}') : (\mathit{req}(\mathtt{O}')) \mid \mathit{req}(\mathtt{N}) & \\ \mathtt{O} & ::= \mathtt{G} \mid \mathtt{X} \mid \chi & \text{open types} \end{array}$$

Fig. 9. Constraints syntax

breaking encapsulation by passing domains as parameters, which are not accessible by the first domain parameter, i.e. the domain of `this`, is impossible.

Constraint-based Ownership Typing for WBTJ. The constraint-based ownership type system for WBTJ can be understood as a refinement of the type system (for a Java-like calculus with traits) proposed in [4], to keep box and ownership annotations into account. The type-checking of each trait definition, in isolation from the classes or traits that use it, is realized by collecting, for each method definition in the trait, the constraints on the use of `this` within the method body. Each method $\mathtt{M} = \mathtt{S}\,\{\,\mathtt{return\,e;}\,\}$ defined within a basic trait expression $\{\,\bar{\mathtt{F}};\ \bar{\mathtt{S}};\ \bar{\mathtt{M}}\}$ is type-checked by assuming for `this` the structural type $\langle\ \bar{\mathtt{F}}\ \mid\ \bar{\mathtt{S}}'\ \rangle$, where $\bar{\mathtt{F}}$ and $\bar{\mathtt{S}}'$ are the required fields and the headers of the required/provided methods of the basic trait expression, respectively. The typing judgment for method definitions has the form: $\mathtt{this} : \langle\ \bar{\mathtt{F}}\ \mid\ \bar{\mathtt{S}}'\ \rangle \vdash_{\mathsf{co}} \mathtt{M} : \mathtt{S}\ \mid\ \langle\ \bar{\mathtt{F}}'\ \mid\ \bar{\mathtt{S}}''\ \mid\ \bar{\mathtt{N}}\ \rangle \mid \Phi$, where S is the header of the method; the triple $\langle\ \bar{\mathtt{F}}'\ \mid\ \bar{\mathtt{S}}''\ \mid\ \bar{\mathtt{N}}\ \rangle$ specifies that the body of the method (the expression e) selects the fields $\bar{\mathtt{F}}'$ ($\subseteq \bar{\mathtt{F}}$) and the methods with headers $\bar{\mathtt{S}}''$ ($\subseteq \bar{\mathtt{S}}'$) on `this`, requires that `this` has the types $\bar{\mathtt{N}}$; and Φ is the set of the validity ownership type-checks that can be performed only when the class or box class that is using the method is known. In particular: (*i*) $\bar{\mathtt{N}}$ contains the types of the formal parameters of methods to which `this` is passed as argument and, when the method returns `this`, also the return type of the method; (*ii*) the elements of Φ, ranged over by ψ, represent the ownership type-checks that would be performed by the ownership type system for FWBTJ when type-checking a class or box class containing the method definition M.

Let μ range over the the types assigned to method definitions. The typing judgment for trait expressions has the form $\vdash_{\mathsf{co}} \mathtt{TE} : \mu_1 ... \mu_n$, where $\mu_1, ..., \mu_n$ (with $n \geq 0$) are the types of the n methods defined by the trait expression TE.

The typing rule for class definitions $\mathtt{class}\ \mathtt{C}\langle\overline{\alpha}\rangle\ \mathtt{implements}\ \mathtt{I}\langle\bar{\mathtt{d}}\rangle\ \mathtt{by}\ \mathtt{TE}\ \{\ \bar{\mathtt{F}};\}$ checks that the constraints in the types of the methods provided by TE are satisfied, that is: class C provides all fields and methods required by the trait expression TE; the trait expression TE has no required methods and provides all the methods of the interfaces implemented by C; each interface required by TE is a superinterface of some interface implemented by C; and all the constraints inferred for the methods provided by TE are satisfied within class C. The typing rule for box class definitions is similar.

The syntax of the constraints ψ representing the ownership type-checks is given in Figure 9, where X ranges over type variables that will be instantiated to types and χ is a distinguished type variable that will be instantiated to the type of `this`. A constraint can be: a type validity check ($\mathit{isValid}(\mathtt{O})$); an annotated trait name validity check ($\mathit{isValid}(\mathtt{T}\langle\bar{\mathtt{d}}\rangle)$); a subtype or type equality check; the binding of type variable to types generated by the *trans* function; a conditional constraint, depending on the type of `this`; or a required type for `this` ($\mathit{req}(\mathtt{N})$). Given a context $\Gamma;\mathtt{T}_{\mathsf{cb}};\mathtt{b}$, all the type variables occurring in a set of constraints Φ are univocally bound to types. We will write

$\Gamma;\mathtt{T_{cb}};\mathtt{b} \vdash_{\mathsf{co}} \Phi$ to mean that all the constraints in Φ are satisfied in the context $\Gamma;\mathtt{T_{cb}};\mathtt{b}$ according to the subtyping relation (not given for space reasons) and to the relation in Figure 8. Note that rule (V-ANNOTATION) in Figure 8 has to be used also for checking annotated trait names, i.e., the metavariable H occurring in the rule can be also a trait name T. The rule for constraint-based type-checking of field access is the following:

$$\text{(OTC-FIELD)}\quad \frac{\Gamma \vdash_{\mathsf{co}} \mathtt{this} : \langle\, \bar{\mathtt{F}} \mid \bar{\mathtt{S}} \,\rangle \mid \langle\, \bullet \mid \bullet \mid \bullet \,\rangle \mid \{\} \qquad N\mathtt{f} \in \bar{\mathtt{F}} \qquad \mathtt{X}\ \text{fresh} \qquad \Phi = \{\, \mathtt{X} = \mathit{trans}(\chi, \mathtt{this}, N),\ \mathit{isValid}(\mathtt{X}) \,\}}{\Gamma \vdash_{\mathsf{co}} \mathtt{this.f} : \mathtt{X} \mid \langle\, \mathtt{Xf} \mid \bullet \mid \bullet \,\rangle \mid \Phi}$$

Note that the two constraints in the set Φ represent the validity check on the translation of the type of f, which cannot be performed until the class of this will be known.

The type τ of a closed expression e is of the form $\mathtt{H}\langle\bar{\mathtt{d}}\rangle$ where H is an interface, box interface, class or box class name. In fact, although class names and box class names cannot be used as types in the program, they are used by the type system to type object/box creation expressions. We say that a WBTJ program $\mathtt{PROGRAM} = \overline{\mathtt{ID}}\ \overline{\mathtt{ID}}\ \overline{\mathtt{TD}}\ \overline{\mathtt{MODULE}}\ \mathtt{e}$ is *well typed* with type τ to mean that all the interfaces, box interfaces, traits, classes, box classes in the program are well typed and that the expression e has type τ.

Properties. In order to define the properties of our type systems, we need an operational semantics. Thanks to flattening, in order to specify the semantics of WBTJ, it is enough to specify a semantics for FWBTJ. Our operational semantics is mainly a standard semantics with two extensions. First the semantics explicitly represents boxes as runtime entities, which are created whenever an instance of a box class is created. In addition, each object is mapped to the box, which it belongs to. The second extension is the restriction of casts. At runtime casts are checked to prevent illegal downcasts, i.e., casts to types, which are not defined in a box boundary. For more details we refer to [18]. Based on the operational semantics, we have the following central properties for the WBTJ type systems. The first property is *subject reduction*, which is a prerequisite to prove that objects during runtime can only access other objects according to their declared static domains.

Theorem 1 (Subject Reduction for $\vdash_{\mathsf{o}}$). *If an expression e is $\vdash_{\mathsf{o}}$-typable, then e can be reduced to e′ and the type of e′ is a subtype of the type of e.*

The proof is by the standard preservation and progress lemmas, which can be proved by standard structural induction. The main property of the ownership type system is the *accessibility invariant.* It states, which objects can access each other.

Theorem 2 (Accessibility Invariant for $\vdash_{\mathsf{o}}$-typable programs). *Objects can only access other objects which are: (i) in the same box, (ii) in the boundary domain of a box which they can access, (iii) in a surrounding box of their own box.*

The proof is by structural induction with the use of the subject reduction theorem and the accessibility and validity definitions.

Corollary 1 (Encapsulation Invariant for $\vdash_{\mathsf{o}}$-typable programs). *Objects in the local domain of a box cannot be accessed by objects of surrounding boxes.*

The following theorems (that can be proved by structural induction on typing derivations) state that the constraint-based ownership type system for WBTJ ($\vdash_{co}$) satisfies the specification provided by the ownership type system for FWBTJ ($\vdash_{o}$) and the conformance of the constraint-based ownership type system to the flattening principle, respectively. Therefore, $\vdash_{co}$-typable programs enjoy the encapsulation invariant.

Theorem 3 (Equivalence of $\vdash_{co}$-typability and $\vdash_{o}$-typability on FWBTJ **programs).** *For every* FWBTJ *program* PROGRAM *it holds that* PROGRAM *is well typed with type* τ *in* $\vdash_{co}$ *if and only if* PROGRAM *is well typed with type* τ *in* $\vdash_{o}$.

Theorem 4 (Flattening preserves $\vdash_{co}$-typing). *If the* WBTJ *program* PROGRAM *is well typed with type* τ *then the* FWBTJ *program* $[\![$PROGRAM$]\!]$ *is well typed with type* τ.

4 Conclusion, Related and Future Work

The literature on traits and boxes has been partially quoted throughout the paper. Here we briefly discuss the relation with ownership type systems. The basic idea of the box component model, namely to hierarchically structure the heap into dynamically created regions, originated from ownership disciplines. They were originally developed to check confinement properties by type systems (see [7] for an introduction and overview; [5] for a system to check concurrency properties; [10,22] for generic ownership type systems). Several different variants of ownership types exist, with varying expressiveness and flexibility. The original ownership type system by Clarke et al. [8] and similar systems [6,9] enforces a so-called *owners-as-dominators* property, which states that all accesses from external objects to owned objects must go through the owner object. This property does not allow for multiple objects at the boundary of a component. The Universe type system [16,10] is more flexible by permitting read-only references to owned objects. The ownership type system of Lu et al. [15] generalize this by using an additional accessibility modifier. Most closest to the ownership system presented in this paper is the general *Ownership Domains* [1] approach. The ownership system of this paper without traits together with an inference algorithm is presented in [19].

Currently we are working on the implementation of the programming language based on the WBTJ calculus (both on the constraint-based type system as well as on an runtime environment supporting boxes). Moreover, we are planning to extend the type system to deal with generics.

Acknowledgment. We thank the anonymous referees and Susan Eisenbach for comments and suggestions for improving the paper. The authors of this work have been partially supported by the German-Italian University Centre (Vigoni program).

References

1. Aldrich, J., Chambers, C.: Ownership domains: Separating aliasing policy from mechanism. In: Odersky, M. (ed.) ECOOP 2004. LNCS, vol. 3086, pp. 1–25. Springer, Heidelberg (2004)
2. Bettini, L., Damiani, F., Schaefer, I.: Implementing Software Product Lines using Traits. In: SAC, pp. 2096–2102. ACM, New York (2010)
3. Bono, V., Damiani, F., Giachino, E.: Separating Type, Behavior, and State to Achieve Very Fine-grained Reuse. In: FTfJP (2007), `http://www.cs.ru.nl/ftfjp/`

4. Bono, V., Damiani, F., Giachino, E.: On Traits and Types in a Java-like setting. In: TCS (Track B). IFIP, vol. 273, pp. 367–382. Springer, Heidelberg (2008)
5. Boyapati, C.: SafeJava: A Unified Type System for Safe Programming. PhD thesis, Massachusetts Institute of Technology (February 2004)
6. Boyapati, C., Liskov, B., Shrira, L.: Ownership types for object encapsulation. In: POPL, pp. 213–223. ACM Press, New York (2003)
7. Clarke, D.: Object Ownership and Containment. PhD thesis, Univ. New South Wales (2001)
8. Clarke, D., Potter, J., Noble, J.: Ownership types for flexible alias protection. In: OOPSLA, pp. 48–64. ACM Press, New York (1998)
9. Cunningham, D., Dietl, W., Drossopoulou, S., Francalanza, A., Müller, P., Summers, A.J.: Universe types for topology and encapsulation. In: de Boer, F.S., Bonsangue, M.M., Graf, S., de Roever, W.-P. (eds.) FMCO 2007. LNCS, vol. 5382, pp. 72–112. Springer, Heidelberg (2008)
10. Dietl, W., Drossopoulou, S., Müller, P.: Generic Universe Types. In: Ernst, E. (ed.) ECOOP 2007. LNCS, vol. 4609, pp. 28–53. Springer, Heidelberg (2007)
11. Ducasse, S., Nierstrasz, O., Schärli, N., Wuyts, R., Black, A.P.: Traits: A mechanism for fine-grained reuse. ACM TOPLAS 28(2), 331–388 (2006)
12. Igarashi, A., Pierce, B., Wadler, P.: Featherweight Java: A minimal core calculus for Java and GJ. ACM TOPLAS 23(3), 396–450 (2001)
13. Lagorio, G., Servetto, M., Zucca, E.: Flattening versus direct semantics for Featherweight Jigsaw. In: FOOL (2009), `http://www.cs.hmc.edu/~stone/FOOL/`
14. Liquori, L., Spiwack, A.: FeatherTrait: A Modest Extension of Featherweight Java. ACM TOPLAS 30(2), 1–32 (2008)
15. Lu, Y., Potter, J.: On ownership and accessibility. In: Thomas, D. (ed.) ECOOP 2006. LNCS, vol. 4067, pp. 99–123. Springer, Heidelberg (2006)
16. Müller, P., Poetzsch-Heffter, A.: A type system for controlling representation exposure in Java. In: FTfJP (2000), `http://www.cs.ru.nl/ftfjp/`
17. Nierstrasz, O., Ducasse, S., Schärli, N.: Flattening traits. JOT 5(4), 129–148 (2006)
18. Poetzsch-Heffter, A., Gaillourdet, J.-M., Schäfer, J.: Towards a fully abstract semantics for object-oriented program components (July 2008), `http://softech.cs.uni-kl.de/pub?id=129`
19. Poetzsch-Heffter, A., Geilmann, K., Schäfer, J.: Infering ownership types for encapsulated object-oriented program components. In: Reps, T., Sagiv, M., Bauer, J. (eds.) Wilhelm Festschrift. LNCS, vol. 4444, pp. 120–144. Springer, Heidelberg (2007)
20. Poetzsch-Heffter, A., Schäfer, J.: Modular specification of encapuslated object-oriented components. In: de Boer, F.S., Bonsangue, M.M., Graf, S., de Roever, W.-P. (eds.) FMCO 2005. LNCS, vol. 4111, pp. 313–341. Springer, Heidelberg (2006)
21. Poetzsch-Heffter, A., Schäfer, J.: A representation-independent behavioral semantics for object-oriented components. In: Bonsangue, M.M., Johnsen, E.B. (eds.) FMOODS 2007. LNCS, vol. 4468, pp. 157–173. Springer, Heidelberg (2007)
22. Potanin, A., Noble, J., Clarke, D., Biddle, R.: Generic ownership for generic java. In: OOPSLA, pp. 311–324. ACM Press, New York (2006)
23. Reppy, J., Turon, A.: Metaprogramming with traits. In: Ernst, E. (ed.) ECOOP 2007. LNCS, vol. 4609, pp. 373–398. Springer, Heidelberg (2007)
24. Schäfer, J., Poetzsch-Heffter, A.: A parameterized type system for simple loose ownership domains. Journal of Object Technology (JOT) 5(6), 71–100 (2007)
25. Smith, C., Drossopoulou, S.: *Chai*: Traits for Java-like languages. In: Black, A.P. (ed.) ECOOP 2005. LNCS, vol. 3586, pp. 453–478. Springer, Heidelberg (2005)
26. Szyperski, C., Gruntz, D., Murer, S.: Component Software – Beyond Object-Oriented Programming, 2nd edn. Addison-Wesley, Reading (2002)
27. Ungar, D., Chambers, C., Chang, B.-W., Hölzle, U.: Organizing Programs Without Classes. Lisp and Symbolic Computation 4(3), 223–242 (1991)

JErlang: Erlang with Joins

Hubert Ploriniczak[1,*] and Susan Eisenbach[2]

[1] École Polytechnique Fédérale de Lausanne
hubert.plociniczak@epfl.ch
[2] Imperial College London
s.eisenbach@imperial.ac.uk
http://www.doc.ic.ac.uk/~susan/jerlang/

Abstract. ERLANG is an industrially successful functional language that uses the Actor model for concurrency. It supports the message-passing paradigm by providing pattern-matching over received messages. Unfortunately coding synchronisation between multiple processes is not straightforward. To overcome this limitation we designed and implemented JERLANG, a JOIN-CALCULUS inspired extension to ERLANG. We provide a rich set of language features with our *joins*. We present implementation details of our two alternative solutions, a library and an altered VM. Our optimisations provide JERLANG with good performance.

Keywords: Concurrency, Join-Calculus, Erlang, Static Analysis.

1 Introduction

Writing concurrent and distributed applications is at the heart of current software development. Even though these problems are not new, language development has yet to catch up with the current reality and programmers still have to use error prone techniques such as primitive locking mechanisms. An effort that improves on this situation is the single assignment functional language, ERLANG [1], for the development of concurrent, distributed, fault-tolerant and now multi-core systems. ERLANG, designed by Joe Armstrong from Ericsson, was aimed at tackling telecom problems, such as building zero downtime systems, which manage millions of concurrent processes.

For concurrency and distribution ERLANG relies on the message passing, Actor paradigm, which defines the communication between processes. However synchronisation is required in many concurrent problems and Actors are not the most natural paradigm for providing it. Our aim is to extend the choice of constructs provided to the programmer, without threatening the safety that a non-shared memory language provides. For this we chose the *join*, a synchronisation construct from the JOIN-CALCULUS [2], a calculus designed with implementation in mind, which with its firm formal foundation fits well with ERLANG, while providing elegant, powerful and expressive constructs. In

* The author worked on this research during his studies at Imperial College London.

D. Clarke and G. Agha (Eds.): COORDINATION 2010, LNCS 6116, pp. 61–75, 2010.

this paper we introduce our ERLANG extension, JERLANG, which is available with the companion technical report, source code and many examples from `http://www.doc.ic.ac.uk/~susan/jerlang/`.

In Section 2 we show the need for adding joins with an ERLANG example that is problematical. Section 3 is devoted to the definition and design decisions for JERLANG. We wanted it to remain backward-compatible with the original version and introduce features which current ERLANG programmers would want to use. Hence we couldn't just copy the ideas from existing implementations of JOCAML [3], Cϖ [4], or SCALA [5], but adapted *joins* to ERLANG's powerful message receive and pattern matching. ERLANG wouldn't have become so popular without the existence of its Open Telecom Platform (OTP) design patterns that provide customisable solutions for client-server, fault-tolerant applications development. Therefore in order to attract the ERLANG audience we provide *join* inspired client-server `behaviour` that we call **gen_joins**, for building synchronisation patterns within server applications.

We provide our *joins* implementation in the form of a stand-alone library, which contains transformation functions, available for the compiler, that convert JERLANG into ERLANG source code before it is actually checked. We have also developed a second version of JERLANG which uses ERLANG's Virtual Machine in modified form for performance reasons. In Section 4 we describe both implementations. We also present the algorithms used in the non-trivial implementation of our join-solver. Section 5 explains novel optimisations in the implementation done in order to boost the performance.

Our analysis in Section 6 has shown acceptable performance in most of the shown situations and more importantly an improved expressiveness and clarity in comparison with the original language. Finally we present related work in Section 7 and conclude in Section 8. A formal definition of our extension, included in the companion technical report, gave us a better understanding of how joins should fit into the ERLANG language and what semantics we should chose for it.

2 From Erlang to JErlang

Central to ERLANG is the notion of a *process*, created with a **spawn** statement which upon successful execution returns a process id (*PID*). To enable inter-process communication, each ERLANG process has a single mailbox containing a queue for incoming messages. Sending asynchronous messages to other processes is done through a **!** (send) operator: `Pid ! Value`.

```
receive
  {msg, Val1, Res} when (Val1 == test) -> Res; %% pattern with guard
  {error, Error} -> none
after DefaultTimeout -> timeout end
```

Listing 1. Typical actor programming in ERLANG

A *process* analyses the contents of the mailbox using the *Selective Receive* construct, as shown in listing 1. The incoming messages are tested against all patterns until a match is found (with satisfied guards) or the timeout limit is reached. Only the idle time of waiting for new messages contributes towards the latter.

The **receive** construct has its limitations. Consider synchronising on two messages that match the patterns {**get, A**} and {**set, B**}, where A and B are equal, given the following mailbox (the oldest message is on the left): ({**get, 1**} · {**set, 4**} · {**set, 2**} · {**get, 2**}). A typical implementation by a beginner ERLANG programmer is presented below:

```
receive
  {get, X} ->  receive {set, Y} when (X == Y) -> {found, X} end;
  {set, X} ->  receive {get, Y} when (X == Y) -> {found, X} end
end
```

When retrieving messages from a mailbox, the operation will match the first {**get, X**} pattern and get stuck, since there is no message {**set, 1**} in the mailbox, as X is now bounded. The programmers must consider the possible layouts of the mailbox and how the processes would interact.

Listing 2 presents a refined program where we continuously fetch messages from the queue and at the stage when no synchronisation can be fulfilled with the first message (**after 0**), we resend it (**self() !**) and call the function again until successful (**Func(Func)**). The order of the messages in the queue is not preserved, the solution is error prone and inefficient and wastes computational power, whenever the second pattern cannot be satisfied. ERLANG programmers also lack the language support they need in several other areas, such as matching on multiple messages that convey priority values. This limitation of the language leads to complicated code, which in turn leads to the re-invention of the mailbox mechanism at the application level.

```
A = fun(Func) ->
  receive
    {get, X} -> receive {set, Y} when (X == Y) -> {found, X}
                after 0 -> self() ! {get, X}, Func(Func) end
    {set, X} -> receive {get, Y} when (X == Y) -> {found, X}
                after 0 -> self() ! {set, X}, Func(Func) end
  end,
A(A)
```

Listing 2. Synchronisation on two messages without order preservation

The JOIN-CALCULUS [2] is a process calculus, computationally equivalent to the π-CALCULUS [2], but designed to be a basis for a concurrent programming language. The JOIN-CALCULUS introduces *multi-way join patterns* that enable synchronisation of multiple message patterns on different communication channels. It is this construct that made it our choice for adding to ERLANG. As a

JOIN-CALCULUS example program consider a single-cell stack. In this buffer you can only **push** an item if the buffer is empty. If the buffer is full and a **pop** occurs, the **pop** and **push** *join* is reduced, and the item is retrieved, making the buffer empty.

$$def\ pop\langle\mu\rangle \mid s\langle\nu\rangle \triangleright empty\langle\rangle \mid \mu\langle\nu\rangle \wedge push\langle t\rangle \mid empty\langle\rangle \triangleright s\langle t\rangle$$

Symbol | defines the *and* semantics in the join operation, symbol $\wedge$ combines the related join definitions together and $\triangleright$ precedes the join's action definition.

3 JErlang Language Features

JERLANG provides synchronisation semantics with a **receive**-like join construct. Using the guards in listing 3 we end up with the intuitive (and correct) solution to the motivating problem from listing 2 which reduces the eight lines to one.

```
receive {get, X} and {set, Y} when (X == Y) -> {found, X} end
```

Listing 3. Synchronisation on two messages with guards in JERLANG

In the JOIN-CALCULUS implementations of JOCAML [3] and Cϖ [4] whenever there is more than one satisfiable join then the execution is non-deterministic. In the implementation of **receive** in JERLANG we assume that the semantics of *First-Match* [6] provides more predictable behaviour. With *First-Match* strategy we gradually increase the "window" of the mailbox which is used to analyse deterministically if any join can be satisfied with it. The strategy ensures that whenever a join is satisfied by a strict prefix of the original mailbox then it is the smallest prefix that can satisfy any join. Whenever the current mailbox prefix is able to satisfy more than a single join, then the order of declaration of the joins determines the successful one. Obviously, the order of messages for such prefix is significant for matching, but here it is enough to assume that the matching of the messages follows the total ordering scheme.

```
self() ! {foo, one}, self() ! {error, 404}, self() ! {bar, two},
receive
    {foo, A} and {bar, B} -> {error, {A, B}};
    {error, 404}          -> {ok, error_expected};
    {error, Reason}       -> {error, Reason}        %% general error
end
```

Listing 4. Impact of First-match semantics on joins

Example 4 underlines the consequence of our matching strategy where the result of the joins depends on the ordering of the messages. JERLANG's priority is to preserve the original sequence of the messages during each pattern-matching attempt. By looking only at the first two messages of the mailbox in the example (starting with an empty mailbox), the second join is satisfied after the analysis of the first two messages, whereas the first join at this stage still misses one more successful pattern. By ensuring this deterministic behaviour in our implementation we believe that developers gain more control. *First-Match* also allows for having the typical design schema where patterns are described from the least to the most general.

```
receive
  {amount, Transaction, Money} and {limit, LowerLimit, UpperLimit}
      when (Money < UpperLimit and Money > LowerLimit) ->
    commit_withdrawal(Money, Limit);
  {abort, Trans} and {amount, Transaction, Money}
      when (Trans == Transaction) ->
    abort_withdrawal(Transaction, Money)
after Timeout -> abort_withdrawal_timeout(Transaction) end
```

Listing 5. Guards and timeout used in cash withdrawal in JErlang

Guards and timeouts in joins have often been omitted in Join-Calculus implementations due to complexity and performance issues. Yet it was important to include them in our work as they are commonly used in Erlang. In listing 5 we use guards (using **when**) to perform sanity checks for the withdrawal transaction that was requested by an external user and a timeout (**after**) to abort withdrawal actions that take too long. As in Erlang, guards in JErlang cannot contain side effects, therefore assignments or user-defined functions are prohibited.

Unlike all of the other Join-Calculus's implementations JErlang allows for non-linear patterns. In other words patterns in joins can contain the same unbound variables and therefore synchronise on their values as well (due to Erlang's single value assignment) in a structural equivalence manner. Listing 6 presents a shorter version of example 3. Non-linear patterns are often used by Erlang programmers in function headers or simple matching with variables. Non Erlang programmers might initially regard it as a possible source of confusion when mixing bound and unbound variables, yet as we said its usage is very common in the original language.

```
receive {get, X} and {set, X} -> {found, X} end
```

Listing 6. A one-cell buffer in JErlang

JErlang introduces an optional propagation attribute which allows developers to say that whenever a pattern matches, all the unbound variables in it should become bound in the join's body but the message itself should not be removed from the mailbox. To enable it, the programmer wraps the pattern with the **prop** closure. Propagation is not known in the Join-Calculus world but introduced successfully in Constraint Handling Rules[7,6]. It can obviously be implemented by implicitly sending the same message in the body of the join (see Haskell prototype by Lam and Sulzmann in [8]), however we are convinced that our feature is more readable and less error prone. More importantly, whenever a search is performed on the mailbox again, the message will not be placed at the end of the queue, and thus will get higher priority so that the matching should be performed faster. Dynamic propagation within the body would significantly deteriorate the clarity of the matching logic, as for example it is unclear at which point the other messages should be discarded. Listing 7 presents an authorisation procedure using propagation.

```
receive
    prop({session, Id}) and {action, A, Id} -> doAction(A, Id);
    {session, Id} and {logout, Id}          -> logout_user(Id)
end
```

Listing 7. Session support using propagation in JErlang

JErlang, as in Erlang, allows for the creation of synchronous calls. This can be achieved by appending a process identifier value to the message, so that the receiver knows where to send the reply.

```
accept(Key) -> jerlang_gen_joins:call(dest, {accept, self(), Key}).
enter(Value) -> jerlang_gen_joins:call(dest, {enter, Value}).
valid(Amount) -> jerlang_gen_joins:cast(dest, {valid, Amount}).

handle_join({accept, PidA, Key} and {enter, Pid1, Val1} and
            {enter, Pid2, Val2} and {valid, 2}, State) ->
  {[{reply, {ok, 2}}, {reply, {ok, Key}}, {reply, {ok, Key}}, noreply],
     [{Key, Pid, Val1, Val2} | State] }      %% new state
```

Listing 8. Barrier synchronisation in **gen_joins** with combination of synchronous and asynchronous messages

To provide full conformance with the Erlang infrastructure we decided to implement an extension of **gen_server**[1], a popular design pattern used for building complex, fault-tolerant client-server applications. **gen_joins** is a natural extension of the **gen_server** design pattern that allows for the definition of joins, i.e. for synchronisation on multiple synchronous and asynchronous messages (calls). Listing 8 shows an extract of a JErlang program that has synchronous (**accept, enter**) and asynchronous (**valid**) tuple messages in the join. We follow Erlang's standards, where the former is represented by execution of **call** and the latter by **cast**. Functions for sending the messages (**dest** is just the name of the target process) and a separate callback function **handle_join** allow for clear separation of the API from the server implementation. The callback function mirrors the action of **receive** with the additional parameter (here named **State**) representing the internal state of the server process. Asynchronous messages should always return a **noreply** value,

[1] See http://erlang.org/doc/man/gen_server.html

whereas synchronous ones can either return a value (that conforms to the structure {**reply, ReplyVal**}) or **noreply**. In the latter case the caller will stall forever or timeout.

4 Implementation

The main problem with implementing joins inside ERLANG's VM was the lack of the necessary operators to enable us to manipulate and inspect the processes' mailboxes. Apart from that we were constrained by consistency, intuitiveness and determinism of execution of the standard ERLANG, so that current programmers feel eager to try out our extension. We decided to implement two different systems, both of which include a transformation module (**parse_transform**, explained later) that can produce valid ERLANG code:

- The pure library version. It supports an internal queue that fetches, analyses and stores messages in the same order as they appear in the VM mailbox. The main drawback lies in its performance.
- We provide low-level functions, constructs and logic to manipulate the mailboxes inside ERLANG's VM and then use them from a higher-level JERLANG library (different from the above) to provide the necessary joins logic. The main drawback lies in it providing a non-standard VM.

Join constructs are written using the familiar **receive** (or **handle_join**) construct. In order to facilitate this feature we use **parse_transform**, an experimental module available in ERLANG's standard library, that allows the developers to use ERLANG syntax, but with different semantics. The transform-function receives syntactically valid ERLANG abstract syntax tree (AST), JERLANG in our case, and creates a new semantically valid AST. The aim of our transformation is to find joins patterns, create necessary tests for patterns and joins (in the form of multiple anonymous functions) and the code that initiates the call to the library modules, which perform the actual join operations. This allows the programmers to write clear and intuitive join definitions without studying a library API.

```
test_receive(Input) ->
    A = 12,
    receive {ok, Input} and [A, Rest] -> valid end.
-------------------
FirstPartialTest  = fun({ok, Input}) -> true end,
SecondPartialTest = fun([A, _]) -> true end,
FinalTest  = fun([{ok, Input}, [A, Rest]]) -> true end.
```

Listing 9. Simple joins in JERLANG and corresponding tests

Since in the implementation of JERLANG, we perform isolated tests only for patterns, without taking into consideration the body of the join, the former would create multiple false *unused variable* warnings by the compiler. Therefore we perform a simplified (syntax) *Reaching Definitions Analysis* [9]. This allows us to create valid test functions for patterns: we leave the original name for the bound variables and substitute the unbound variables with the neutral _ as presented in listing 9. Without this analysis, line 6 would create an *unused variable* warning for header **`[A, Rest]`**.

In **`gen_joins`** behaviour joins are specified in the header of the function instead of in the body and hence do not require any past knowledge of the variables. To avoid *unbound variable* errors and execute the partial matching tests on non-linear patterns as soon as possible, we perform a variant of static *Live Variable Analysis* [9]. This enables us to determine whether the variable in the test for partial joins should be substituted with the neutral _ or left unchanged because it used more than once in the join. This way we can also eliminate the unsatisfiable branches in the joins solver quickly and still create valid code.

The ERLANG VM executes the bytecode, called BEAM, which is the result of a few transformation phases on the initial Abstract Syntax Tree. As an example of execution we consider accessing the process' mailbox using the **`receive`** construct, which results roughly in the following set of steps:

1. Each process maintains a pointer to the last tested message within the mailbox. The pointer is re-set to the beginning of the queue only when first entering the **`receive`** construct.
2. Take the next message as the operand for matching.
3. Take the current instruction representing the pattern, and try to match it with the message from step 2.
   If matching is not successful, we go to step 4, otherwise we go to step 6.
4. If there are more patterns then we increment the current program counter (PC) and go to step 3. If we reached the last pattern and there are still some messages left then we update the pointer of the mailbox to the next message, update the PC to the first pattern of **`receive`** and execute step 2. Otherwise we go to step 5.
5. The VM sets up the timeout counter (if this were not done already), and the process is suspended. It will either be awakened by the timer (and jump to the timeout action) or by a new message (go to step 1).
6. A successful match frees the memory associated with the currently pointed-to message, sets the mailbox pointer to the head of the queue and jumps to the BEAM instruction associated with the pattern.

One of the constructs that we incorporated into the modified VM and which enabled us to parse the message queues more freely without immediate discards (and duplicate queues), is **`search`**. It follows the same syntax as a standard **`receive`**, yet has slightly different semantics. Namely it maintains a separate *search pointer* on the mailbox that is independent from the original mailbox's *pointer*. For large mailboxes and complicated join combinations, it could be the case that a large number of calls to the mailbox need to be made to do pattern tests. To improve the performance over a queue based implementation, we use orthogonally the *uthash*[2] hash tables for each JERLANG process, which maps identifiers to the addresses of the messages.

To reduce the number of repeated (and often unnecessary) pattern matching, which most other JOIN-CALCULUS implementations do not do, we added a new data structure that serves as a cache for storage and retrieval of the partial results of the matching. The overhead is acceptable, because we store only the messages' indices. We also had to modify the already presented ERLANG **receive** algorithm to incorporate the joins resolution mechanism. The simplified description, which follows the formal definition of the operational semantics, is given below:

1. Take the message from the queue and the first join.
2. Take the list of tests associated with the join and check the message on each of the patterns. For each successful test, we store the message's index in the cache of the corresponding pattern.
3. We go to step 6 if none of the patterns' caches was updated, otherwise to step 4.
4. We take the final test function, i.e. the one that checks all the patterns and guards together, associated with the join and run it on all possible permutations of the satisfying messages. We go to step 5 if there is at least one successful run, or step 6 otherwise.
5. Retrieve the associated messages for each pattern and execute the join's body in the new context that updates the previously unbound variables.
6. We take the next join and go to step 2. If the current join is the last one and there are still some messages left in the queue, we update the message pointer to the next message and go to step 1, otherwise we stall until a new message arrives to the process.[3]

In JERLANG with the modified VM, step 1 uses the **search** construct. In the non-VM version we use a standard **receive** construct that matches any message and puts it into the "internal" library queue for analysis.

Joins that exist in the **gen_joins** behaviour offer more optimisation possibilities because unlike in **receive**, they are defined only once, during compile time, and there is the possibility of reusing gathered knowledge. The joins solver doesn't have to repeat the tests for the patterns for the already parsed messages since successful running of the test function is independent of other factors. Another challenge introduced by **gen_joins** is the addition of the *status* variable[4]. Since the execution of a join may have side-effects on its value, joins that previously couldn't be fired may now have become successful. Our algorithm takes into account the possibility of a chain of join actions that does not involve analysis of any new messages (similar to [10]).

---

[2] http://uthash.sourceforge.net

[3] *Timeout* is treated as in the description of **receive**.

[4] The status variable allows for internal storage in the client-server pattern.

5 Optimisations

For performance reasons we incorporated ideas from the RETE algorithm [11], used for efficient solving of *Production Rule Systems*. RETE reduces the amount of redundant operations through partial evaluation, thus allowing for steady building of knowledge. RETE uses so called alpha- and beta-reductions to build an efficient network of information nodes representing knowledge. The former focuses on testing independent nodes, irrespective of any connections they can have, whereas the latter gradually, from the left-hand side, tries to find a satisfying connection. As a simplified example assume the existence of a statement consisting of *A, B, C* and *D* predicates. The alpha-reduction will correspond to testing *A*, *B*, *C* and *D* individually, and beta-reduction will incrementally check *A and B*, *A and B and C* and *A and B and C and D*.
We implemented the algorithm sequentially because:

- We still can profit from *First-Match* semantics.
- The order of the messages in the mailbox is preserved.
- JERLANG has to preserve the no-shared-memory principle between processes.

JERLANG's alpha-reduction is performed by having local test functions for each of the patterns of the joins. Beta-reduction has to be performed by having multiple test functions that perform partial checks of the joins. Checking for consistency is performed through the matching of the headers. Joins of length 1 would have a single beta function and for joins with *n* patterns, we produce *n - 1* beta functions. Listing 10 presents a **`handle_join`** function with 4 patterns and the corresponding beta-functions for the RETE algorithm.

```
handle_join( {operation, Id, Op} and {num, Id, A} and {num, Id, B}
                and {num, Id, C}, State) when (A > B) ->
   Res = Op([A,B,C]),
  {[{reply, {ok, Res}}, noreply, noreply, noreply], [Res | State]}.
 %% -------------------------------
 [fun([{operation, Id, _}, {num, Id, _}], _) -> true end,
  fun([{operation, Id, _}, {num, Id, _}, {num, Id, _}], _)
                                                 -> true end,
  fun([{operation, Id, _}, {num, Id, A}, {num, Id, B},
         {num, Id, _}], Status) when (A > B)    -> true end]
```

Listing 10. Multi-pattern join in **`gen_joins`** and the corresponding beta-reduction tests

In **`gen_joins`**, the internal state can be changed during the execution of the body of the join so care is taken to preserve possible knowledge instead of repeating all the partial tests when not necessary.

To improve the efficiency of the algorithm we prune branches of the search space that cannot be satisfied or that are satisfiable by some previous branches in the search order. Hence sequences of messages that only permute equal messages are pruned. This radically increased the performance of the Santa Claus problem solution (see Section 6). In example 10 guards and the status variable are applied only to the last test function. We believe that this (typical) construction insufficiently uses knowledge about the patterns, because variables **A** and **B** in line 7 already provide information necessary to use the guard **A** > **B**. Therefore we check the earliest beta-function to which we can apply guards and additional variables, so that the filtering of invalid message combinations is done as soon as possible. This feature is especially interesting for the case when JERLANG has to handle very large mailboxes, an Achilles' heel of ERLANG.

We decided to investigate the dependency between ordering of the patterns and efficiency of the joins solver, especially in the context of the RETE algorithm. It is important to remember that each set of messages that satisfies a partial test from the joins increases the time to solve it. Therefore it is crucial to abort any incorrect sequence of messages as soon as it is possible. The analysis of the structure of the joins assigns a rank to each pattern, which depends on the number of variables that it shares with other patterns, taking into account the occurrence of the variables inside guards and the status parameter (if available). Using this information we can reorder the patterns in the join during compile time, without actually losing the deterministic ordering guarantee, gaining reasonable speed-ups for joins with multiple dependencies. This feature worked well along with the guard optimisations described above.

6 Evaluation

With JERLANG we aimed to increase the expressiveness of ERLANG for handling concurrency problems while keeping negative effects on performance as small as possible. One of the problems that drove the development of JERLANG is the *Santa Claus* problem first defined by Trono [12]. In this synchronisation problem, *Santa* sleeps at the North Pole waiting to be awakened by nine *reindeer* or three *elves* and then performs work with them. However the waiting group of the former has higher priority if both full groups gather at the same time.

```
receive
    {reindeer, Pid1} and {reindeer, Pid2} and {reindeer, Pid3}
      and {reindeer, Pid4} and {reindeer, Pid5} and {reindeer, Pid6}
      and {reindeer, Pid7} and {reindeer, Pid8} and {reindeer, Pid9} ->
        io:format("Ho, ho, ho! Let's deliver presents!~n"),
        [Pid1, Pid2, Pid3, Pid4, Pid5, Pid6, Pid7, Pid8, Pid9];
    {elf, Pid1} and {elf, Pid2} and {elf, Pid3} ->
        io:format("Ho, ho, ho! Let's discuss R&D possibilities!~n"),
        [Pid1, Pid2, Pid3]
end
```

Listing 11. Santa Claus solution in JERLANG

Many solutions were proposed, using semaphores (or similar), but since the advent of the JOIN-CALCULUS a more elegant solution is possible. We compare our JERLANG solution with one provided by Richard A. O'Keefe [5] written in ERLANG. Listing 11 presents an extract from our solution (the pids allow us to reply to the processes representing the *reindeer* and *elves*). With JERLANG we are able to say: "Synchronise on 9 *reindeer* or 3 *elves*, with the priority given to the former". Typically the priority remains the hardest part to solve but with our *First-Match* semantics we get it for free. An ERLANG solution contains multiple nested receive statements therefore it is hard to understand immediately what is the aim of the code and how the priority is resolved. The JERLANG version of *Santa Claus* is half the size of the original ERLANG version.

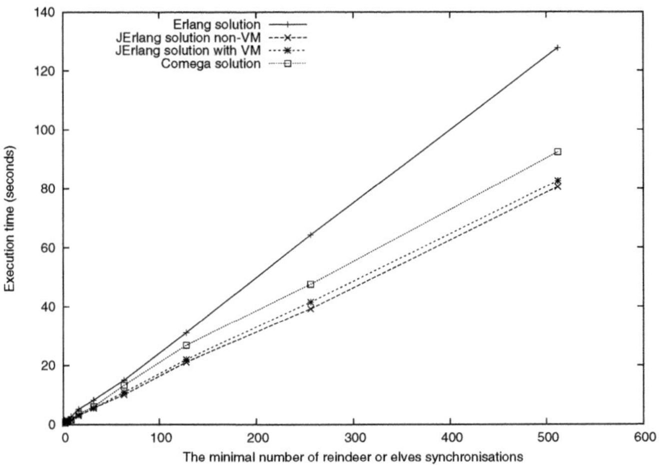

Fig. 1. Execution of the *Santa Claus* problem in **gen_joins**, implemented in ERLANG as well as JERLANG with and without VM support. The problem artificially limits the synchronisation to measure the correct time of execution.

Our tests have shown that VM-supported JERLANG gives better results but only for larger mailboxes. The overhead that we introduce is too big for small mailboxes. Figure 1 presents an average time of execution of the *Santa Claus* problem in ERLANG, Cϖ(using implementation from [4]), JERLANG with and without the VM support. The difference between the two JERLANG versions is minimal because consumers work at a similar rate as producers. Unsurprisingly, the time of execution of the simulation increases linearly with the number of required synchronisations. It is interesting that the optimised JERLANG is faster than the one implemented using ERLANG, as a result of our optimisations, as one would expect a manual, specific and overhead-free implementation to be more efficient.

[5] http://www.cs.otago.ac.nz/staffpriv/ok/santa

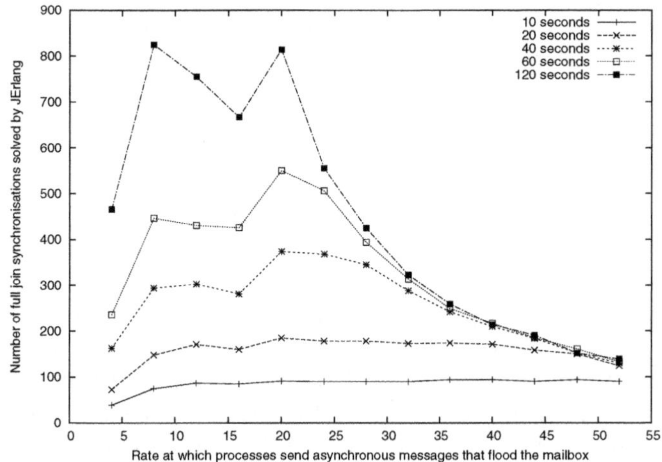

Fig. 2. VM supported JERLANG benchmark. The effect of increasing the rate at which the processes produce asynchronous messages on the number of synchronisations that the join solver is able to analyse in a given quantity of time (different lines). We introduced random delays to clearly mark the tendency in the performance and therefore the real numbers of synchronisations are higher.

To experiment with the performance of joins we developed tests that create competitive, heavy-load client-server scenarios. Our aim was to develop situations where the numerous producers contributed to a sudden increase in the size of the mailbox. Additionally, we generated messages that do not necessarily match the specific patterns or won't match the full join, which is much closer to real systems. Figure 2 shows the drop in the number of synchronisations that our joins-solver was able to find, as we kept increasing the rate at which the messages were produced (exponentially), with the rate of messages that can actually perform a join remaining constant. The empirical results have shown that the difference between using the non-VM JERLANG and a hash-map data structure inside the VM is negligible for small mailboxes, but for this benchmark we were seeing at least double boost in the performance for VM supported JERLANG (omitted on the graphs). Additionally for simple benchmarking we compared different implementations of a single cell buffer (using the example from [4]) and the performance of JERLANG was better from its Cϖ's equivalent (roughly 20%) but worse than the SCALA version (10%), due to its speed for simple matching.

7 Related Work

The JOIN-CALCULUS has inspired many implementations, the first being JOCAML[3], an extension of OCAML. Compilation of patterns is described in [10] in the JOCAML implementation. In comparison to our work, JOCAML requires the uniqueness of patterns in the joins and forces an awkward syntax when using the same patterns in different join definitions. Guards are disallowed in JOCAML.

Cϖ (previously POLYPHONIC C#) [4] was introduced as an extension of the popular C# language where it introduces an object-oriented version of joins, known as *chords*. JERLANG's **gen_joins** is similar if we want to synchronise on multiple function calls but Cϖ allows for at most one synchronous method call in the whole *chord* and suffers from similar feature limitations as JOCAML. A Cϖ variant has been implemented as a library and can be used on the .NET platform with languages like VISUAL BASIC or C# itself.

In HASKELLJOINRULES[6] project the authors designed efficient implementation of *Constraint Handling Rules*(CHR), concepts which were shown in [13] to be comparable to JOIN-CALCULUS. HASKELLJOINRULES was one of the first to propose guards along with the join patterns. It also inspired us to include a propagation feature (included in CHR), however JERLANG, unlike HASKELLJOINRULES, proposes a more efficient approach instead of primitive re-send semantics. Sulzmann and Lam proposed a join construct for ERLANG in [6], but the semantics of their approach was vague and no prototype was built. For their HASKELL extension they focused on the implementation of a parallel solver for their *Constraints*[14,8] a possible approach for future development of JERLANG. This way though they lose some of the important guarantee like deterministic behaviour.

Eugster and Jayaram presented an extension of *Java* for creating efficient event-based systems. *EventJava* [15] allows for powerful expressions in guards, which enables it to build complex relations between asynchronous-only messages. In JERLANG, guard conditions can also span over multiple messages, but we are limited by ERLANG functionality to disallow new variables or control constructs in them. In *EventJava* the messages are transformed into a format acceptable by the off-the-shelf RETE framework. In our implementation we have focused on introducing optimisations which specifically target joins resolutions, because of better control and a lack of existing solutions in ERLANG. The *Java* extension has the option of streams yet no event can appear in more than one correlation pattern, which is reasonable for solving the problems presented in their work, but opposite to our implementation. Finally *EventJava* allows for assigning timeouts to specific events unlike JERLANG, which forces timeouts on whole joins on the receiver side. We believe that the former option would be more suitable to message queueing systems rather than JERLANG. Nevertheless the synchronous calls in **gen_joins** modules can specify timouts, therefore avoiding stalling for long running operations.

8 Conclusions and Future Work

This paper presents JERLANG, a JOIN-CALCULUS inspired extension of ERLANG. A number of examples have shown typical actor synchronisation problems that programmers encounter while writing concurrent applications, and how they can be solved using JERLANG primitives. Unlike other JOIN-CALCULUS implementations we tightly integrated joins semantics, by adding guards, timeouts, non-linear patterns and propagation to the original idea. The implementation of

[6] http://taichi.ddns.comp.nus.edu.sg/taichiwiki/HaskellJoinRules/

these features allowed us to explore the role of *First-Match* semantics in JERLANG programs.

We intend to experiment further with the various join techniques to explore the performance optimisations possibilities. It would be interesting to compare the limits of the sequential algorithms to the parallel, out-of-order joins solver and find a reasonable trade-off between JERLANG's performance and expressiveness. More in-depth static analysis of the patterns, as well as better data structures for mailboxes, promises further optimisations.

Acknowledgements. We would like to thank our shepherd, Patrick Eugster, and the reviewers for their helpful comments.

References

1. Armstrong, J.: Programming Erlang: Software for a Concurrent World. Pragmatic Bookshelf (July 2007)
2. Gonthier, G., Rocquencourt, I.: The reflexive CHAM and the Join-Calculus. In: Proceedings of the 23rd ACM Symposium on Principles of Programming Languages, pp. 372–385. ACM Press, New York (1996)
3. Mandel, L., Maranget, L.: JoCaml Documentation and Manual (Release 3.11). INRA (2008)
4. Benton, N., Cardelli, L., Polyphonic, C.: Modern Concurrency Abstractions for C#. ACM Trans. Program. Lang. Syst., 415–440 (2002)
5. Haller, P., Van Cutsem, T.: Implementing Joins using Extensible Pattern Matching. In: Lea, D., Zavattaro, G. (eds.) COORDINATION 2008. LNCS, vol. 5052, pp. 135–152. Springer, Heidelberg (2008)
6. Sulzmann, M., Lam, E.S.L., Weert, P.V.: Actors with multi-headed message receive patterns. In: Lea, D., Zavattaro, G. (eds.) COORDINATION 2008. LNCS, vol. 5052, pp. 315–330. Springer, Heidelberg (2008)
7. Sulzmann, M., Lam, E.S.: Haskell - join - rules. In: Chitil, O., Horváth, Z., Zsók, V. (eds.) IFL 2007. LNCS, vol. 5083, pp. 195–210. Springer, Heidelberg (2008)
8. Lam, E.S., Sulzmann, M.: Parallel join patterns with guards and propagation (2009)
9. Nielson, F., Nielson, H.R., Hankin, C.: Principles of Program Analysis. Springer, New York (1999)
10. Maranget, L., Fessant, F.L.: Compiling join-patterns. Electronic Notes in Computer Science. Elsevier Science Publishers, Amsterdam (1998)
11. Forgy, C.: RETE: a fast algorithm for the many pattern/many object pattern match problem. Artificial Intelligence 19, 17–37 (1982)
12. Trono, J.A.: A new exercise in concurrency. SIGCSE Bull. 26(3), 8–10 (1994)
13. Lam, E., Sulzmann, M.: Finally, a comparison between Constraint Handling Rules and Join-Calculus. In: Fifth Workshop on Constraint Handling Rules, CHR 2008 (2008)
14. Sulzmann, M., Lam, E.S.: Compiling Constraint Handling Rules with lazy and concurrent search techniques. In: CHR 2007, pp. 139–149 (2007)
15. Eugster, P., Jayaram, K.R.: Eventjava: An extension of java for event correlation. In: Drossopoulou, S. (ed.) ECOOP 2009. LNCS, vol. 5653, pp. 570–594. Springer, Heidelberg (2009)

A Hybrid Visual Dataflow Language for Coordination in Mobile Ad Hoc Networks

Andoni Lombide Carreton* and Theo D'Hondt

Software Languages Lab,
Vrije Universiteit Brussel, Pleinlaan 2 1050 Brussel, Belgium
{alombide,tjdhondt}@vub.ac.be

Abstract. Because of the dynamic nature of mobile ad hoc networks and the applications running on top of them, these applications have to be conceived as event-driven architectures. Such architectures are hard to program because coordination between concurrent and distributed mobile components has to be expressed by means of event handlers or callbacks. Applications consisting of disjoint event handlers that are independently triggered (possibly by their environment) exhibit a very implicit control flow that is hard to grasp. This paper presents a visual dataflow language tailored towards mobile applications to express the interaction between mobile components that operate on data streams. By using a visual dataflow language as a separate coordination language, the coarse grained control flow of a mobile application can be specified visually and separately from the fine grained control flow. In its turn, this allows a very explicit view on the control flow of the entire mobile application.

Keywords: dataflow programming, coordination languages, visual programming, mobile ad hoc networks.

1 Introduction

When developing pervasive applications for mobile ad hoc networks, the programmer has to deal with a number of characteristics of both the underlying network infrastructure and the applications running on top of them.

1. Devices in mobile networks often experience intermittent connectivity with nearby peers. Because devices are mobile, they can move out of and back into range of each other at any point in time. Hence, connections between devices are volatile.
2. Applications deployed on mobile ad hoc networks cannot rely on fixed infrastructure such as servers.
3. Mobile applications moving through different ad hoc networks should be able to discard unavailable services and find replacement services at runtime. Applications should remain functional on roaming devices.

* Funded by a doctoral scholarship of the "Institute for the Promotion of Innovation through Science and Technology in Flanders" (IWT Vlaanderen).

D. Clarke and G. Agha (Eds.): COORDINATION 2010, LNCS 6116, pp. 76–91, 2010.

4. Services offered by nearby devices in the network should be discovered at runtime and trigger the appropriate actions without requiring prior knowledge about these devices or services.
5. The data that is interchanged between different parties often takes the form of a stream, for example a stream of sensor readings or a stream of scanned RFID tags.

These characteristics make it impossible to structure pervasive applications as monolithic programs which accept a fixed input and compute it into some output. Instead, to allow responsiveness to changes in the mobile ad hoc network, programming paradigms targeting pervasive applications propose the adoption of event-driven architectures [1,2,3,4]. In such event-driven architectures, the programmer no longer steers the application's control flow explicitly. Rather, control is handed over to the application logic whenever an event is detected by means of callbacks. By adopting such an event-driven architecture, the application logic becomes scattered over different event handlers or callbacks which may be triggered independently [5]. This is the phenomenon known as *inversion of control* [6]. Control flow among event handlers has to be expressed implicitly through manipulation of shared state. Unlike subsequent function calls, code triggered by different event handlers cannot use the runtime stack to make local variables visible to other executions (*stack ripping* [7]), such that these variables have to be made instance variables, global variables, etc. This is why in complex systems such an event-driven architecture can become hard to develop, understand and maintain [8,9]. Coordination of distributed and concurrent activities can be done on a higher level by means of a separate coordination language. However, current coordination languages lack support to deal with all the characteristics of mobile ad hoc network applications pointed out above.

The visual dataflow language presented in this paper is geared towards applications running on mobile ad hoc networks in the following ways:

1. Application components that move out of range are either treated as temporarily or permanently disconnected. In the latter case, replacement components can be discovered and automatically plugged into the distributed application.
2. Mobile application components are dynamically discovered based on broadcasted role names - acting as topics in a decentralized publish/subscribe architecture - that describe their behavior, and require no additional infrastructure to discover each other.
3. Distributed application components interact by means of reactive scripts that propagate events to dataflow variables and depend on their own set of dataflow variables. This is a straight-forward interface that allows such distributed components to be made dependent on changes in their environment without relying on an explicit callback-style that would introduce the problems mentioned above.
4. The basic dataflow coordination model is extended with infrastructure to allow different strategies of dataflow event propagation tweaked towards a

mobile ad hoc network setting, offering one-to-one, one-to-many, many-to-one, and many-to-many communication among a volatile set of communication partners.

1.1 Coordination in Mobile Ad Hoc Networks

Gelernter and Carriero [10] argue that a complete programming model consists of both a *computation model* and a *coordination model*. The computation model allows programmers to build a single computational activity (e.g., a process, a thread, an actor in an actor language). The coordination model is the glue that binds separate activities into a concurrent application. An ordinary computation language embodies a computation model. Different concurrent languages provide in addition a coordination model that ranges over different levels of abstraction, from manual thread creation and locking to event-based communication among distributed processes. An example of the latter will be discussed in Section 2. A coordination language embodies a coordination model; it provides operations to *create* computational activities and to support *communication* among them. We require the coordination model to be applicable in mobile ad hoc networks, meaning that the model should be resilient to network partitioning and reactive to network topology changes. In the remainder of this section, we discuss some related work in the form of existing coordination and visual (dataflow) languages.

Coordination Languages. Thanks to their decoupling both in space and time of the different communicating processes, coordination based on tuple spaces is quite popular for mobile ad hoc network applications. Both the LIME [3] and TOTA [11] middleware implement variations on the original tuple space model targeted towards mobile ad hoc network applications. In both systems however, devices respond to the appearance of such tuples by registering *reactions*. Reactions are an advanced form of callbacks, where the callback gets executed as soon as a tuple in the tuple space is successfully pattern-matched.

Reo [12] is a glue language that allows the orchestration of different heterogeneous, distributed and concurrent software components. Reo is based on the notion of mobile channels and has a coordination model wherein complex coordinators, called connectors, are compositionally built out of simpler ones (where the simplest ones are channels). These different types of connectors hierarchically coordinate their constituent connectors, which eventually coordinate the software components that they interconnect. The mobility of the channels refers in this case to a user-invoked migration of a software component along with all its connected channels to a different host. This is not the automatic runtime adaptation to the frequently changing network topology in a mobile ad hoc network that we require.

Visual Languages. LabVIEW was the first software program to include graphical, iconic programming techniques to make programming more transparent and the sequence of processing visible to the user [13]. LabVIEW is based on the G visual dataflow language and the concrete implementation in the LabVIEW environment is primarily used for data acquisition, processing and monitoring in a lab setting. LabVIEW does not use dataflow for expressing distribution and/or parallelism, but for the graphical composition of software components that interact with lab hardware.

Another language that does use dataflow for expressing distribution and concurrency is Distributed Prograph [14]. Distributed Prograph is very similar to our approach in the sense that the program code of dataflow operators is dynamically sent to remote processing units. The scheduling of the execution of these operators happens at runtime, but the processing units themselves have to be known at compile time, which is unrealistic in mobile ad hoc networks. In our approach, the processing units are dynamically discovered at runtime in the mobile ad hoc network.

NesC. nesC [15] is a programming language for networked embedded systems (such as sensor networks) offering event-driven execution, a flexible concurrency model, and component-oriented application design. These components, however, are statically linked to each other via their interfaces. This makes nesC programs better statically analyzable, but restricts the language to networks of static devices instead of entirely mobile networks.

2 Fine-Grained Programming with AmbientTalk

The visual dataflow language that we propose in this paper is a hybrid language: it uses a host language to implement the dataflow operators and allows expressing the coordination among these operators visually. In our case, this host language is AmbientTalk [16,17], a distributed scripting language embedded in Java that can be used to compose Java components which are distributed across a mobile ad hoc network. The language is developed on top of the J2ME platform and runs on handheld devices such as smart phones and PDAs. Even though AmbientTalk is embedded in Java, it is a separate programming language. The embedding ensures that AmbientTalk applications can access Java objects running in the same JVM. These Java objects can also call back on AmbientTalk objects as if these were plain Java objects. The most important difference between AmbientTalk and Java is the way in which they deal with concurrency and network programming. Java is multithreaded, and provides both a low-level socket API and a high-level RPC API (Java RMI) to enable distributed computing. In contrast, AmbientTalk is a fully event-driven programming language. It provides only event loop concurrency [18] and distributed object communication by means of asynchronous message passing, which are briefly illustrated below. Event loops deal with concurrency similar to GUI frameworks (e.g. Java AWT or Swing): all concurrent activities are represented as events which are handled sequentially by an event loop thread.

To be synchronized with changes in one's environment, AmbientTalk uses a classic event-handling style by relying on closures to function as event handlers. This has two advantages: firstly closures can be used in-line and can be nested and secondly closures have access to their enclosing lexical scope. Event handlers are (by convention) registered by a call to a function that starts with **`when`**. The following code snippet illustrates how AmbientTalk can be used to discover a `LocationService` and `WeatherService` in the ad hoc network.

```
when: LocationService discovered: { |locationSvc|
 when: locationSvc<-getLocation(gpsModule.getCoordinates())
   becomes: { |myLocation|
     when: WeatherService discovered: { |weatherSvc|
       when: weatherSvc<-getWeather(myLocation)
         becomes: { |weatherInfo|
           GUI.updateWithWeatherInfo(weatherInfo);
         }}}}
```

Once the `LocationService` is discovered, it is sent a message along with the current GPS coordinates to determine the current location of the user. As soon as a reply is received, the lookup for the `WeatherService` starts. When such a service is discovered, it is sent the `getWeather` message along with the current location that was received from the `LocationService`.

The above code consists of four event handlers. The first event handler, registered by means of the **`when:discovered:`** control structure, is invoked when the language runtime discovers a `LocationService` component. Here, `LocationService` refers to a Java interface. The discovered object is accessible via the `locationSvc` variable, which denotes a remote AmbientTalk object that wraps a Java component implementing the weather service. The syntax `obj<-msg()` denotes an asynchronous message send and is used here to query the `LocationService` object for the current location of the user (e.g., city) given her GPS coordinates.

When the query message is received by the remote `locationSvc` object, that object's `getLocation` method is invoked. The return value of this method is used as the reply to the query. This reply is signaled asynchronously to the caller. The **`when:becomes:`** control structure is used to install an event handler that can process this reply. The return value is passed to this event handler (cf. the `myLocation` variable in the example). As soon as this value is received, this event handler registers two new event handlers (following the same pattern) to query a `WeatherService` about the weather at `myLocation`. Therefore, as soon as the `WeatherService` signals a reply, the user interface is updated.

As can be seen from the above example, service discovery and replies to remote queries (to causally connect the program with the outside world) are represented in AmbientTalk as events that trigger the appropriate event handlers. Care must be taken when coordinating and synchronizing asynchronous invocations: nesting callbacks (like in the example presented above) introduces simple synchronization (the discovery of the `WeatherService` only starts when a `LocationService` is discovered and has replied to the `getLocation` message), but more complex synchronization and coordination patterns require more complicated structures (the lookup of a `WeatherService` could happen, for example, in parallel without waiting for the `LocationService` to reply). While in this simple example the control flow remains apparent enough to understand, the control flow of large-scale event-driven applications can quickly become puzzling.

3 Coordinating Distributed AmbientTalk Components Using a Visual Dataflow Language

Before the Von Neumann architectures took over the parallel programming world as well, dataflow languages were popular to program massively parallel systems that used a dataflow hardware architecture [19]. By making data dependencies explicit, these languages and hardware architectures allowed a high degree of parallelization while preventing race conditions and other problems arising when parallelizing programs intended for Von Neumann architectures. Moreover, the resulting dataflow graphs are easy to visualize, allowing a visual representation of the data dependencies and the coordination they imply on the different parallel components of the application. The dataflow coordination model can be informally described as follows:

- Dataflow programs consist of *dataflow operators* that take a number of input values and return a single output value. These dataflow operators are best compared to functions or procedures in functional or imperative programming languages that always run in parallel.
- Dataflow operators communicate with each other over *dataflow edges*. These edges represent data dependencies and always flow from the output of a dataflow operator (corresponding to its output value) to one of the inputs of a dataflow operator (corresponding to one if its input values).
- When a dataflow operator is fired depends on the concrete coordination model used. Some languages only fire dataflow operators once as soon as *all* its input values have received a value. Other languages repeatedly fire the dataflow operator as soon as *one* of its input values received a *new* value

Such a coordination model allows that different dataflow operators in the dataflow graph can execute in parallel as long as their data dependencies are satisfied. For example a number of operators in a pipeline execute in parallel when the first operator is fed a stream of data. In such a pipeline the first operator is being applied to new data from the stream while operators later in the sequence are being applied to data already processed by earlier dataflow operators in the pipeline.

Currently, the dataflow paradigm is mostly used in the form of the *coarse-grained* dataflow model, as can be seen from the systems discussed in Section 1.1. In such models, the dataflow paradigm is used to orchestrate the control flow between different modules (possibly running in parallel) that can be of an arbitrary level of abstraction, usually implemented in a conventional programming language. When looking at the characteristics and requirements of mobile networks and the applications running on top of them (discussed earlier in Section 1), we have observed that the dataflow model may provide a very suitable coordination model for this kind of applications. These applications consist of different distributed components running in parallel that in many cases have to be invoked whenever some external data is fed to them (event-driven architectures). Hence, the driving force for program execution in such applications is not the control flow, which is explicitized by the order of statements in an imperative textual program, but the data flow, which is implicit in an imperative textual program. Furthermore, in many cases these data come in the form of streams, such as continuous sensor readings. These observations, combined with the basic coordination model of the AmbientTalk programming language, led us to the integration of AmbientTalk with a coarse grained dataflow coordination model, that explicitizes the data flow, and a graphical language embodying this model. The main advantage above implementing everything in plain AmbientTalk, is that the coarse-grained control flow, which in AmbientTalk would become very implicit in a complex interplay of different event handlers, is now represented in a very explicit visual notation based on the dataflow coordination model. In this section, this visual dataflow language is explained.

3.1 Visual Dataflow Programming

Figure 1 shows the general idea behind our visual dataflow language. The languages uses the boxes-and-arrows notation to denote dataflow operators and dataflow dependencies between them respectively. The identifier before the -> symbol denotes the *role* of the operator (for now, it suffices to think of a role as a procedure name). The code after the -> symbol can be any list of AmbientTalk expressions and comprises the code of the dataflow operator, which serves as its implementation. This code can be parametrized by variables that are bound to the input values of the dataflow operator. This is achieved by naming the edges, such that these names can be used as the names of the dataflow parameters in the dataflow operator implementation. The dataflow operator firing rule in our visual languages is the following: *any new value propagated along an incoming dataflow edge results in reapplying the dataflow operator with the new value of the dataflow variable.*

Executing a dataflow program happens by distributing the dataflow operator code to devices that match the roles designated to the operators in the graph and

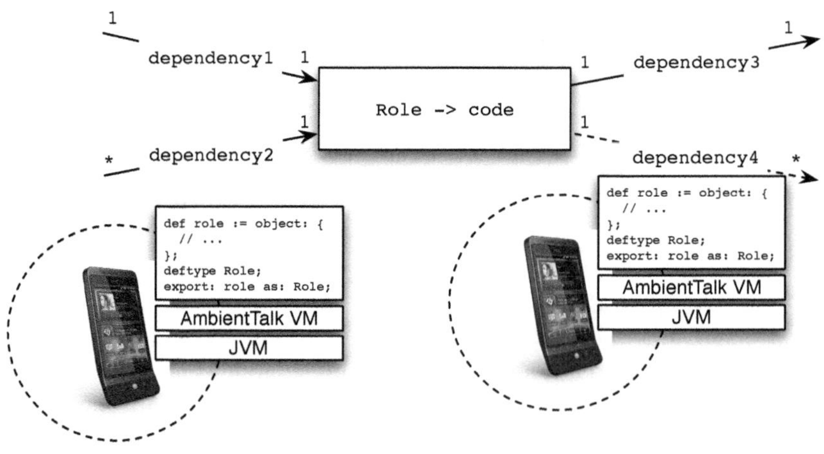

Fig. 1. Basic architecture of a dataflow program

installing communication channels that represent the dependency edges between them. Dependency edges can be either *fixed* (uninterrupted lines) or *rebinding* (dashed lines). The service discovery needed for this is further explained in Section 3.2. For this, these devices should have an AmbientTalk virtual machine running on top of a Java virtual machine, and additionally host the necessary library code to execute their role code. The code associated with a role is mobile AmbientTalk code that can call any AmbientTalk or Java library code that is made visible to it by the device. This is further explained in Section 3.3.

Finally, to cater for group communication in mobile ad hoc networks, we extended the basic dataflow coordination model with dependency arities that allow dataflow dependencies to be one-to-one, one-to-many, many-to-one, many-to-many. This is indicated by the programmer by changing the annotations at the start point or end point of the graph edges and is further explained in Section 3.5.

Before going further into detail, we sketch a small scenario. Envision the shop of the future where every product is tagged with an RFID tag. Customers pick up these products and carry them to certain locations in the shop where the tagged products can be scanned. In a CD shop for example, one could install an RFID reader below the listening stations where customers can listen to the albums they are carrying before buying them. Based on the list of scanned products, the device scanning the products requests a list of recommended products from a remote party. In the CD shop demo application that we have implemented this remote party is the LastFM web service[1]. The resulting list of recommended products is passed to a software service representing the shop and is filtered to only contain the products that are currently in stock, extended with their location in the shop (based on products that are scanned by RFID devices in the shop's shelves). Given these three pieces of information (the list of scanned products carried by the user, the list of recommended products, and the list of recommended products available in the shop), a small application on the user's PDA or smartphone is updated to show this information and help the user in getting the products he wants. As soon as the user removes a product from the range of the device scanning the products (for example by putting it back in the shelves) or brings another product in range of the device, this change is reflected on the application running on his PDA or smartphone.

In this scenario, we consider the user's PDA or smartphone a mobile device moving throughout the shop and being dynamically discovered by multiple RFID readers running the dataflow program. Interaction between the user's mobile device and other devices present in the shop happens entirely spontaneous over wireless connections that can break at any point in time when the user moves out of range of one of the components. However, such intermittent connections as the the user roams the shop should be tolerated and not break the application. The continuous flow of RFID data generated by the different components of the application is usually processed by representing this data as data streams [20,21]. The screenshot shown in figure 2 shows the scenario implemented in our

[1] `http://www.last.fm/api/intro`

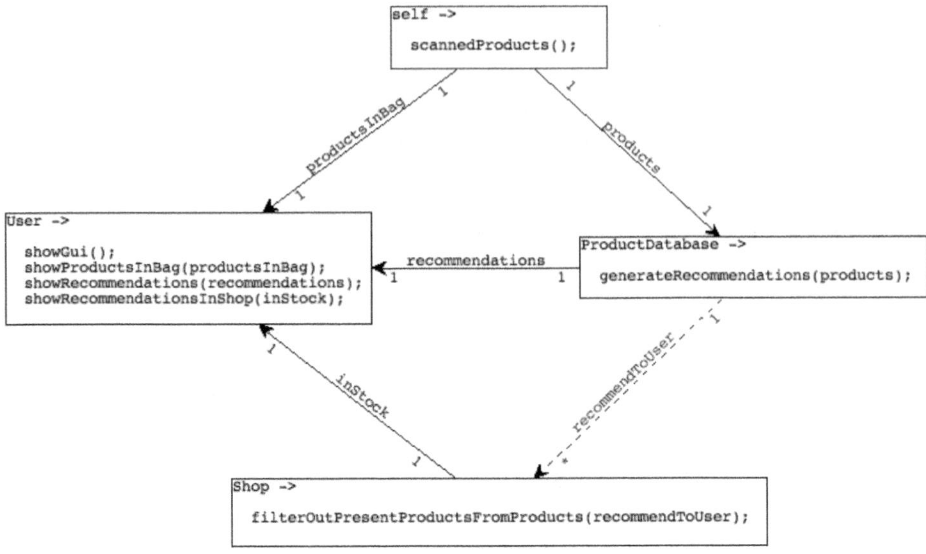

Fig. 2. AmbientTalk visual dataflow example

visual dataflow language. In this example, the Java package paths to the methods that are invoked in the code are omitted for the sake of brevity, but other than that the program shown here is entirely functional. Dataflow operators are represented as boxes while the directed edges connecting these boxes represent data dependencies.

3.2 Discovering Operator Nodes

Our visual dataflow language serves the purpose of coordinating application components running in parallel and distributed over a mobile network. Because the devices hosting these application components can move out of range and back into range of each other at any point in time, our dataflow engine has to discover these application components at runtime without relying on naming servers or other fixed infrastructure. In our visual dataflow language, mobile application components that play a role in a dataflow program are discovered based on their roles. These roles actually have the same use (and in fact are implemented this way) as the Java interfaces that are used by AmbientTalk to discover remote objects and hence act as the *topics* that are being used by the underlying distributed publish/subscribe architecture. The system uses UDP broadcasting to both advertise dataflow nodes and devices willing to execute one or more of the roles in the dataflow program. This an entirely decentralized approach that does not assume any other infrastructure but the mobile devices themselves.

Depending on what kind of dataflow dependency edge there is between two operators, the discovery mechanism works differently. In case of *fixed* dataflow edges, such as between the `Shop` node and the `User` node, once the `User` node is discovered, the same instance of the dataflow program expects always the same instance of a `User` node. This means concretely that when the connection is lost with the `User` node, the `Shop` node will wait until the connection is restored to resume the execution of the dataflow program. This makes sense if there is a stateful aspect over the different distributed nodes in the dataflow program, for example if users should receive personalized recommendations and not recommended products from different users. To detect a permanent disconnection the dataflow dependency edge can be annotated with a timeout period. Event messages are buffered until the timeout is signaled[2].

On the other hand, in some cases a different operator node encoding the same role can be used as a replacement, typically when there is no state associated with the operator's execution. This is catered for by *rebinding* dataflow edges, which are represented by a dashed line, such as the one between the `ProductDatabase` node and the `Shop` node. In this scenario, the shop may consist of different shelves which are all represented as `Shop` nodes. Concretely, a rebinding dataflow edge allows rebinding the dataflow dependency to another destination operator at runtime, because the network topology has changed for example. Again, a timeout can be specified that determines how long event messages are buffered. In this example, the user might have moved out of range of shelf in the shop and moved into communication range of a different shelf. How the group communication to the different shelves is handled is discussed later in Section 3.5.

3.3 Executing Mobile AmbientTalk Code

Dataflow operators operate on data streams. In most cases, it makes sense to process the stream on the device, through which the stream flows, to reduce communication overhead and to avoid a performance bottleneck when all the processing happens on a single device. In such scenarios, it is thus cheaper to move the processing code towards the data than the data stream itself. In the shopping assistant example, the scaling of album cover images can happen directly on the server hosting the images which is better suited for such a CPU-intensive job than a mobile device. Furthermore, in the face of intermittent network connections, long-lasting computations can continue while the network connections with other nodes is temporarily broken, and flush buffered return values when the network connection is restored. This is why the implementation of dataflow operators is in fact mobile AmbientTalk code that is sent to application components playing a role in the dataflow program. To be able to execute this mobile code, these application components need to provide some already present infrastructure in the form of some pre-implemented AmbientTalk or Java methods. Currently, this means that services playing a role in our coarse-grained dataflow model are usually implemented as objects that provide an interface that can be called by the mobile code (as shown in our example

[2] Buffer overflows can happen in theory for very large timeout periods and will raise a Java exception.

where the filterOutPresentProducts method is assumed to be implemented by the Shop node[3]). To allow objects to be easily extended with the necessary methods for accepting and executing their mobile dataflow operator code in the correct way, we provide a basic OperatorHostInterface object. Custom implementations specific to the device hosting the service can be used as well (e.g., to impose restrictions on the received mobile code to prevent security issues) by overriding specific methods on the OperatorHostInterface.

The code snippet below shows how a certain host can advertise itself as a User by simply exporting a service object implementing the User role (hence, this is local code present on the user's machine). The userService object extends from the OperatorHostInterface discussed above and simply implements the necessary methods to fulfill its role in the application. The last two lines declare a Java interface that will be used for service discovery and publish the user service into the network such that it can be discovered by other remote application components.

```
def userService := extend: OperatorHostInterface with: {
  // ... Private fields...
  def showGui() {
    // Show the user interface
  };
  def showProductsInBag(products) {
    // Update GUI with new shopping bag contents
  };
  def showRecommendations(products) {
    // Update GUI with new recommendations
  };
  def showRecommendationsInShop(products) {
    // Update GUI with new recommendations in stock
  };
};
deftype User;
export: userService as: User;
```

Note that the same device hosting a number of application components can play a role in different dataflow programs. However, race conditions cannot occur because the communication between all dataflow operator nodes happens by means of asynchronous AmbientTalk messages that are scheduled in the event loop of each host, and are sequentially executed by a single thread (causing the sequential execution of the operator code as well).

3.4 Propagating Events and Reacting to Events

Until this point, we have not elaborated yet on how the actual dataflow program is executed by our dataflow engine. This is based on the reactive programming

[3] One can designate a dedicated namespace that is visible to the mobile code and organize the library code to be called by the mobile code in Java packages.

paradigm [22,23,24], which requires a reactive version of the AmbientTalk interpreter [25]. Concretely, the dataflow variables in the operator code denote reactive values. These reactive values are updated each time their respective input value changes (by new data objects flowing over the dataflow edges corresponding to the input values). Analogous to the reactive programming paradigm, a dataflow operator is re-executed as soon as one of the reactive values it depends on changes. Dataflow updates are signaled simply by executing a dataflow operator, which results in a new return value for the executed dataflow operator and which is propagated over all the outgoing dataflow edges. For example in the **self** role, the scanned products could be periodically updated by the RFID reader by for example periodically scanning its surroundings for tags and updating a reactive value. The events signaled by this reactive value will in this case be propagated along the `products` and `productsInBag` dataflow dependencies, invoking the rest of the dataflow graph. In the other direction, the `User` node will receive updates to its `productsInBag`, `recommendations` and `inStock` dataflow variables, which will result in the re-execution of the dataflow operator, leading to the necessary updates to the user interface.

The names identifying the dataflow dependency edges are again used for service discovery, but this time only for enabling the communication (initiated behind the scenes by the dataflow engine) to update the reactive values used in the dataflow operator code: no additional semantics are attached to them (in contrast to the role names). Important to note is that the propagation of dataflow events happens by means of the underlying reliable asynchronous messages of AmbientTalk. This means that intermittent connections between dataflow operators do not cause errors, instead the event messages are buffered and resent when the same dataflow operator host comes back in range or a replacement host is found. Per dataflow dependency, a timeout can be specified that determines how long these messages are buffered. In case of a timeout, an exception is raised on both disconnected application components, which can trigger cleanup actions in response.

3.5 Dependency Arities

In mobile ad hoc networks, it is in many cases necessary to gather information from and/or propagate information to a multitude of peers (that can move out of range and back into range at any point in time). For example, a mobile application may want to query other mobile applications about their GPS coordinates to show the location of their users on a map. On the other hand, an application may also want to periodically broadcast the new GPS coordinates of its host device to nearby peers. To cater for this kind of remote communication with a number of equivalent peers, we have extended the original dataflow coordination model with *dependency arities*. These dependency arities can be one-to-one, one-to-many, many-to-one or many-to-many. This is depicted graphically in our visual dataflow language on the end points of edges (i.e., `1-1`, `1-*`, `*-1` and `*-*`, respectively).

Table 1. Dependency arity semantics

	Incoming 1	**Incoming** *
Outgoing 1	Send one value to a single (rebound or fixed) node	Send one value to all reachable nodes of same role
Outgoing *	Send list of values to a single (rebound or fixed) node	Send list of values to all reachable nodes of same role

In the example given above, there is a one-to-many dataflow dependency between the `ProductDatabase` and `Shop` nodes. This will cause the dataflow engine not only to look for a single `Shop` operator host (representing a shelf in our shop scenario), but to all hosts able to play this role in the dataflow program. They will all receive the mobile operator code and will all receive the events propagated along the `recommendToUser` edge. Now it is up to the dataflow programmer to decide what will happen with all the different return values from the replicated `Shop` nodes running in parallel. One could either choose to receive the events propagated by a single `Shop` (although other ones are running in parallel) by installing a one-to-one dependency between the `Shop` and the `User` node. In our scenario this means that the user only receives recommended products from a single shelf, although multiple ones are filtering recommended product lists based on their contents. The alternative would be to install a many-to-one dependency between these components. In that case, the `User` node will receive *all* the events of *all* the replicated `ProductDatabase` nodes that are in communication range. The result here is that the user receives recommended products from all shelves in communication range, i.e., a dynamically changing list of product lists. The programmer can specify a timeout to determine how long values received from non-responding nodes should be kept in the list. Hence, the list changes not only when dataflow values change, but also when values are added (because new nodes were discovered) or removed (when nodes time out). The processing code that operates on this reactive list should of course take into account that the dataflow variable represents such a changing list. Note that declaring a dataflow dependency one-to-many or many-to-many will automatically convert the respective dataflow edge into a rebinding edge (see Section 3.2). The reason is that when broadcasting events to all nodes playing the same role, a fixed dataflow dependency simply makes no sense: events are propagated to a dynamically changing collection of listeners as the network topology changes. This is not always desirable: the dataflow dependency between the `Shop` node and `User` node should clearly be fixed: one instance of the dataflow program should send personalized recommendations always to the same user. Table 1 summarizes the semantics of the different combinations of dataflow nodes and dependency arities connecting them.

4 Limitations and Future Work

The naming and discovery of dataflow nodes happens via Java interfaces acting as role names. We make the underlying assumption that the name of such Java interfaces represents a unique service and is known by all participating services in the immediate neighbourhood. This discovery mechanism also does not take versioning into account explicitly. For example, if the `ProductDatabase` service from the example in Section 3.1 is updated, older clients may discover the updated service, and clients that want to use only the updated service may still discover older versions. Clients and services are thus themselves responsible to check versioning constraints. A similar issue can be observed with respect to security: currently, dataflow operator hosts are responsible themselves for providing a secure infrastructure to execute the mobile AmbientTalk code that is being sent to them by the dataflow engine. This infrastructure currently has to be implemented by the programmer of the service: there is no ready to use framework for this purpose.

Finally, we are working on a more advanced visual dataflow editor and debugger. The current editor[4] is a very early prototype which we would like to extend with debugging support (currently it only offers syntactic error checking and undefined variables checking of the mobile AmbientTalk scripts in dataflow operators). We are currently working on a prototype that allows the stepwise execution of the dataflow graph, similar to the way one would step through invocation stack frames in a stack-based language. This is not trivial since the execution of the dataflow program is distributed over a mobile ad hoc network, of which the nodes have to communicate with the debugger. The approach we are currently pursuing is to integrate a simulator with the debugger that simulates network communication and also allows simulating failures, for example arbitrary network partitions, during the simulated execution of the dataflow program.

5 Conclusions

In this paper, we have introduced a visual dataflow language for coordinating mobile ad hoc network applications. The motivation for using a dataflow language for coordination is that the language offers a coordination model that is very well suited to the dynamic and inherently parallel nature of mobile ad hoc network applications and allows separating the coarse-grained coordination behavior from the fine-grained application logic. The language represents data dependencies between distributed mobile application components very explicitly and allows them to be visualized and edited graphically. Since its coordination model is purely based on the satisfaction of these data dependencies, it maps very well on a mobile ad hoc network environment where distributed application components are running in parallel, react to events coming from the outside world, and are interconnected by peer-to-peer connections over which data can only flow when the connection is not broken (which may frequently happen due to the limited communication range and the mobility of the devices). Our implementation of a dataflow coordination language is made resilient to these

[4] It can be downloaded as a library for the AmbientTalk language from: `http://code.google.com/p/ambienttalk/` ("rfid" SVN branch).

intermittent connections by either buffering dataflow events between different nodes while communication partners are (temporarily) unavailable, or by allowing new reachable nodes to be dynamically selected. The resulting dataflow graph instance is entirely decentralized and does not rely on a fixed infrastructure, but instead only on peer-to-peer connections. To provide the programmer with abstractions to encode different communication strategies that we deem useful in such a mobile context, we have extended the basic dataflow model with *rebinding* data dependency edges and dependency *arities.*

References

1. Kaminsky, A., Bischof, H.P.: Many-to-many invocation: a new object oriented paradigm for ad hoc collaborative systems. In: 17th annual ACM SIGPLAN conference on Object-oriented programming, systems, languages, and applications, pp. 72–73. ACM, New York (2002)
2. Meier, R., Cahill, V.: Steam: Event-based middleware for wireless ad hoc networks. In: 22nd International Conference on Distributed Computing Systems, Washington, DC, USA, pp. 639–644. IEEE Computer Society, Los Alamitos (2002)
3. Murphy, A., Picco, G., Roman, G.C.: Lime: A middleware for physical and logical mobility. In: Proceedings of the The 21st International Conference on Distributed Computing Systems, pp. 524–536. IEEE Computer Society, Los Alamitos (2001)
4. Grimm, R.: One.world: Experiences with a pervasive computing architecture. IEEE Pervasive Computing 3(3), 22–30 (2004)
5. Chin, B., Millstein, T.: Responders: Language support for interactive applications. In: Thomas, D. (ed.) ECOOP 2006. LNCS, vol. 4067, pp. 255–278. Springer, Heidelberg (2006)
6. Haller, P., Odersky, M.: Event-based programming without inversion of control. In: Lightfoot, D.E., Szyperski, C. (eds.) JMLC 2006. LNCS, vol. 4228, pp. 4–22. Springer, Heidelberg (2006)
7. Adya, A., Howell, J., Theimer, M., Bolosky, W.J., Douceur, J.R.: Cooperative task management without manual stack management. In: USENIX Annual Technical Conference, Berkeley, CA, USA, pp. 289–302. USENIX Association (2002)
8. Levis, P., Culler, D.: Mate: A tiny virtual machine for sensor networks. In: International Conference on Architectural Support for Programming Languages and Operating Systems, San Jose, CA, USA (October 2002)
9. Kasten, O., Römer, K.: Beyond event handlers: programming wireless sensors with attributed state machines. In: 4th international symposium on Information processing in sensor networks, Piscataway, NJ, USA, p. 7. IEEE Press, Los Alamitos (2005)
10. Gelernter, D., Carriero, N.: Coordination languages and their significance. Commun. ACM 35(2), 97–107 (1992)
11. Mamei, M., Zambonelli, F.: Programming pervasive and mobile computing applications with the TOTA middleware. In: IEEE International Conference on Pervasive Computing and Communications, Washington, DC, USA, p. 263. IEEE Computer Society, Los Alamitos (2004)
12. Arbab, F.: Reo: a channel-based coordination model for component composition. Mathematical Structures in Comp. Sci. 14(3), 329–366 (2004)
13. Kalkman, C.: Labview: A software system for data acquisition, data analysis, and instrument control. Journal of Clinical Monitoring and Computing 11(1), 51–58 (1995)

14. Cox, P.T., Glaser, H., Lanaspre, B.: Distributed prograph: Extended abstract. In: Queinnec, C., Halstead Jr., R.H., Ito, T. (eds.) PSLS 1995. LNCS, vol. 1068, pp. 128–133. Springer, Heidelberg (1996)
15. Gay, D., Levis, P., von Behren, R., Welsh, M., Brewer, E., Culler, D.: The nesc language: A holistic approach to networked embedded systems. In: ACM SIGPLAN conference on Programming language design and implementation, pp. 1–11. ACM, New York (2003)
16. Van Cutsem, T., Mostinckx, S., Gonzalez Boix, E., Dedecker, J., De Meuter, W.: Ambienttalk: object-oriented event-driven programming in mobile ad hoc networks. In: XXVI International Conference of the Chilean Computer Science Society, pp. 3–12. IEEE Computer Society, Los Alamitos (2007)
17. Van Cutsem, T., Mostinckx, S., De Meuter, W.: Linguistic symbiosis between event loop actors and threads. Computer Languages Systems & Structures 35(1) (2008)
18. Miller, M., Tribble, E.D., Shapiro, J.: Concurrency among strangers: Programming in E as plan coordination. In: De Nicola, R., Sangiorgi, D. (eds.) TGC 2005. LNCS, vol. 3705, pp. 195–229. Springer, Heidelberg (2005)
19. Johnston, W.M., Hanna, J.R.P., Millar, R.J.: Advances in dataflow programming languages. ACM Comput. Surv. 36(1), 1–34 (2004)
20. Park, K., Kim, Y., Chang, J., Rhee, D., Lee, J.: The prototype of the massive events streams service architecture and its application. In: 9th ACIS International Conference on Software Engineering, Artificial Intelligence, Networking, and Parallel/Distributed Computing, Washington, DC, USA, pp. 846–851. IEEE Computer Society, Los Alamitos (2008)
21. Jin, X., Lee, X., Kong, N., Yan, B.: Efficient complex event processing over rfid data stream. In: 7th IEEE/ACIS International Conference on Computer and Information Science, Washington, DC, USA, pp. 75–81. IEEE Computer Society, Los Alamitos (2008)
22. Elliott, C., Hudak, P.: Functional reactive animation. In: ACM SIGPLAN International Conference on Functional Programming, vol. 32(8), pp. 263–273 (1997)
23. Wan, Z., Taha, W., Hudak, P.: Real-time FRP. In: International Conference on Functional Programming, ICFP 2001 (2001)
24. Peterson, J., Hudak, P., Elliott, C.: Lambda in motion: Controlling robots with Haskell. In: Gupta, G. (ed.) PADL 1999. LNCS, vol. 1551, p. 91. Springer, Heidelberg (1999)
25. Mostinckx, S., Lombide Carreton, A., De Meuter, W.: Reactive context-aware programming. In: Workshop on Context-Aware Adaptation Mechanisms for Pervasive and Ubiquitous Services (CAMPUS 2008). Electronic Communications of the EASST, DisCoTec, June 2008, vol. 10 (2008)

Compositional Construction of Real-Time Dataflow Networks

Stephanie Kemper*

CWI, Amsterdam, The Netherlands
S.Kemper@cwi.nl

Abstract. Increasing sizes of present-day distributed software systems call for coordination models which are both *modular* and *scalable*. Precise modelling of real-life applications further requires the notion of *real-time*.

In this paper, we present a modular formal development of a compositional model for real-time coordination in dataflow networks. While real-time dataflow networks are typically asynchronous, our approach includes coordination patterns which combine, but are not limited to, synchrony and asynchrony. We define a constraint- and SAT-based encoding, which allows us to benefit from high-end constraint solving techniques when inspecting valid interactions of the system.

Keywords: Real-Time Dataflow Networks, Component-Based Software Construction, Coordination, Constraint Solving, SAT.

1 Introduction

The size of present-day distributed software systems increases constantly, demanding for adequate scalable methods, which assist developers in constructing large systems, by composing individual components. This in turn creates the need for well-defined formal coordination languages to integrate and, more importantly, orchestrate the distributed system components. Such coordination languages must handle temporal and other nonfunctional interactive properties that cannot be expressed algorithmically [18]. In this paper, we take the view that concurrent interacting software systems are variants of real-time dataflow networks. Distributed software components are components of the network, their timed behaviour is orchestrated by component connectors, such that coordination amounts to composing the behavioural constraints of individual components and their connectors. Traditionally, communication between components and connectors is asynchronous, resembling the idea that connections are realised by unbounded FIFO buffers.

Separation of concerns allows us to consider computation (i.e., concrete data values) and coordination (i.e., presence and absence of dataflow) in real-time dataflow networks separately. In this paper, we focus on the latter; in particular, we do not handle concrete data values. Yet, the integration of these data values is

* Part of this research has been funded by the Dutch BSIK/BRICKS project AFM3.

D. Clarke and G. Agha (Eds.): COORDINATION 2010, LNCS 6116, pp. 92–106, 2010.

straightforward. We extend the untimed asynchronous communication model by adding *timed connectors*, which orchestrate the network behaviour. Connectors consist of a number of distinctly named ports, through which they communicate with the environment (i.e., components), by transmitting data items. The ports are of three different types: *read ports* read data items from the environment, *write ports* write data items to the environment, and *internal ports* (not visible to the environment) transmit data items within the connector. Components are no longer connected to each other, but to a connector, such that communication between components becomes anonymous. The connector imposes a certain coordination pattern on the network, for example by delaying or reordering.

As a second extension of real-time dataflow networks, we take into account environmental constraints, cf. [8]: in traditional approaches, the possible states of ports are *active* (i.e. communicating) and *inactive* (i.e. idle). In this paper, we assume that whenever the internal state of a connector permits communication, it must not refuse communication requests from the environment (e.g., a simple empty buffer can always accept data). Thus, a port in a connector may only be inactive if there is a reason to delay the communication, coming from either the connector or the environment (or both). We therefore split the inactive state of ports into two, based on where the reason for the delay comes from.

In the end, we represent a network as a number of constraints, which can be solved using well-studied constraint solving techniques [2]. A single solution to these constraints corresponds to a valid interaction between a connector and its environment, and the set of all solutions precisely describes the imposed coordination pattern.

1.1 Contributions

The main contributions of this paper can be summarised as follows: we provide a modular framework for compositional construction of a real-time generalisation of dataflow networks. We use a new type of transition systems to describe the behaviour of connectors. We provide a *direct* definition of the behavioural constraints of the connectors in terms of these transition systems, which makes it easy to understand the incorporated coordination pattern. The approach is suitable to model both the "algorithmic" behaviour of connectors (i.e. the internal implementation of the coordination pattern) and the inter-component coordination behaviour. In addition, it can also be used to model the behaviour of the components, such that complete networks can be described with our formalism.

We define a constraint-based encoding of real-time networks, using propositional logic with linear arithmetic. These constraints capture the current state of connectors, how connectors are plugged together, and possible synchronisations with the environment. In this way, we can benefit from existing constraint solving techniques [2] to determine the possible coordination patterns of a connector, or the valid interactions within a network, since these correspond to solutions of the constraints. Starting from the transition systems describing the behaviour, the translation from networks to constraints is fully automatic, such that new connectors (incorporating new coordination patterns) can be easily introduced simply by defining the underlying transition system.

1.2 Related Work

Dataflow networks have first been defined by Kahn [13], as a set of nodes—containing arbitrary sequential processes—which communicate via unbounded FIFO buffers. All processes need to be deterministic; the straightforward extension of the framework to nondeterministic processes is not compositional anymore [7]. Jonsson [12] showed that to regain compositionality, the model needs to contain information about *all* possible interleavings of *all* communication events in the system (Kahn considers the sequential order on each port in isolation). For this reason, we define the semantics of networks based on traces of LTSs (similar to Jonsson), which contain the necessary information about the possible interleavings. Beyond that, our communication model is more refined, in that we take into account not only presence and absence of dataflow, but in addition require a reason for the absence of dataflow, coming from either the network or the environment. Moreover, all the abovementioned approaches assume *asynchronous* communication over *unbounded FIFOs*. In contrast, we allow both asynchronous and synchronous communication—the latter being needed for global coordination (through synchronisation)—and we allow the nodes to be connected by arbitrary channels, including for example reordering and delay.

Clarke *et al.* [9] and Bonsangue *et al.* [6] present approaches for modelling and verifying connectors in the channel-based coordination language $\mathcal{R}$eo. The basic ideas are similar to ours: [9] represents connectors as constraints, and [6] uses an automata-based formal model, which takes into account environmental constraints by modelling presence and absence of requests. Yet, our framework is more general, in that neither of them considers timing constraints, or distinguishes between input and output ports. In fact, $\mathcal{R}$eo networks and connectors are an untimed subclass of networks in our framework.

The work of Ren and Agha [17] describes real-time systems as compositions of actors (the components), together with timing relations on the occurrence of events between them. The behaviour of the actors is orchestrated by so-called *RTsynchronizers.* These are collections of declarative real-time constraints, which restrict the temporal behaviour of events over groups of actors. The major drawbacks of the approach are that the declarative constraints do not allow to reason about sequential occurrences of events, and therefore are unable to express coordination patterns like for example buffering (for buffer sizes >1) or reordering (while this is possible in our approach). Moreover, RTsynchronizers describe a high-level programming language construct rather than a concrete implementation, so ordinary programming languages first need to (be able to) implement the construct in order to use it.

Kemper and Platzer [14] have presented an encoding of timed automata [1] (TA) in propositional logic with linear arithmetic, the nature of which is close to the constraints defined in this paper. Yet, due to the liberal notion of networks and connectors presented here, and since we take into account environmental constraints, we may consider TA to be a subclass of those systems covered here. The same is true for earlier work on timed constraint automata [15] (modulo data values, but this is a straightforward extension of the work presented here).

Example (Introduction). Fig. 1 (left side) shows our graphical representation of the external interface of a connector C, with n read ports $r_1, \dots, r_n$, and m write ports $w_1, \dots, w_m$. Our running example in the paper is a connector S_q of a timed sequencer, cf. Fig. 1 (right side). The idea of S_q is to cyclically communicate through ports w_1, r_1, w_2, r_2. For components C_i, i=1, 2, connected to S_q via the pair (w_i, r_i), S_q in fact works as a token ring: it offers the token to C_i through w_i, accepts it back through r_i, then offers it to the next component. We assume a timeout for each component, i.e., if a component fails to accept the token in time, S_q skips that component in the current round, and offers the token to the next component. We formalise this internal behaviour in Sect. 2.1, and we compose several instances of S_q to build a larger token ring in Sect. 2.2 (cf. also Fig. 3).

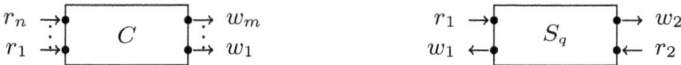

Fig. 1. Graphical Representation of Connector Interfaces

Structure of the Paper. In the next section, we provide the formal definitions for syntax and semantics of real-time components and networks. In Sect. 3, we present our encoding of real-time networks in propositional logic with linear arithmetic, show how to use constraint solving techniques to determine possible coordination patterns, and depict some preliminary experimental results. Finally, Sect. 4 concludes the paper and discusses some directions of future work.

2 Compositional Real-Time Networks

In this section, we present the formal definitions underlying our real-time networks, and illustrate them by means of our running example. In Sect. 2.1, we define simple real-time connectors and how they capture environmental constraints, then we show how to compose these to generate networks and how to propagate the environmental constraints (Sect. 2.2). In Sect. 2.3, we define the semantics of real-time networks by means of transition systems.

2.1 Primitive Connectors

The behaviour of a port, i.e., whether data flows or not, not only depends on the internal state of the connector, but also on the environment in which the connector occurs. In particular, "no dataflow" requires a reason from either the connector or the environment. This in turn means that if both connector and environment are ready to communicate, then dataflow cannot be delayed. Following the three-colouring idea from [8], we define three different states of ports—called colours—which in the case of no dataflow capture where the reason for delaying the communication comes from.

The *set of possible colours* of a port a is { a: ——, a: –!–, a: –?– }. A *colouring over a set of ports* P is a function c assigning a colour to each port in P. The set of *all possible colourings of* P is $\mathbb{C}(P)$. The colourings denote *dataflow through* a (a: ——) and *delay on* a, with the underlying connector either providing (a: –!–) or getting (a: –?–) a reason for the delay on a. Intuitively, a: –?– means that the connector cannot actively delay dataflow through a, instead, delay requires a reason from the *outside*. On the other hand, a: –!– denotes that the connector *itself* delays the communication. We write colourings in either orientation (e.g. a: —— or —— :a), and we omit port name a if it is clear from the context.

We describe the internal behaviour of connectors by means of labelled transition systems (LTS), which we call *Network Transition Automata* (NTA). We use clock constraints to describe enabling conditions of transitions: clock constraints $\varphi{\in}\Phi(X)$ over a finite set of real-valued clocks X are conjunctions of `true` and atoms $x{\sim}c$, with $x{\in}X$, $c{\in}\mathbb{Q}$, and ${\sim}{\in}\{<, \leq, =, \geq, >\}$. For simplicity, we assume dataflow to be instantaneous. Time may only elapse while the NTA remains in one of its states. Yet, it is straightforward to model duration of data flow, by for example adding a fresh clock and appropriate clock guards >0 on transitions.

Definition 1 (Network Transition Automaton). *An* NTA T *over a finite set of ports* P *is a tuple* $T{=}(S, s_0, X, E)$*, with* S *a finite set of states,* s_0 *the initial state,* X *a finite set of real-valued clocks, and* $E{\subseteq}S{\times}\Phi(X){\times}\mathbb{C}(P){\times}2^X{\times}S$ *the finite transition relation. An element* $(s, \varphi, c, Y, s'){\in}E$ *describes a transition from state* s *to state* s'*, enabled under* guard φ*, with dataflow/delay according to colouring* c*, and resetting all clocks in the set* Y*; it is called* delay *iff* $s'{=}s$*,* $Y{=}\emptyset$ *and* $c(a){\neq}$—— *for all* $a{\in}P$*, and* communication *otherwise. Two NTAs are called* disjoint *if the respective subsets (i.e, ports, states and clocks) are disjoint.*

A communication (s, φ, Y, c, s') describes conditions on presence/absence of dataflow and on clocks which trigger a state change, while a delay $(s, \varphi, \emptyset, c, s)$ describes the conditions under which T may delay in s, namely, as long as guard φ is satisfied, and a reason for delay exists which satisfies colouring c.

Definition 2 (Connector). *A* connector C *is a tuple* $C{=}(P^r, P^w, T)$*, with* T *an NTA over a set of ports* P*,* $P^r{\subseteq}P$ *and* $P^w{\subseteq}P$ *finite disjoint sets of read respectively write ports. The set* $\mathcal{I}_C \stackrel{\text{def}}{=} P^r{\cup}P^w{\neq}\emptyset$*, with* $\mathcal{I}_C{\subseteq}P$*, called* external interface *of* C*, contains all externally visible ports, while* P *may contain additional internal ports. Two connectors are called* disjoint *if the respective subsets (i.e., ports and NTAs) are disjoint.*

Example (Primitive Connector). Using Def. 2, the S_q connector from Sect. 1 is $S_q{=}(\{r_1, r_2\}, \{w_1, w_2\}, T)$, with NTA $T{=}(\{ot_1, wf_1, ot_2, wf_2\}, ot_1, \{x\}, E)$. The details of E—with a deadline of 3 time units on the availability of the token—are shown in Fig. 2. Communications are denoted by solid lines, delays by dashed

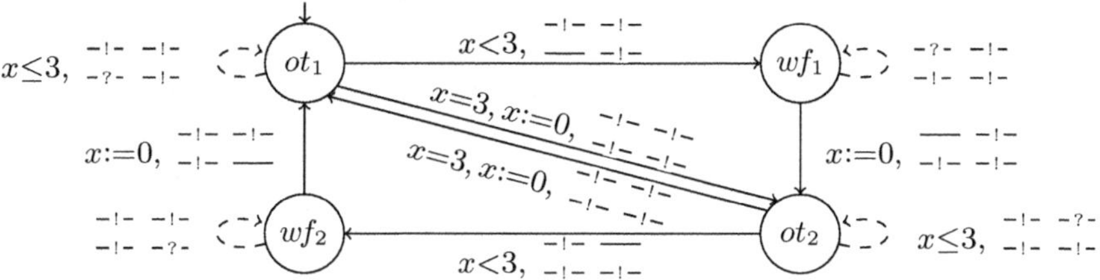

Fig. 2. NTA of the Two-Token Ring Connector

lines. We omit empty clock sets and clock constraints equal to `true`, and we use assignment rather than set notation for clock sets. We arrange the colourings so that they reflect the layout in Fig. 1 (r_1 and w_1 on the left, w_2 and r_2 on the right), and then omit the port names. For explanatory purposes, we assume component C_i is connected to S_q through w_i and r_i, $i = 1, 2$.

S_q starts in ot_1, where it offers the token to C_1. It may delay in this state (delay loop) as long as the deadline of 3 time units is not violated and C_1 is not ready to accept the token (w_1 requires a reason). If C_1 accepts the token in time ($x{<}3$), S_q moves to wf_1 and waits for C_1 to return the token. Otherwise ($x{=}3$), S_q moves directly to ot_2. In wf_1, S_q delays until C_1 returns the token (r_1 requires a reason); then (with dataflow through r_1) moves to ot_2 to offer the token to C_2, thereby resetting clock x to start a new deadline for C_2. The behaviour in ot_2 and wf_2 is symmetric.

2.2 Compositional Construction of Networks

We define composition of connectors by joining sets of (read and write) ports, which yields "invisible" *internal ports.* This is depicted as

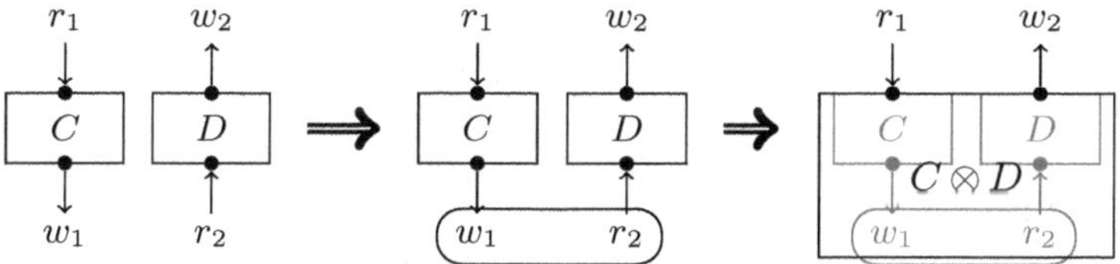

Joining write port w_1 (from C) with read port r_2 (from D) yields a new connector $C{\otimes}D$ with a read port r_1, a write port w_2, and an invisible internal port. For a set of ports P, we call a set $P'{\subseteq}P$ of ports intended to be joined a *merge set (over P)*, the resulting internal port is denoted as $p_{\prec P'}$. Ports in P' become invisible to the environment (i.e., are removed from the external interface).

The intended behaviour of internal ports is to act as self-contained, stateless "pumping stations" [4], *merging* data from write ports, and *replicating* data to read ports. If data flows, then it flows through *exactly one* write port and through *all* read ports. Absence of dataflow is subject to environmental constraints on the involved ports: if there is a reason for delay (-!-) on at least one read port or on all write ports, data cannot flow. Stated differently, a valid colouring of an internal port must not involve the colour -?- only. While other approaches restrict composition to one-to-one relations [3,8,9], we do not impose any restriction on the number, type (read/write) or origin (which connector) of ports in a merge set; the only condition is that merge sets are pairwise disjoint. Though the composition of colourings would be slightly simpler, our many-to-many composition provides a direct and more intuitive way of specifying compositions for for example mergers, replicators or multi-synchronisations.

A colouring $c \in \mathbb{C}(P)$ is *valid over a merge set P'/an internal port $p_{\prec P'}$* if it satisfies the following conditions for all ports $p, p', q \in P'$ (where P^r and P^w are the subsets of P of read respectively write ports):

1. If $\exists p \in P^w : c(p) =$ ——, then $\forall q \in P^r : c(q) =$ ——, and $\forall p' \in P^w, p' \neq p : c(p') \neq$ ——
2. If $\exists q \in P^r : c(q) =$ ——, then $\exists p \in P^w : c(p) =$ ——
3. If $\nexists p \in P' : c(p) =$ ——, then $((\forall p' \in P^w : c(p') =$ -!-$)$ or $(\exists q \in P^r : c(q) =$ -!-$))$

Only valid colourings correctly model the aforementioned behaviour: conditions 1 and 2 describe simultaneous dataflow through exactly one write port and all read ports of $p_{\prec P'}$. Condition 3 describes the propagation of environmental constraints (delays): no dataflow is possible only if either all write ports or at least one read port in P' provide a reason to delay.

The *flip rule* [8] is used to reduce the size of NTAs by identifying redundant (with respect to compositionality) colourings. If for some set of ports P and a port $p \in P$, two colourings $c_1 \in \mathbb{C}(P)$ and $c_2 \in \mathbb{C}(P)$ are identical except for $c_1(p) =$ -!- and $c_2(p) =$ -?-, then c_2 is redundant and can be removed: the set of colourings with which c_2 can compose over p is a strict subset of the set of colourings with which c_1 can compose over p. The valid colourings (after applying the flip rule) of an internal port $p_{\prec\{r_1, r_2, w_1, w_2\}}$ are given by

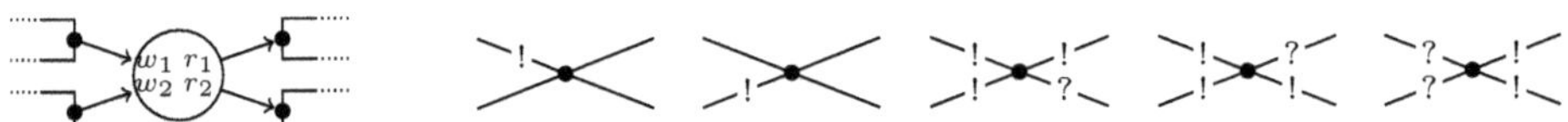

(for clarity, the internal port is conceptually depicted on the left). The colouring on the right, for example, can be read as follows: if all write ports get a reason (-?-), the reason propagates to the read ports, which then provide a reason (-!-), and dataflow is not possible.

The behaviour of a composed connector $C \otimes D$ is described by the composition $T_C \bowtie T_D$ of the underlying NTAs. The basic idea is along the same lines as the standard cross product in other automata models. Yet, to ensure the composed NTA correctly models the propagation of reasons for delay on internal ports, we need to ensure that colourings satisfy the above conditions. Colourings in $T_C \bowtie T_D$ are compositions of colourings from T_C and T_D. The *composition $c_1 \cup c_2$ of colourings $c_1 \in \mathbb{C}(P_1)$ and $c_2 \in \mathbb{C}(P_2)$*, with P_1 and P_2 disjoint, is a new colouring $c = c_1 \cup c_2 \in \mathbb{C}(P_1 \dot{\cup} P_2)$, with $c(p) = c_1(p)$ iff $p \in P_1$, and $c(p) = c_2(p)$ iff $p \in P_2$ for all ports $p \in P_1 \cup P_2$.

Definition 3 (NTA Composition). *Let $\mathcal{T} = \{T_1, \ldots, T_k\}$, $k \geq 1$, be a set of disjoint NTA, $T_i = (S_i, s_{0,i}, X_i, E_i)$, $i \leq k$, an NTA over port set P_i, $\mathcal{Q} = \{Q_1, \ldots, Q_n\}$,*

$n \geq 1$, a set of disjoint merge sets over $\bigcup P_i$. The composition of the T_i over Q, *denoted $T_1 \bowtie_Q \ldots \bowtie_Q T_k$ (or simply $\mathcal{T} \bowtie_Q$), is a new NTA $\mathcal{T} \bowtie_Q = (S, s_0, X, E)$ over $P \stackrel{\text{def}}{=} \bigcup P_i$, with $S = \prod S_i$ (Cartesian product), $s_0 = (s_{0,1}, \ldots, s_{0,k})$, $X = \bigcup X_i$, and transitions in E are given by*

$$\frac{(s_1, \varphi_1, c_1, Y_1, s_1') \in E_1, \ldots, (s_k, \varphi_k, c_k, Y_k, s_k') \in E_k, \quad c = c_1 \cup \ldots \cup c_k \text{ valid over } P}{((s_1, \ldots, s_k), \varphi_1 \wedge \ldots \wedge \varphi_k, c, Y_1 \cup \ldots \cup Y_k, (s_1', \ldots, s_k')) \in E}$$

The definition of connector composition is now straightforward. The basic idea is to compose the NTAs, join the sets of read and write ports, and remove the ports in the merge sets from the external interface.

Definition 4 (Connector Composition). *Let $\mathcal{C} = \{C_1, \ldots, C_k\}$, $k \geq 1$, be a set of disjoint connectors, with $C_i = (P_i^r, P_i^w, T_i)$, $i \leq k$. Let $R \stackrel{\text{def}}{=} \bigcup P_i^r$, $W \stackrel{\text{def}}{=} \bigcup P_i^w$, let $\mathcal{Q} = \{Q_1, \ldots, Q_n\}$, $n \geq 1$, a set of disjoint merge sets over $R \cup W$. The* composition of the C_i over $\mathcal{Q}$, *denoted $C_1 \otimes_{\mathcal{Q}} \ldots \otimes_{\mathcal{Q}} C_k$ (or simply $\mathcal{C} \otimes_{\mathcal{Q}}$), is a new connector $\mathcal{C} \otimes_{\mathcal{Q}} = (P^r, P^w, T)$, with $P^r = R \setminus \bigcup Q_i$, $P^w = W \setminus \bigcup Q_i$, and $T = \bigcup T_i \bowtie_{\mathcal{Q}}$. We call the C_i the* underlying connectors *of $\mathcal{C} \otimes_{\mathcal{Q}}$.*

Connector composition is commutative and—after applying the flip rule to remove redundant colourings—associative (modulo state names).

Though the ports contained in merge sets are removed from the external interface $\mathcal{I}_C$ during composition, they are still contained in the underlying NTA T. We define the *reduction of $C = (P^r, P^w, T)$ to $\mathcal{I}_C$* , denoted $C_\downarrow$, to be a new connector $C_\downarrow = (P^r, P^w, T_\downarrow)$, where transitions (s, φ, c', Y, s') in $T_\downarrow$ are obtained from transitions (s, φ, c, Y, s') in T by restricting the colourings to the external interface—i.e. $c' = c|_{\mathcal{I}_C}$—and removing duplicates if necessary

Example (Connector Composition). Consider a set $\mathcal{S} = \{S_{q,0}, S_{q,1}, S_{q,2}\}$ of three instances of the S_q connector from Sect. 2.1. The connectors are identical, except that we add an additional index $0, 1, 2$ to all names (ports, states, clocks) to make clear which connector they belong to, and we change the start state of the NTAs of $S_{q,1}$ and $S_{q,2}$ to be $wf_{2,1}$ and $wf_{2,2}$, respectively (to ensure initially only $S_{q,0}$ offers a token). Composing $\mathcal{S}$ over $\mathcal{Q} = \{\{w_{2,0}, r_{2,1}\}, \{w_{2,1}, r_{2,2}\}, \{w_{2,2}, r_{2,0}\}\}$, we create a token ring for mutual exclusion for three components, as depicted in Fig. 3 (left side). The reachable part of the NTA of the resulting connector $\mathcal{S} \otimes_{\mathcal{Q}}$ is shown in Fig. 4. Again, we omit port names in the colourings, and we

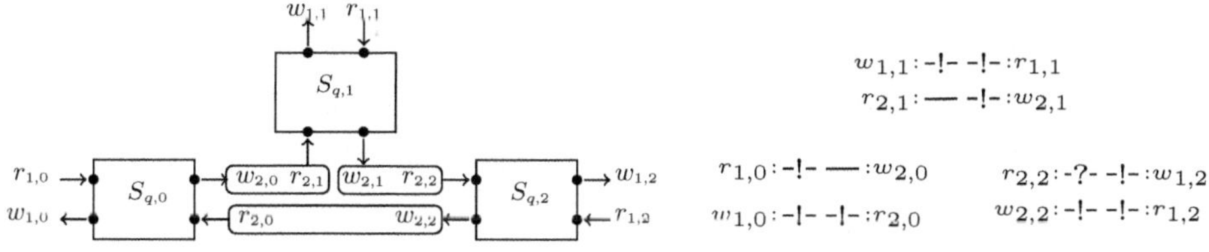

Fig. 3. Connector Composition: Three-Token Ring Connector

arrange the colourings so that they reflect the graphical layout. See the right side of Fig. 3 for an example.

In the initial state, $\mathcal{S} \otimes_{\mathcal{Q}}$ offers the token to the environment through $w_{1,0}$. If the token is taken in time, $\mathcal{S} \otimes_{\mathcal{Q}}$ moves to $(wf_{1,0}wf_{2,1}wf_{2,2})$, where it waits for the token to be returned through $r_{1,0}$. Otherwise (i.e., if the value of x_0 reaches the timeout), $\mathcal{S} \otimes_{\mathcal{Q}}$ moves to state $(ot_{2,0}wf_{2,1}wf_{2,2})$. Note that it is not possible to delay in this state. This is due to the fact that in state $ot_{2,0}$, $S_{q,0}$ offers the token to the environment through $w_{2,0}$, cf. Fig. 2. A delay in $ot_{2,0}$ is only possible if $S_{q,0}$ *gets* a reason to delay on $w_{2,0}$. But $S_{q,1}$, which is connected to $w_{2,0}$ via $r_{2,1}$, never provides a reason for delay on $r_{2,1}$ in state $wf_{2,1}$ (cf. Fig. 2 again). Therefore, the only possible transition from $(ot_{2,0}wf_{2,1}wf_{2,2})$ is to move to $(wf_{2,0}ot_{1,1}wf_{2,2})$, which correctly corresponds to passing the token from $S_{q,0}$ to $S_{q,1}$ without delay. This shows the importance of taking into account environmental constraints, since without these (i.e., when having only one unconstrained "no flow" colour) it would wrongly be possible to delay in $(ot_{2,0}wf_{2,1}wf_{2,2})$. The explanation for the rest of the connector is symmetric. Hiding the three internal ports, that means reducing $\mathcal{S} \otimes_{\mathcal{Q}}$ to $\mathcal{I}_{\mathcal{S} \otimes_{\mathcal{Q}}}$, yields a similar NTA, where blue colourings are removed.

Note that we have removed transitions with unsatisfiable guards. For example, there is a transition from $(ot_{2,0}wf_{2,1}wf_{2,2})$ back to $(ot_{1,0}wf_{2,1}wf_{2,2})$, with guard $x_0{=}3$. But since clock x_0 is reset on both incoming transitions of $(ot_{2,0}wf_{2,1}wf_{2,2})$, and $\mathcal{S} \otimes_{\mathcal{Q}}$ cannot delay in that state (see above), this guard can never be satisfied.

Remark 5 (Size of the Composition). While the NTA of $\mathcal{S} \otimes_{\mathcal{Q}}$ still has a reasonable size, the number of states of the NTA of a composed connector can be

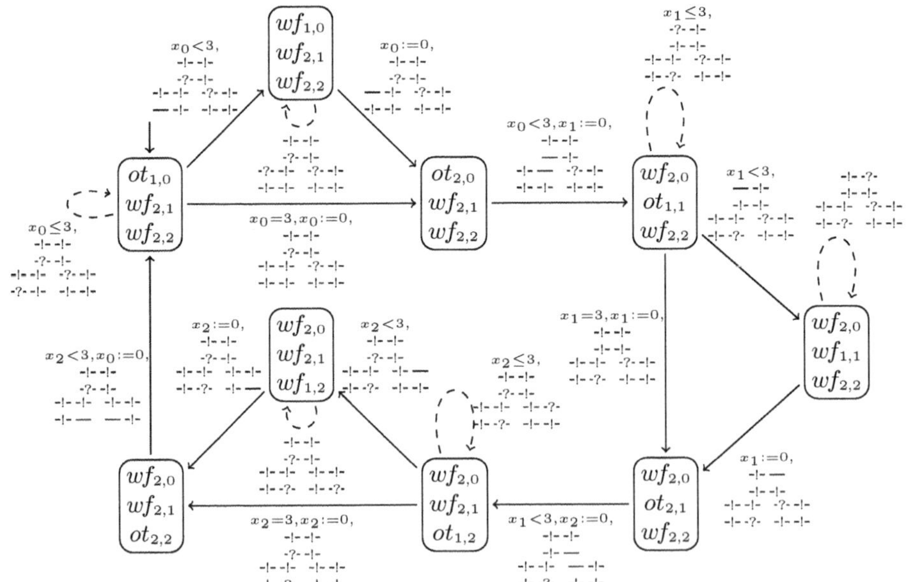

Fig. 4. Connector Composition: NTA of the Three-Token Ring Connector

exponential in the worst case. In Sect. 3.3, we define an encoding of the composition of connectors, which avoids the explicit construction of the composition, and is *linear* in the number of underlying connectors.

2.3 Semantics

We define the semantics of a connector $C=(P^r, P^w, T)$, with $T=(S, s_0, X, E)$, as the set of runs of the associated LTS $\mathcal{L}_C$, which describes transition sequences of T. A configuration q of $\mathcal{L}_C$ is a pair $\langle s, \nu\rangle$ of a state $s\in S$ and a clock valuation ν. A clock valuation is a mapping $\nu{:}X\to\mathbb{R}_{\geq 0}$ assigning a real value to each clock, its current value. $\mathcal{V}(X)$ denotes the set of all clock valuations over X, and we use $\models$ for the standard satisfaction relation.

The initial configuration of $\mathcal{L}_C$ is $\langle s_0, \mathbf{0}\rangle$, with $\mathbf{0}(x)=0$ for all $x\in X$. Transitions of $\mathcal{L}_C$ directly correspond to the two types of transitions of NTA. An *action transition* $\langle s,\nu\rangle\xrightarrow{c}\langle s',\nu'\rangle$ describes the firing of an instantaneous communication $(s,\varphi,Y,c,s')\in E$, with $\nu\models\varphi$, and ν' resulting from ν by resetting all clocks in the set Y to zero. A *delayed action transition* $\langle s,\nu\rangle\xrightarrow{t,c}\langle s,\nu{+}t\rangle$, with delay $t\geq 0$, describes the firing of a delay $(s,\varphi,\emptyset,c,s)\in E$, where $\nu{+}t'\models\varphi$ for all $0\leq t'\leq t$ (that means the guard has to be satisfied at all times during the delay). In both cases, data flows according to colouring c.

An *execution of C of length k* is given by a *k-run of $\mathcal{L}_C$*, which is a sequence of k transitions, starting in the initial configuration: $\langle s,\mathbf{0}\rangle\xrightarrow{\gamma_1}q_1\xrightarrow{\gamma_2}\ldots\xrightarrow{\gamma_k}q_k$, with $\gamma_i\in\mathbb{C}(P^r\cup P^w)\cup(\mathbb{C}(P^r\cup P^w)\times\mathbb{R}_{\geq 0})$, and $q_i\in(S\times\mathcal{V}(X))$, for all $1\leq i\leq k$. The *semantics of C* is given by the set Run_C of k-runs of $\mathcal{L}_C$, for all $k\geq 0$.

Example (Semantics). Consider again the connector $\mathcal{S}\otimes_{\mathcal{Q}}$ in Fig. 4, after hiding. A run of length 6 is given as[1]

$$\left\langle\begin{pmatrix} ot_{1,0}\\ wf_{2,1}\\ wf_{2,2}\end{pmatrix},\mathbf{0}\right\rangle \xrightarrow{\substack{\texttt{-!--!-}\\ \texttt{-!--!-}\\ 1,\texttt{-?--!-}}} \left\langle\begin{pmatrix} ot_{1,0}\\ wf_{2,1}\\ wf_{2,2}\end{pmatrix},\begin{matrix}x_0{=}1\\ x_1{=}1\\ x_2{=}1\end{matrix}\right\rangle \xrightarrow{\substack{\texttt{-!--!-}\\ \texttt{-!--!-}\\ \texttt{----!-}}} \left\langle\begin{pmatrix} wf_{1,0}\\ wf_{2,1}\\ wf_{2,2}\end{pmatrix},\begin{matrix}x_0{=}1\\ x_1{=}1\\ x_2{=}1\end{matrix}\right\rangle \xrightarrow{\substack{\texttt{-!--!-}\\ \texttt{----!-}\\ \texttt{-!--!-}}} \left\langle\begin{pmatrix} ot_{2,0}\\ wf_{2,1}\\ wf_{2,2}\end{pmatrix},\begin{matrix}x_0{=}0\\ x_1{=}1\\ x_2{=}1\end{matrix}\right\rangle$$

$$\xrightarrow{\substack{\texttt{-!--!-}\\ \texttt{-!--!-}\\ \texttt{-!--!-}}} \left\langle\begin{pmatrix} wf_{2,0}\\ ot_{1,1}\\ wf_{2,2}\end{pmatrix},\begin{matrix}x_0{=}0\\ x_1{=}0\\ x_2{=}1\end{matrix}\right\rangle \xrightarrow{\substack{\texttt{-?--!-}\\ \texttt{-!--!-}\\ 3,\texttt{-!--!-}}} \left\langle\begin{pmatrix} wf_{2,0}\\ ot_{1,1}\\ wf_{2,2}\end{pmatrix},\begin{matrix}x_0{=}3\\ x_1{=}3\\ x_2{=}4\end{matrix}\right\rangle \xrightarrow{\substack{\texttt{-!--!-}\\ \texttt{-!--!-}\\ \texttt{-!--!-}}} \left\langle\begin{pmatrix} wf_{2,0}\\ ot_{2,1}\\ wf_{2,2}\end{pmatrix},\begin{matrix}x_0{=}3\\ x_1{=}0\\ x_2{=}4\end{matrix}\right\rangle$$

After a delay of 1, the token is delivered to the environment through $w_{1,0}$, and accepted back immediately through $r_{1,0}$. The next transition corresponds to the token being transmitted from $S_{q,0}$ to $S_{q,1}$ (since internal ports are hidden, there is no visible dataflow). Next, $\mathcal{S}\otimes_{\mathcal{Q}}$ delays in state $(wf_{2,0}ot_{1,1}wf_{2,2})$ for 3 time units, then, due to the timeout condition $x_1{=}3$, moves to $(wf_{2,0}ot_{2,1}wf_{2,2})$.

3 Encoding

In this section, we construct a formula $\varphi(C)$ in propositional logic with linear arithmetic, that encodes the transition relation of an NTA T of a connector C,

[1] The colourings—reflecting the layout in Fig. 4 after hiding—correspond to $w_{1,1}$, $r_{1,0}$, $w_{1,0}$ on the left (top to bottom) and $r_{1,1}$, $w_{1,2}$, $r_{1,2}$ on the right (top to bottom).

and we present an encoding of connector composition which is *linear* in the number of involved connectors. In the sequel, let $C{=}(P^r, P^w, T)$ be a connector, with $T{=}(S, s_0, X, E)$ over $P{\supseteq}\mathcal{I}_C$ (cf. Def. 2).

3.1 Basic Concepts

The presence (and absence) of dataflow through the ports of C depends on the state of T and the values of its clocks. We encode these concepts as follows.

For every port $p{\in}P$, we introduce two Boolean variables $\mathtt{p}^0$ and $\mathtt{p}^1$, to encode the three possible colours of p: the *encoding* $\mathtt{p}_{\langle c\rangle}$ *of* p *under colouring* c is $\neg\mathtt{p}^0{\wedge}\neg\mathtt{p}^1$ iff $c(p){=}$-?-, $\neg\mathtt{p}^0{\wedge}\mathtt{p}^1$ iff $c(p){=}$-!-, and $\mathtt{p}^0$ iff $c(p){=}$——.

We use logarithmic encoding for states: for $|S|{=}n$, we introduce a vector $\boldsymbol{s}$ of $j{=}\lceil\log_2(n)\rceil$ Boolean variables, encoding a j-digit Boolean value. The intended meaning is that $\boldsymbol{s}$ encodes the value i, denoted by $\boldsymbol{s}_\mathtt{i}$, iff the connector is in state s_i; $\boldsymbol{s}_\mathtt{i}$ is called the *encoding of* s_i.

For every clock $x{\in}X$, we introduce a rational variable $\mathtt{x}$ (*clock reference*),[2] such that $\mathtt{x}$ holds the absolute point in time when x was last reset prior to the current step. An additional rational variable $\mathtt{z}$ (*absolute time reference*) denotes the absolute amount of time that has passed, such that the *clock value* of clock x is given by $\mathtt{z}{-}\mathtt{x}$, and the encoding $\upphi$ of a clock constraint $\varphi{=}x{\sim}c$ is $\upphi{=}(\mathtt{z}{-}\mathtt{x}){\sim}c$. This temporal difference representation significantly reduces the number of arithmetic operations [14].

3.2 Transition Relation

The transition relation of T describes the possibilities to evolve to the next step, based on the configuration in the current step. In the sequel, the variables introduced in the previous section refer to the values *before* the firing of a transition, and primed variants refer to the values *after* the firing.

Definition 6 (Connector Encoding). *Let C and T be a connector and NTA as before, $f{=}(s_i, \varphi, Y, c, s_j)$ and $d{=}(s_k, \varphi, \emptyset, c, s_k)$ a communication respectively delay in E. The* encoding $\upphi(C)$ of C *is given in* (5) *(on the facing page).*

The encoding of a communication (1) ensures that the connector is in state s_i before firing, guard φ is satisfied, and data can flow according to colouring c. After firing, the connector is in state s_j, the values of the absolute time reference and clock references of $X\backslash Y$ have not changed, while all other clock references have been set to the actual point in time. The encoding of a delay (2) is similar, except that the value of the absolute time reference increases, while all other clocks keep their value. In addition, guard φ still needs to be satisfied after the time delay. The disjunction of these formulas expresses (nondeterministic) transition choice (3). The connector starts in its initial state, and initially all clocks start at zero (4).

[2] Linear arithmetic is equisatisfiable for rational and real variables [14], so rational variables are sufficient to encode real-valued clocks.

$$\varphi^f(f) = \boldsymbol{s}_{\mathtt{i}} \wedge \upphi \wedge (\mathbf{z}'{=}\mathbf{z}) \wedge \bigwedge_{x \in Y} (\mathtt{x}'{=}\mathbf{z}') \wedge \quad (1)$$

$$\bigwedge_{x \in X \setminus Y} (\mathtt{x}'{=}\mathtt{x}) \wedge \bigwedge_{p \in \mathcal{I}_C} \mathtt{p}_{\langle \mathtt{c} \rangle} \wedge \boldsymbol{s}_{\mathtt{j}}{}'$$

$$\varphi^d(d) = \boldsymbol{s}_{\mathtt{k}} \wedge \upphi \wedge (\mathbf{z}'{\geq}\mathbf{z}) \wedge \bigwedge_{x \in X} (\mathtt{x}'{=}\mathtt{x}) \wedge \quad (2)$$

$$\bigwedge_{p \in \mathcal{I}_C} \mathtt{p}_{\langle \mathtt{c} \rangle} \wedge \boldsymbol{s}_{\mathtt{k}}{}' \wedge \upphi'$$

$$\varphi^E(C) = \bigvee_{f \text{ comm.}} \varphi^f(f) \vee \bigvee_{d \text{ delay}} \varphi^d(d) \quad (3)$$

$$\varphi^i(C) = \boldsymbol{s}_0 \wedge (\mathbf{z}{=}0) \wedge \bigwedge_{x \in X} (\mathtt{x}{=}0) \quad (4)$$

$$\varphi(C) = \varphi^i(C) \wedge \varphi^E(C) \quad (5)$$

$$\varphi(C)^k = \varphi^i(C) \wedge \bigwedge_{0 \leq j \leq k} \varphi^E(C)^{j \cdot \prime} \quad (6)$$

$$\varphi^1(P) = \bigvee_{w \in P^w} \mathtt{w}^0 \rightarrow \Big(\bigwedge_{r \in P^r} \mathtt{r}^0 \wedge \bigwedge_{\substack{w_h, w_i \in P^w, \\ w_h \neq w_i}} \neg(\mathtt{w_h}^0 \wedge \mathtt{w_i}^0) \Big) \quad (7)$$

$$\varphi^2(P) = \bigvee_{r \in P^r} \mathtt{r}^0 \rightarrow \bigvee_{w \in P^w} \mathtt{w}^0 \quad (8)$$

$$\varphi^3(P) = \bigwedge_{p \in P} \neg \mathtt{p}^0 \rightarrow \Big(\bigwedge_{w \in P^w} \mathtt{w}^1 \vee \bigvee_{r \in P^r} \mathtt{r}^1 \Big) \quad (9)$$

$$\varphi(P) = \varphi^1(P) \wedge \varphi^2(P) \wedge \varphi^3(P) \quad (10)$$

$$\varphi(\mathcal{C} \otimes_{\mathcal{Q}}) = \bigwedge_{C \in \mathcal{C}} \varphi(C) \wedge \bigwedge_{Q \in \mathcal{Q}} \varphi(Q) \quad (11)$$

3.3 Connector Composition

Though the flip rule (Sect. 2.2) reduces the size of NTAs, the size of the NTA of a composed connector is still exponential in the worst case. Here, we define a *linear size* logical encoding of the composition of connectors. The basic idea is to define composition via conjunction of the encodings of the single connectors. In addition, we need to encode the constraints on internal ports, to ensure the encoding of the composition correctly models internal ports.

For a merge set P, the *encoding* $\varphi(P)$ *of internal port* $p_{\prec P}$ is given in (10). The constituents of $\varphi(P)$ directly correspond to the conditions in Sect. 2.2 (on Page 98). For example, (9) corresponds to condition 3: if there is no flow at all (left side of the implication), then (right side) either all write ports, or at least one read port provide a reason for delay (first respectively second disjunct). Using this, the *encoding of a composition* $\mathcal{C} \otimes_{\mathcal{Q}}$, for sets $\mathcal{C}$ and $\mathcal{Q}$ of disjoint connectors respectively merge sets (over the ports of connectors in $\mathcal{C}$), is defined in (11).

Hiding the internal ports amounts to existential quantification over the variables representing ports in $\mathcal{Q}$: the *reduction of* $\varphi(\mathcal{C} \otimes_{\mathcal{Q}})$ *to* $\mathcal{I}_{\mathcal{C}}$ is defined as $\exists \bigcup Q_i (\varphi(\mathcal{C} \otimes_{\mathcal{Q}}))$.

Example (Encoding). Consider again the connector $\mathcal{S} \otimes_{\mathcal{Q}}$ from Sect. 2.2, and the definition of its encoding (11). Due to space limitations, we do not show the complete encoding, but restrict this example to two instructive transitions of $\mathcal{S} \otimes_{\mathcal{Q}}$. For each of the underlying connectors $S_{q,i}$, $i{=}0,1,2$, we introduce a vector $\boldsymbol{si}$ of two Boolean variables, where $\boldsymbol{si}_0$, $\boldsymbol{si}_1$ and $\boldsymbol{si}_2$ are the encodings of states $ot_{1,i}$, $ot_{2,i}$ and $wf_{2,i}$, respectively. We show the encoding of the communication from $ot_{1,0}$ to $ot_{2,0}$ (12), and the delays in $ot_{1,0}$ (13), $wf_{2,1}$ (14) and $wf_{2,2}$ (15). The communication from $(ot_{1,0} wf_{2,1} wf_{2,2})$ to $(ot_{2,0} wf_{2,1} wf_{2,2})$ (in $\mathcal{S} \otimes_{\mathcal{Q}}$) is then given by the conjunction of (12), (14) and (15), and the delay in $(ot_{1,1} wf_{2,1} wf_{2,2})$ by the conjunction of (13), (14) and (15).

$$\boldsymbol{s0}_0 \wedge ((\mathtt{z}-\mathtt{x}_0)=3) \wedge (\mathtt{z}'=\mathtt{z}) \wedge (\mathtt{x}_0'=\mathtt{z}') \wedge \\ \neg \mathtt{r}_{1,0}{}^0 \wedge \mathtt{r}_{1,0}{}^1 \wedge \neg \mathtt{w}_{1,0}{}^0 \wedge \mathtt{w}_{1,0}{}^1 \wedge \neg \mathtt{r}_{2,0}{}^0 \wedge \mathtt{r}_{2,0}{}^1 \wedge \neg \mathtt{w}_{2,0}{}^0 \wedge \mathtt{w}_{2,0}{}^1 \wedge \boldsymbol{s0}_1{}' \tag{12}$$

$$\boldsymbol{s0}_0 \wedge ((\mathtt{z}-\mathtt{x}_0)\leq 3) \wedge (\mathtt{z}'\geq\mathtt{z}) \wedge (\mathtt{x}_0'=\mathtt{x}_0) \wedge \\ \neg \mathtt{r}_{1,0}{}^0 \wedge \mathtt{r}_{1,0}{}^1 \wedge \neg \mathtt{w}_{1,0}{}^0 \wedge \neg \mathtt{w}_{1,0}{}^1 \wedge \neg \mathtt{r}_{2,0}{}^0 \wedge \mathtt{r}_{2,0}{}^1 \wedge \neg \mathtt{w}_{2,0}{}^0 \wedge \mathtt{w}_{2,0}{}^1 \wedge \boldsymbol{s0}_0 \wedge ((\mathtt{z}'-\mathtt{x}_0')\leq 3) \tag{13}$$

$$\boldsymbol{s1}_2 \wedge (\mathtt{z}'\geq\mathtt{z}) \wedge (\mathtt{x}_1'=\mathtt{x}_1) \wedge \neg \mathtt{r}_{1,1}{}^0 \wedge \neg \mathtt{r}_{1,1}{}^1 \wedge \neg \mathtt{w}_{1,1}{}^0 \wedge \mathtt{w}_{1,1}{}^1 \wedge \neg \mathtt{r}_{2,1}{}^0 \wedge \mathtt{r}_{2,1}{}^1 \wedge \neg \mathtt{w}_{2,1}{}^0 \wedge \mathtt{w}_{2,1}{}^1 \wedge \boldsymbol{s1}_2 \tag{14}$$

$$\boldsymbol{s2}_2 \wedge (\mathtt{z}'\geq\mathtt{z}) \wedge (\mathtt{x}_2'=\mathtt{x}_2) \wedge \neg \mathtt{r}_{1,2}{}^0 \wedge \neg \mathtt{r}_{1,2}{}^1 \wedge \neg \mathtt{w}_{1,2}{}^0 \wedge \mathtt{w}_{1,2}{}^1 \wedge \neg \mathtt{r}_{2,2}{}^0 \wedge \mathtt{r}_{2,2}{}^1 \wedge \neg \mathtt{w}_{2,2}{}^0 \wedge \mathtt{w}_{2,2}{}^1 \wedge \boldsymbol{s2}_2 \tag{15}$$

3.4 Coordination as Constraint Satisfaction

With the encoding $\varphi(C)$ of a connector C (5), traditional constraint solving techniques [2] and tools (e.g. MathSAT [16] or HySAT [11]) are used to model check the behaviour and verify properties of C. To inspect executions of C of length k (cf. Sect. 2.3), the encoding $\varphi(C)$ of C is *unfolded* k times, i.e., instantiated for all steps up to k. The resulting formula is shown in (6). The formula $\varphi^E(C)^{j\cdot\prime}$ denotes the variant of $\varphi^E(C)$, where j primes have been added to all variable symbols (e.g., $\varphi^E(C)^{3\cdot\prime}$ contains $\mathtt{z}^{3\cdot\prime}=\mathtt{z}'''$). Intuitively, a satisfying valuation (*model*, i.e., a single solution to the satisfiability check) of $\varphi(C)^k$ corresponds to an execution of length k, and the set of all models precisely describes the coordination pattern of C (for executions up to length k).

Other properties used to analyse the behaviour of C include for example whether a certain error state s is reachable within k steps. This amounts to conjoining $\varphi(C)^k$ with $\rho \stackrel{\text{def}}{=} \boldsymbol{s}^{0\cdot\prime} \vee \ldots \vee \boldsymbol{s}^{k\cdot\prime}$, the error state is (un)reachable iff the conjunction is (un)satisfiable. Lifting ρ to reason about configurations (i.e., include timing information) is straightforward. Other bounded LTL properties can be specified using the encoding in [5], for example. The next section shows how to use constraint satisfaction to check the correctness of the $\mathcal{S}\otimes_{\mathcal{Q}}$ connector.

3.5 Preliminary Experimental Results

Some preliminary experimental results (runtime and memory consumption) are shown below. All experiments have been carried out with MathSAT, on an Intel Core 2 Quad with 2.83GHz, 8GB RAM and Fedora 10. The input file, containing the system description and the representation of the properties, can be found at `http://www.cwi.nl/~kemper/ThreeTokenRing/`. For the interested reader, we have added some comments to the file, to ease understanding the encoding.

We checked three correctness properties for the encoding $\varphi(\mathcal{S}\otimes_{\mathcal{Q}})$ of the $\mathcal{S}\otimes_{\mathcal{Q}}$ connector, for executions of length 20 and 50, respectively. Property MoreTokens is satisfiable iff $\mathcal{S}\otimes_{\mathcal{Q}}$ can reach a state where more than one of the underlying connectors is in an "ot" state, i.e., where more than one token is offered at the same time: though $\mathcal{S}\otimes_{\mathcal{Q}}$ is composed from three two-token rings, there must be only one token in the composition (remember that we changed the initial states of $S_{q,1}$ and $S_{q,2}$ for this purpose). The property Shortcut is satisfiable iff it is possible to fire the communication from $ot_{2,i}$ to $ot_{1,i}$ in any of the underlying connectors: firing it in $S_{q,0}$, for example, would wrongly skip the connectors

$S_{q,1}$ and $S_{q,2}$, and immediately offer the token through port $w_{1,0}$ again. Property NoSeqFlow is used to check that every dataflow through a $w_{1,i}$ port is followed by dataflow through the corresponding $r_{1,i}$ port, without dataflow through any other port of the external interface in between; it is satisfiable iff the sequential order is violated. As expected, the result of checking the conjunction of $\varphi(\mathcal{S}\otimes_{\mathcal{Q}})$ with any of the properties is "unsatisfiable".

length	MoreTokens		Shortcut		NoSeqFlow	
20	1.493s	23.465MB	1.481s	23.227MB	4.526s	33.215MB
50	3.300s	29.598MB	2.242s	24.867MB	9.431s	39.484MB

The results clearly show that our approach is tailored towards and profits from using well-optimised, high-end constraint solving techniques, as it scales very well for long executions: the increase in runtime is roughly linear in the increase of the execution length, while at the same time, the number of possible executions that need to be checked increases exponentially.

4 Conclusion and Future Work

In this paper, we have presented a modular framework for *compositional construction of* and *coordination in* real-time dataflow networks, which takes into account environmental constraints from outside the network. We have defined a new type of transition systems (NTA), used to describe the behaviour of components and, since our approach is compositional, whole networks. This *direct* definition of the behaviour makes it easy to understand (and thus, use) our framework. In addition, it also facilitates the introduction of new, user-defined primitives, by just giving the underlying NTA. Liberal notions of components and networks allow to encode many common (coordination) models, like e.g. TA [1] or timed constraint automata (TCA) [15], in our framework.

We have defined a constraint-based encoding of connectors, using propositional logic with linear arithmetic. This enables us to benefit from well-studied, high-end constraint solving techniques, when checking for valid interactions within a network, or inspecting the incorporated coordination pattern. The logical encoding of networks —i.e. composition of connectors—is *linear* in the size of the NTAs of the underlying connectors. In this way, we overcome the omnipresent state explosion problem, and are able to deal with larger systems.

We do not consider concrete data values which are transmitted, but rather focus on the presence and absence of dataflow. However, the integration of handling these data values is straightforward: transitions of NTA are augmented with data constraints in a "TCA-like" style, the basis for encoding these constraints has already been established in [9].

Besides this, future work includes comparisons of our approach on different real-world case studies, possibly using different constraint solvers. So far, no tool support for the full theory presented in this paper exists. Yet, for the trivial case of untimed connectors, our approach is essentially equivalent to the animation of $\mathcal{R}$eo [3] in the ECT framework [10]. We plan to further integrate our work into this framework. In particular, implement an editor for NTA, which provides composition and hiding, such that connectors and networks can be easily defined by users. Adding the translation from NTA to constraints will then offer support for the full theory. We expect some performance gains when using our constraint-based approach as underlying theory for computing the $\mathcal{R}$eo animations in the ECT, which will increase the manageable system size.

References

1. Alur, R.: Timed automata. In: Halbwachs, N., Peled, D.A. (eds.) CAV 1999. LNCS, vol. 1633, pp. 8–22. Springer, Heidelberg (1999)
2. Apt, K.R.: Principles of Constraint Programming. Cambridge Univ. Press, Cambridge (2003)
3. Arbab, F.: $\mathcal{R}$eo: a channel-based coordination model for component composition. Mathematical Structures in Comp. Sci. 14(3), 329–366 (2004)
4. Baier, C., Sirjani, M., Arbab, F., Rutten, J.J.M.M.: Modeling component connectors in $\mathcal{R}$eo by constraint automata. Sci. Comp. Prog. 61(2), 75–113 (2006)
5. Biere, A., Cimatti, A., Clarke, E.M., Zhu, Y.: Symbolic model checking without BDDs. In: Cleaveland, W.R. (ed.) TACAS 1999. LNCS, vol. 1579, pp. 193–207. Springer, Heidelberg (1999)
6. Bonsangue, M., Clarke, D., Silva, A.: Automata for Context-Dependent Connectors. In: Field, J., Vasconcelos, V.T. (eds.) COORDINATION 2009. LNCS, vol. 5521, pp. 184–203. Springer, Heidelberg (2009)
7. Brock, J.D., Ackerman, W.B.: Scenarios: A model of non-determinate computation. In: Díaz, J., Ramos, I. (eds.) Formalization of Programming Concepts. LNCS, vol. 107, pp. 252–259. Springer, Heidelberg (1981)
8. Clarke, D., Costa, D., Arbab, F.: Connector colouring I: Synchronisation and context dependency. Sci. Comp. Prog. 66(3), 205–225 (2007)
9. Clarke, D., Proença, J., Lazovik, A., Arbab, F.: Deconstructing $\mathcal{R}$eo. Electr. Notes Theor. Comput. Sci. 229(2), 43–58 (2009)
10. Eclipse Coordination Tools, `http://reo.project.cwi.nl/`
11. HySAT Bounded Model Checker, `http://hysat.informatik.uni-oldenburg.de`
12. Jonsson, B.: A fully abstract trace model for dataflow networks. In: POPL, pp. 155–165 (1989)
13. Kahn, G.: The semantics of a simple language for parallel programming. In: IFIP Congress, pp. 471–475 (1974)
14. Kemper, S., Platzer, A.: SAT-based abstraction refinement for real-time systems. Electr. Notes Theor. Comput. Sci. 182, 107–122 (2007)
15. Kemper, S.: SAT-based verification for timed component connectors. Electr. Notes Theor. Comput. Sci. 255, 103–118 (2009)
16. The MathSAT 4 SMT solver, `http://mathsat4.disi.unitn.it`
17. Ren, S., Agha, G.: RTsynchronizer: Language support for real-time specifications in distributed systems. In: LCT-RTS, pp. 50–59 (1995)
18. Wegner, P.: Coordination as constrainted interaction (extended abstract). In: Hankin, C., Ciancarini, P. (eds.) COORDINATION 1996. LNCS, vol. 1061, pp. 28–33. Springer, Heidelberg (1996)

Coordinating Resource Usage through Adaptive Service Provisioning in Wireless Sensor Networks

Chien-Liang Fok, Gruia-Catalin Roman, and Chenyang Lu

Dept. of Computer Science and Engineering
Washington University in St. Louis
Saint Louis, MO, 63105, USA
{liang,roman,lu}@cse.wustl.edu

Abstract. Wireless sensor networks (WSNs) exhibit high levels of network dynamics and consist of devices with limited energy. This results in the need to coordinate applications not only at the functional level, as is traditionally done, but also in terms of resource utilization. In this paper, we present a middleware that does this using adaptive service provisioning. Novel service binding strategies automatically adapt application behavior when opportunities for energy savings surface, and switch providers when the network topology changes. The former is accomplished by providing limited information about the energy consumption associated with using various services, systematically exploiting opportunities for sharing service invocations, and exploiting the broadcast nature of wireless communication in WSNs. The middleware has been implemented and evaluated on two disparate WSN platforms, the TelosB and Imote2. Empirical results show that adaptive service provisioning can enable energy-aware service binding decisions that result in increased energy efficiency and significantly increase service availability, while imposing minimal additional burden on the application, service, and device developers. Two applications, medical patient monitoring and structural health monitoring, demonstrate the middleware's efficacy.

1 Introduction

Coordination in wireless sensor networks (WSNs) is critical due to limited resource availability and high levels of network dynamics. The Service-Oriented Computing (SOC) programming model can facilitate this coordination in an elegant and application-transparent manner. It decouples service consumers and providers enabling the bindings between them to be dynamically adjusted in response to resource and network link availability. In this paper, we investigate the use of SOC to coordinate resource utilization in WSNs. This differs markedly from prior research that focuses on the coordination of applications at the functional level.

In this paper, we investigate two novel methods of coordination that increase energy efficiency and service availability in an autonomous and application-transparent manner. First, we propose dynamic service selection strategies that

D. Clarke and G. Agha (Eds.): COORDINATION 2010, LNCS 6116, pp. 107–121, 2010.

enhance energy efficiency. This is important because in a dense WSN, there are often multiple providers available operating at varying levels of energy efficiency. Thus, the selection of a provider affects the application's energy footprint. To account for this, a limited amount of information regarding a provider's energy efficiency is sent to the consumer allowing it to determine and bind to the provider that will result in the highest energy efficiency. Furthermore, opportunities for sharing service executions are automatically identified and exploited to further increase energy efficiency. This is particularly useful when combined with the broadcast nature of wireless communication, which enables the results of a single service execution to be simultaneously delivered to multiple consumers.

Second, we propose adaptive service binding strategies to automatically adjust the binding configurations in response to changes in the network topology. This is important because WSNs exhibit high levels of dynamics due to the use of low-power radios, node mobility, and exposure to a dynamic environment [12]. A key advantage of our adaptive service binding scheme is that it enables *application-transparent* handling of network topology changes in a SOC framework, and thus imposes no additional burden on the application developer.

Significant contributions of this work also lie in the implementation and evaluation of the aforementioned coordination strategies. We have implemented them within a SOC middleware called Servilla [8], which is available under an open-source license from its website.[1] In addition, we have evaluated it on two disparate hardware platforms, the Imote2 [4] and TelosB [17], which highlight the vast differences in energy efficiencies among WSN nodes and demonstrate the need for energy-aware adaptation mechanisms. The evaluation indicates that our midleware does *not* impose undue additional burden on the device, service, and application developers. In addition, two real-world application case studies involving structural health monitoring and medical patient monitoring demonstrate our middleware's ability to enhance energy efficiency and enable perfect invocation success rate despite frequent topology changes due to user mobility.

The remainder of this paper is organized as follows. Section 2 presents related work. Section 3 presents the problem definition. Section 4 presents the mechanisms for coordinating applicaion resource utilization. Section 5 presents the evaluation. The paper ends with conclusions in Section 6.

2 Related Work

Researchers have traditionally focused on the coordination of applications at the functional level. This has generally taken the form of novel abstractions and calculi for sharing and transmitting data among distributed software components. For example, in wireless ad hoc networks, researchers have investigated the use of tuple spaces [3,22], process calculi [21], workflow engines [20], publish-subscribe [9], and ambient references [5]. While such coordination is critical, the unique properties of WSNs like limited resources motivate the coordination of applications in terms of resource utilization. The programming model we use

[1] Servilla's website: http://mobilab.cse.wustl.edu/projects/servilla/

to achieve this is SOC. SOC has been used in MANETs in the form of follow-me sessions [13] that decouple services from providers. Like the aforementioned systems, it does not consider resource utilization when establishing binding configurations.

SOC has been used in WSNs for various purposes [16]. One original use is to integrate WSNs with Internet applications [1,18]. To do this, the WSN is hidden behind services that provide sensor data. Using SOC, traditional Internet applications can bind to these services and access information generated by the WSN. While these systems facilitate the integration of WSNs with the Internet, they are not designed to enhance energy efficiency and service availability within the WSN itself.

Another use of SOC is to enable adaptation to network heterogeneity. To this end, we previously developed Servilla [8], a service-oriented architecture (SOA) facilitating the development of applications that execute efficiently in heterogeneous WSNs. Its key idea was to present platform-specific functionalities as services that are dynamically bound to platform-independent applications. Servilla is *not* energy-ware or adaptive to network topology changes. The changing of binding configurations is done explicitly by the application. Other systems like eSOA [19] and OASiS [15] use SOC within WSNs but perform service matching and binding *off-line.*

Energy efficiency is critical in WSNs because many nodes operate on batteries. As such, making the SOA energy-aware is essential. Unlike previous systems, this paper uniquely focuses on how energy can be saved through careful service selection and opportunistically merging service executions.

3 Problem Definition

The two problems addressed in this paper are how to support coordination by enabling applications to 1) conserve energy and 2) transparently adapt to changing network topologies. Prior to expanding on these, the system model is described. The system consists of a WSN in which there are many types of nodes. Some are more energy efficient. Others are line-powered and not energy constrained. They also differ in their computational and sensing abilities. Regardless of these differences, they all communicate over the same low-power wireless networking technology like IEEE 802.15.4. The result is a heterogeneous and dynamic environment in which devices differ both in terms of hardware capabilities and energy efficiencies.

The WSN runs a SOA in which each device may host one or more service consumers and/or providers. Consumers are typically platform-independent and contain application logic. Platform-specific functionalities are accessed through services that are bound to consumers. Providers are dynamically discovered, bound to, and invoked by, consumers. A consumer and its providers may reside on the same node or on different nodes. Due to variations in network link quality over time, the set of providers that are within range of a consumer is dynamic. The service discovery, matching, and binding process is automatic and done based on service-specifications published by both the consumer and provider. The service specification includes both functional and non-functional properties of the service. For example, a functional property of the sensing service may be the sensor type and its accuracy, while its non-functional property may be its location. By comparing the properties required by the consumer to the ones provided by the provider, a match can be made. The matching process ensures that all matching services are functionally interchangeable from the consumer's perspective and will satisfy the application requirements.

WSNs are not general-purpose computing platforms and, as such, exhibit certain common characteristics that are reflected by the SOA. For example, many WSN applications like habitat monitoring operate periodically, each time performing the same set of operations like sensing and data delivery. Other applications remain idle until a particular event like the detection of a phenomenon occurs. To account for these operational characteristics, the SOA has three forms of service invocations: *on-demand*, *periodic*, and *event-based*. On-demand is what is traditionally provided by most SOAs in which an invocation is similar to a remote procedure call. That is, the consumer initiates a service invocation by sending the provider a message, and waits for the provider to respond with results. Periodic and event-based invocations involve the provider automatically invoking the service periodically. They differ in that periodic invocations send every result whereas event-based invocations only send interesting results, as defined by the provider, back to the consumer. Both of the latter forms of invocations are more energy efficient than on-demand, assuming the same invocation period, since they do not require the consumer to send the provider a message each time the service is executed.

Given the system configuration described above, the primary objectives of our work are to:

- Reduce energy consumption through energy-aware service selection and sharing. The selection of a particular provider affects the amount of energy consumed due to device heterogeneity and differences in wireless link qualities between the consumer and provider. Achieving this objective involves developing a mechanism that determines *which* provider to select among a set of potential providers. In this paper, the objective of the energy-aware selection and sharing mechanism is to reduce an application's "energy footprint," which is the total energy an application consumes invoking services. This includes the energy spent on wireless communication and service execution on all energy-constrained nodes in the network, including the hosts of both consumers and providers.
- Enhance service availability through application-transparent service rebinding. This is necessary due to the transient connectivity between the consumers and providers. Achieving it requires determining *when* to switch providers. Ideally, the adaptation mechanism should prevent the application from being exposed to service invocation failure when there are available providers within range.

In addition to the above two objectives, the following design goals are needed to enhance the usability and practicality of the coordination middleware. The first is how to ensure the system is responsive to network topology changes while remaining energy efficient. This is a challenging problem because rapid proactive detection of network topology changes requires frequent beaconing, which is energy-intensive. Second, the problem of additional overhead for achieving adaptation must be addressed. Specifically, they must not outweigh the energy efficiency gained through adaptation. Finally, the problem of additional burden imposed on the application, device, and service developers must be addressed. Ideally, their software components can be integrated with the adaptive SOA with little to no changes.

4 Adaptation Mechanisms

This section presents the adaptation mechanisms of our coordination middleware for WSNs. Before presenting the details, we first give an overview of the basic service selection and binding process. Service selection involves the consumer analyzing the properties of each known provider and selecting one that best meets its requirements. Upon selection, the consumer binds to the provider by noting its address, which is used to communicate with the provider when it invokes the service. Note that the middleware hides the provider's address from the application by presenting a simple interface for invoking the service.

The remainder of this section is divided into three parts: 1) selecting the most energy-efficient provider, 2) optimizing energy efficiency via shared service invocations, and 3) increasing service availability by adapting to network topology changes.

4.1 Energy-Aware Provider Selection

This section describes *which* provider to select. The selection process must be energy-aware since differences in hardware architectures result in different energy cost. For example, the power draws of the Imote2 and TelosB differ widely, i.e., 145mW versus 9mW, meaning binding to an Imote2 may result greater energy consumption relative to a TelosB. Fundamentally, deciding which provider to select is simple – choose the one that results in the smallest energy footprint. The problem is how the energy footprint of a particular binding can be determined. By calculating the amount of energy each potential binding configuration will consume, the middleware can select the provider that will result in the smallest energy footprint.

Determining the energy footprint of a binding requires analyzing the steps of invocation. First consider on-demand and periodic invocations. Both share the same three steps since on-demand is a special case of periodic in which the number of periods is one. As shown in Figure 1, the three steps are 1) initiation, 2) execution, and 3) results delivery. Initiation involves the consumer telling the provider that it wants to invoke the service. If the provider is remote, this involves

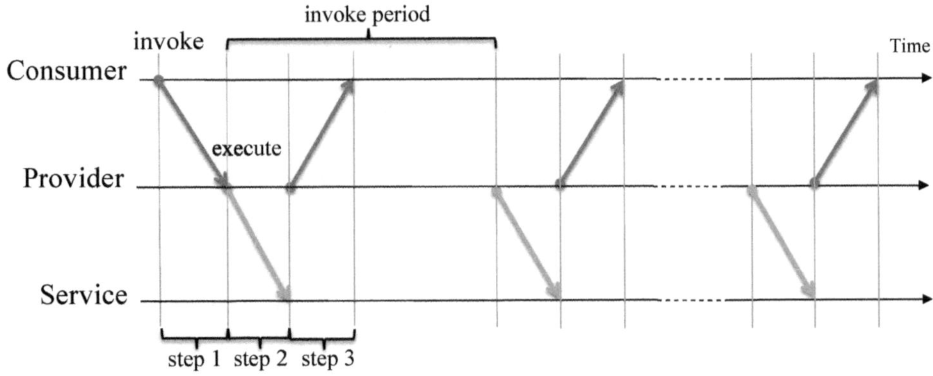

Fig. 1. The actions performed during periodic invocations

sending an `invoke` message. Execution involves running the service. Finally, results delivery involves sending the results of the execution to the consumer. For periodic invocations, the latter two steps are repeated as specified by the consumer.

Each of the aforementioned steps must be analyzed to determine the energy footprint of a particular binding. The variables used are shown in Table 1. The system-defined variables can be directly measured as will be described in Section 5. The estimated energy footprint is given by equation 1. The first line accounts for the energy in step one while lines 2-3 accounts for steps two and three. Finally, line 4 accounts for the energy consumed while idling. Note that the estimator only considers the energy footprint a consumer has on the overall system. It does not consider the implications of concurrent searches or explicit coordination among consumers or providers, which can result in even greater energy savings. The current equation is used due to its simplicity and ability to estimate actual energy consumption in a real system, as will be shown in Section 5.

$$\begin{aligned} E_{periodic} = {} & E_{tx,c} + E_{rx,p} \\ & + \texttt{Count} \cdot (P_{idle,c} \cdot T_{invoke} + T_{invoke} \cdot P_{invoke} + E_{rx,c} + E_{tx,p}) \\ & + (\texttt{Count} - 1) \cdot (P_{idle,c} \cdot (\texttt{Period} - T_{invoke} - T_{rx,c}) \\ & \quad + P_{idle,p} \cdot (\texttt{Period} - T_{invoke} - T_{tx,p})) \end{aligned} \tag{1}$$

When the binding is local, Equation 1 is simplified since there is no wireless communication. Specifically, equation 2 captures the energy footprint of all forms of local invocation, including those that are event-based. A similar analysis can be done for event-based invocations. It is omitted due to space constraints, details can be found in [7].

$$E_{local} = \texttt{Count} \cdot T_{invoke} \cdot P_{invoke} + (\texttt{Count} - 1) \cdot (\texttt{Period} - T_{invoke}) \cdot P_{idle} \tag{2}$$

If a node is not energy-constrained, the energy cost of the node can simply be set to zero. The original equations can be used without modification. For

Table 1. Variables for deriving the energy cost of service invocation

Application Developer

Symbol	Meaning	Units
`Period`	Service execution period	ms
`Count`	Number of service executions	n/a

Service Developer

Symbol	Meaning	Units
T_{invoke}	Latency of service execution	ms
P_{invoke}	Power during service execution	mW

Device Developer

Symbol	Meaning	Units
$T_{rx,c}$	Latency of consumer receiving a message	ms
$T_{tx,p}$	Latency of provider sending a message	ms
$P_{idle,c}$	Consumer idle power	mW
$P_{idle,p}$	Provider idle power	mW
$E_{tx,c}$	Energy cost of consumer sending a message	μJ
$E_{tx,p}$	Energy cost of provider sending a message	μJ
$E_{rx,c}$	Energy cost of consumer receiving a message	μJ
$E_{rx,p}$	Energy cost of provider receiving a message	μJ

example, if the provider is line-powered, $E_{tx,p}$, $E_{rx,p}$, and P_{invoke} should be set to zero. This will effectively remove non-power-constrained nodes from the energy cost calculation.

As mentioned in Section 3, the coordination middleware must not impose an unreasonable burden on the device, application, and service developers. In this case, the additional burden is the derivation of the variables shown in Table 1. To understand the actual amount of additional work required, the variables shown in Table 1 are divided based on who needs to provide them. The device developer needs to specify eight variables related to the energy efficiency and latency of wireless communication and idling. This only needs to be done once for each platform type. The service and application developers each need to specify only two additional variables. In the application developer's case, the two variables, `Count` and `Period`, need to be specified anyway when invoking a service periodically or in an event-based manner. In other words, there is *no additional burden* placed on the application developer when enabling adaptive capabilities.

4.2 Shared Service Invocations

Periodic and event-based invocations predictably execute a service once every period. This enables *service sharing*, a novel mechanism for saving energy. The

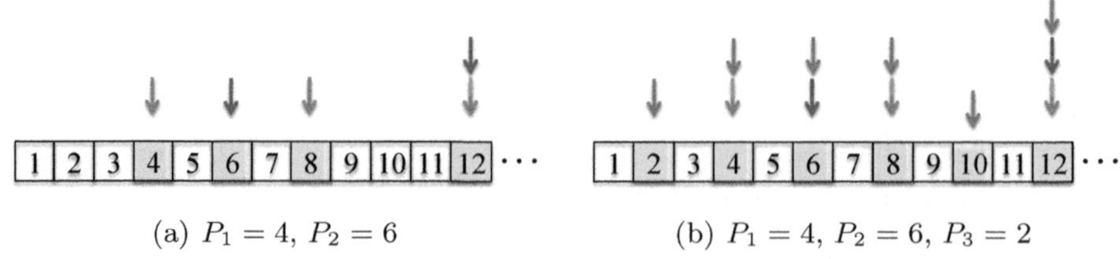

Fig. 2. A visualization of how service utilization is calculated

idea is that multiple service execution requests can be combined into one. In addition, depending on whether reliability is needed, the results can be simultaneously delivered to multiple consumers via wireless broadcast. Energy savings is attained by reducing the number of times a service is executed and the results delivered. This section investigates this possibility.

Before analyzing the details, it is important to note that while not every service is sharable, most are. A service is sharable if its results can be delivered to multiple consumers. This depends on the semantics of the service and whether the invocation parameters are compatible. For example, a sensing service is typically sharable if the invocation periods share common multiples, while a data routing service is usually not. Since the most common service in a WSN is a sensing service, shared service invocation is an important method for increasing energy efficiency. Note that the starting time of a service invocation is assumed to be adjustable to coincide with the discretized time. Most WSN applications, including those that are analyzed in Section 5, meet this assumption since they are only sensitive to the service execution rate.

To understand how energy can be saved via service sharing, consider the impact a particular invocation has on a service's utilization, as shown in Figure 2. Time is discretized and when a consumer invokes a service periodically or in an event-based manner, each service execution will fall into a unique box in the array. A box is shaded gray if at least one invocation occurs during the interval of time represented by the box. The number of arrows pointing at each box is the number of consumers that are sharing the same service execution. Thus, the more arrows pointing at a box, the greater the degree of sharing, and the more energy is saved.

Figure 2(a) shows the service utilization when there are two consumers, C_1 and C_2, invoking at periods $P_1 = 4$ and $P_2 = 6$, respectively. C_1 thus executes the service at times 4, 8 and 12, as indicated by the blue arrows, while C_2 executes the service at times 6 and 12, as indicated by the green arrows. Note that the length of the array is equal to the least common multiple (lcm) of 4 and 6 because the invocation pattern repeats beyond this. Thus, service utilization can be calculated by only considering the block of times leading up to the least common multiple.

Calculating service utilization involves dividing the number of shaded boxes by the total number of boxes, which in this case is $\frac{4}{12} = \frac{1}{3}$. Figure 2(b) shows the utilization when a new consumer, C_3, invoking with period $P_3 = 2$, arrives.

```
Given n periods: P1, P2, ..., Pn;
Let lcm = Least Common Multiple of P1, P2, ..., Pn;
Let list = [P1, P2, ..., Pn]; // These are the base values
Let count = 0;
sort(list);
    while smallest value(s) in list are less lcm
        increment smallest value(s) in list by base value;
        sort(list);
        count++;
utilization = count/lcm
```

Fig. 3. An algorithm for calculating service utilization given service sharing

With this additional consumer, the new utilization is $\frac{1}{2}$, representing an increase of $\frac{1}{2} - \frac{1}{3} = \frac{1}{6}$. Note that this is less than an increase of $\frac{1}{2}$, which would be the case if service invocations could not be shared, demonstrating the benefits of service sharing.

The algorithm for calculating the effects of service invocation sharing is shown in Figure 3. It maintains a sorted list, *list*, that initially contains each period, P_1, P_2, ..., P_n. This initial value is the "base value" that is continuously added to itself until it reaches *lcm*. With each round, the list is sorted and, if the smallest values are less than the *lcm*, they are incremented by their base value. This process repeats until all values in *list* equal *lcm*. The number of rounds in the algorithm is equal to the number of positions in the timeline in which a service execution occurs, meaning the utilization is the number of rounds divided by *lcm*. The time complexity of this algorithm is $O(lcm \cdot utilization \cdot n \cdot log(n))$, which is exponential in the number of invocations. However, it is proportional to the utilization, which is usually small, and the number of consumers is also expected to be small due to the limited wireless range of WSN nodes, meaning this algorithm is feasible in most situations.

The savings achieved through service sharing are incorporated into P_{invoke} and $E_{tx,p}$, which are included in the response to a service discovery message. For example, if adding a consumer results in no change in the utilization of the service, and the results can be delivered via broadcast, then $P_{invoke} = 0$ and $E_{tx,p} = 0$ for that consumer. This results in a consumer preferring providers that are better able to share service executions and thus save energy. One limitation is that future changes to the set of bound consumers are not accounted for. This can be remedied by having the provider notify its consumers whenever the degree of sharing has decreased.

4.3 Adapting to Network Topology Changes

The mechanism for adapting to network topology changes is responsible for switching providers to enhance service availability. As shown in Figure 4, it has only four states imposing minimal overhead. The mechanism only adjusts a service binding when the current one fails. This conservative policy is used due to

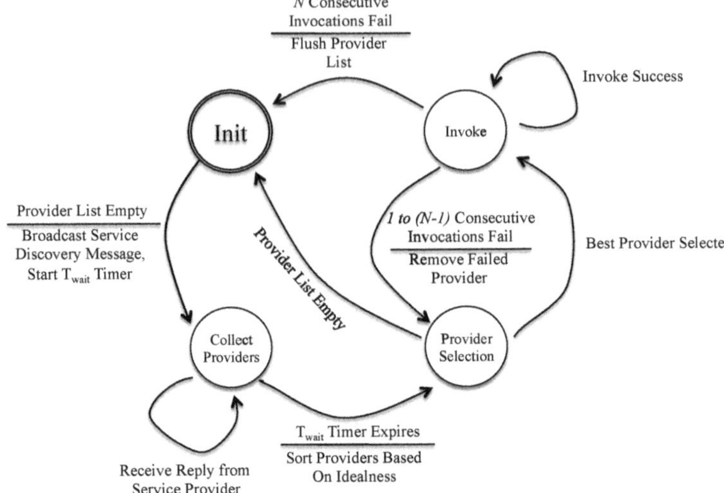

Fig. 4. A finite state machine capturing the behavior of the mechanism used to adapt to network topology changes

energy considerations, i.e., to avoid beaconing overhead and needlessly switching providers. For the same reason, the mechanism does not perform service discovery until N previously discovered providers are tried. Note that N must be carefully selected to maximize the likelihood that the energy spent trying to find an alternate provider is less than simply re-running service discovery. Recall that any matching provider is assumed to be interchangeable, enabling the middleware to switch providers transparently from the application. In addition, switching providers is assumed to involve no state transfer from the old provider to the new. This is the common case since typical services like sensing meets this assumption. In the future, this assumption can be removed by including the overhead of state transfer in the energy consumption computations.

The entire adaptation mechanism shown in Figure 4 is conducted by the middleware and hidden from the application developer. By presenting such a simple interface, application development is simplified.

5 Evaluation

We implemented the coordination model by modifying Servilla as shown in Figure 5. The key changes are highlighted in black. Services are augmented with their energy efficiency profiles, which include T_{invoke} and P_{invoke}, and various components are modified to enable the coordination of resource utilization. These changes impose minimal memory and network bandwidth overhead. On the TelosB, they consume $20kb$ of ROM and $6.5kb$ of RAM, while on the Imote2, they consume $187kb$ of ROM and $10kb$ of RAM. These are small relative to the amounts of memory available.

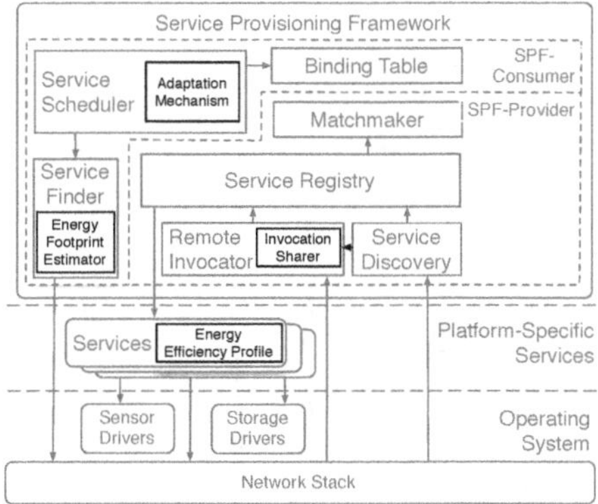

Fig. 5. The middleware architecture

In terms of network bandwidth, the service discovery message must contain four additional variables: the invocation type, period, and count, and whether the results need to be delivered reliably, ie., whether the results can be delivered via broadcast. These variables amount to only eight bytes. The reply message to a service discovery must include six additional variables: $T_{tx,p}$, $E_{tx,p}$, $P_{idle,p}$, $E_{rx,p}$, T_{invoke}, and P_{invoke}. This amounts to twelve bytes and can easily fit within a single TinyOS [14] packet. In addition to the messages, the service specifications must include three additional variables: whether it is sharable, T_{invoke}, and P_{invoke}. This amounts to six bytes and can also fit in a single packet.

Recall that the additional burden placed on the developers consists of obtaining the values in Table 1. This can be done using numerous methods the most basic of which is to use an oscilloscope. In this evaluation, this was done for both the TelosB and Imote2 devices. The actual measurements are omitted for brevity, details are available in [7]. Note that this only needs to be done once for each platform or service. In subsequent usages or when an oscilloscope is unavailable, the values can be looked up or estimated [6].

The remainder of this section presents two application case studies: medical patient monitoring and structural health monitoring. They demonstrate the efficacy of our programing model in terms of coordinating resource utilization. While the evaluations are simplified in that they only contain one consumer, they illustrate how our adaptive SOA can (1) increase service availability and (2) enable energy-awareness in applications.

5.1 Medical Patient Monitoring

This application was originally deployed at Barnes-Jewish Hospital in St. Louis, Missouri and underwent a successful clinical trial with real patients [2]. It consists of an ambulatory patient wearing a WSN device that monitors and delivers vital sign data to a nurse's monitoring station via a multi-hop WSN

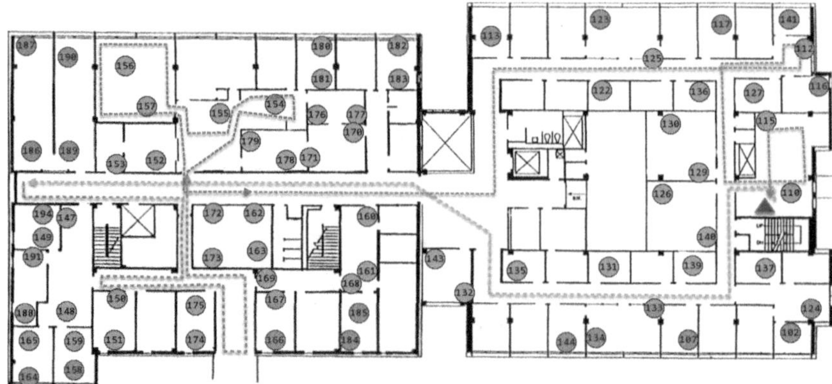

Fig. 6. A map of the WSN testbed at Washington University in St. Louis used in the medical patient monitoring application. The testbed nodes (circles) relay patient data to the monitoring station (triangle). The patient traverses the dotted lines.

infrastructure. The key challenge is overcoming the dynamic network topology caused by patient mobility. Failure to adapt will result in the loss of critical vital sign data jeopardizing the patient's care.

The aforementioned system was implemented in NesC [10] using TinyOS. For this evaluation, we reimplemented it using our adaptive SOA. By using our middleware, the implementation becomes trivial because adaptation to network topology changes is hidden. It consists of a single loop with two lines of code: one for obtaining the patient data, another for invoking a relay service that is provided by the infrastructure nodes. The relay service delivers the data to the monitoring station and is identical to the one used in the original deployment.

We reproduced the results of the clinical deployment using a WSN testbed, a map of which is shown in Figure 6. It runs the Collection Tree Protocol (CTP) [11] to deliver patient data to the monitoring station, which was used in the original implementation. CTP is exposed through our middleware as a service. For each experiment, the patient traversed a fixed $359m$ path as shown in Figure 6. Two walking speeds were used, a slow walk averaging $0.68m/s$ and a fast walk averaging $1.33m/s$.

For a base-line comparison, the application was also implemented using just CTP. Both the adaptive SOA and CTP versions of the application were evaluated using the fixed path shown in Figure 6. While traversing this path, the medical patient's node would attempt to send patient data every 15 seconds, which is sufficient for monitoring most vital signs [2].

The success rates of the adaptive SOA and CTP implementations are shown in Table 2. For all results, the average and 95% confidence intervals over ten rounds are given. The adaptive SOA was able to maintain 100% success rate while the CTP version frequently failed because it was not designed to handle the high level of dynamics due to mobility. In addition the adaptive SOA approach was more energy efficient transmitting an average of 5 packets per invocation

Table 2. Medical patient monitoring service invocation success rate

	Adaptive SOA	CTP
Fast Walk	$100\% \pm 0\%$	$31.16\% \pm 7.6\%$
Slow Walk	$100\% \pm 0\%$	$40.47\% \pm 11.2\%$

relative to CTP's 20. This demonstrates the efficacy of our middleware in terms of coordinating adaptation to network topology changes.

5.2 Structural Health Monitoring

A key challenge of structural health monitoring (SHM) is the need to run for long intervals despite the fact that most SHM algorithms are complex and energy intensive. To address this, a low-power state may be used that simply monitors the structure's vibrations and signals an event whenever they exceed a certain threshold. While previous results demonstrated that this technique saves energy [8], the binding configurations were set manually. This section presents how an adaptive SOA can improve on this technique by automatically determining the energy footprints. The results are validated by comparing the estimated and actual energy consumptions.

The system consists of Imote2s and TelosBs. Both provide a service called `AccelTrigger` that performs low-power monitoring. Among the two, only the Imote2 can perform the complex algorithms for localizing damage. To save energy, the Imote2 relies on `AccelTrigger` during idle periods. Given this setup, there are two binding states: 1) the Imote2 can bind to the *AccelTrigger*

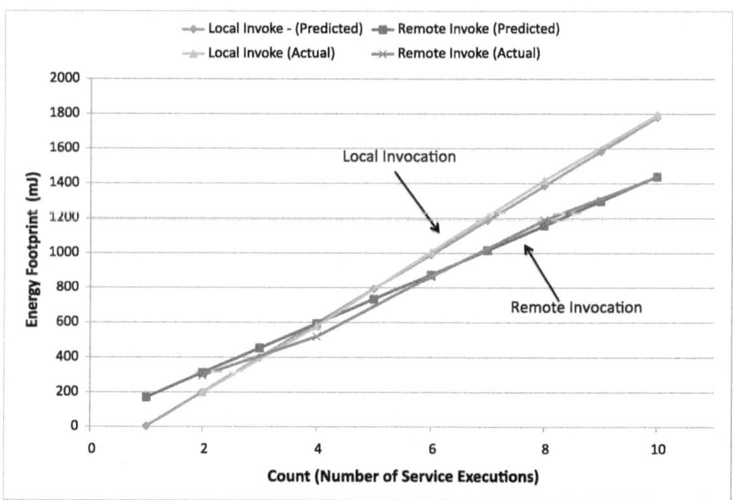

Fig. 7. The predicted and actual energy footprints of the structural health monitoring application when the radio operates at a 10% duty cycle and `Period` = $1000ms$

service locally, or 2) it can bind to the service remotely by using the TelosB. In this evaluation, we determine how well our middleware predicts the energy footprints of the two binding configurations.

Assuming the service is invoked every second using event-based invocation, the Imote2 must determine the energy footprint of each binding configuration relative to the number of times it is invoked (`Count`). Ultimately, the objective is to determine when remote invocations are more energy-efficient than local invocations. The results are shown in Figure 7. The actual values were obtained using an oscilloscope. Note that the predicted and actual energy footprints closely match, and that both result in the same conclusion: that `Count` must be at least 4 for remote binding to be more efficient. Since `Count` is specified by the application during service invocation, the middleware is able to automatically determine which binding configuration is best.

Implementing this application using the adaptive SOA is simple. It consists of a single call to invoke the `AccelTrigger` service, followed by a callback function implementing the normal energy-intensive SHM algorithm. As intended, the process of binding to the most energy efficient provider is hidden from the application.

6 Conclusion

We present a middleware for coordinating resource utilization among WSN applications through the use of an adaptive service provisioning framework. The framework enhances service availability and energy efficiency automatically imposing minimal additional burden to the developer. Our framework features three novel adaptation strategies specifically designed for service provisioning in WSNs: 1) energy-aware service selection, 2) opportunistic service sharing, and 3) adaptive service rebinding in response to network dynamics. Naturally incorporated into an SOC paradigm, our adaptive strategies are hidden from the device, service, and application developers and thereby simplify application development. Empirical results from implementations on TelosB and Imote2 platforms and an evaluation of two applications, medical patient monitoring and structural health monitoring, demonstrate the systems efficiency and efficacy.

Acknowledgment

This research was supported by the NSF under grants CNS-0520220 and CNS-0708460.

References

1. Rock, A.: Arch Rock PhyNet^{TM}, `http://www.archrock.com/product/`
2. Chipara, O., Brooks, C., Bhattacharya, S., Lu, C., Chamberlain, R., Roman, G.-C., Bailey, T.C.: Reliable data collection from mobile users for real-time clinical monitoring. In: AMIA Annual Symp. (November 2009)
3. Costa, P., Mottola, L., Murphy, A.L., Picco, G.P.: TeenyLIME: transiently shared tuple space middleware for wireless sensor networks. In: MidSens 2006, pp. 43–48 (2006)

4. Crossbow Technologies. Imote2 datasheet, `http://tinyurl.com/5jrw85`
5. Cutsem, T.V., Dedecker, J., Meuter, W.D.: Object-oriented coordination in mobile ad hoc networks. In: Murphy, A.L., Vitek, J. (eds.) COORDINATION 2007. LNCS, vol. 4467, pp. 231–248. Springer, Heidelberg (2007)
6. Dutta, P., Feldmeier, M., Paradiso, J., Culler, D.: Energy metering for free: Augmenting switching regulators for real-time monitoring. In: IPSN 2008, pp. 283–294 (2008)
7. Fok, C.-L., Roman, G.-C., Lu, C.: Adaptive service provisioning for wireless sensor networks. Technical Report WUCSE-2009-83, Washington University in St. Louis (December 2009)
8. Fok, C.-L., Roman, G.-C., Lu, C.: Enhanced Coordination in Sensor Networks through Flexible Service Provisioning. In: Field, J., Vasconcelos, V.T. (eds.) COORDINATION 2009. LNCS, vol. 5521, pp. 66–85. Springer, Heidelberg (2009)
9. Frey, D., Roman, G.-C.: Context-aware publish subscribe in mobile ad hoc networks. In: Murphy, A.L., Vitek, J. (eds.) COORDINATION 2007. LNCS, vol. 4467, pp. 37–55. Springer, Heidelberg (2007)
10. Gay, D., Levis, P., von Behren, R., Welsh, M., Brewer, E., Culler, D.: The nesc language: A holistic approach to networked embedded systems. In: PLDI 2003, pp. 1–11. ACM, New York (2003)
11. Gnawali, O., Fonseca, R., Jamieson, K., Moss, D., Levis, P.: Collection tree protocol. In: SenSys 2009 (November 2009)
12. Hackmann, G., Chipara, O., Lu, C.: Robust topology control for indoor wireless sensor networks. In: SenSys 2008, pp. 57–70 (2008)
13. Handorean, R., Sen, R., Hackmann, G., Roman, G.-C.: Supporting predictable service provision in manets via context aware session management. Int. Journal of Web Services Research 3(3), 1–26 (2006)
14. Hill, J., Szewczyk, R., Woo, A., Hollar, S., Culler, D., Pister, K.: System architecture directions for networked sensors. SIGPLAN Not. 35(11), 93–104 (2000)
15. Kushwaha, M., Amundson, I., Koutsoukos, X., Neema, S., Sztipanovits, J.: Oasis: A programming framework for service-oriented sensor networks. In: COMSWARE 2007 (2007)
16. Meshkova, E., Riihijarvi, J., Oldewurtel, F., Jardak, C., Mahonen, P.: Service-oriented design methodology for wireless sensor networks: A view through case studies. In: SUTC 2008, pp. 146–153 (2008)
17. Polastre, J., Szewczyk, R., Culler, D.: Telos: enabling ultra-low power wireless research. In: IPSN 2005, p. 48 (2005)
18. Priyantha, N.B., Kansal, A., Goraczko, M., Zhao, F.: Tiny web services: design and implementation of interoperable and evolvable sensor networks. In: SenSys 2008, pp. 253–266 (2008)
19. Scholz, A., Buckl, C., Sommer, S., Kemper, A., Knoll, A., Heuer, J., Schmitt, A.: eSOA - service oriented architectures adapted for embedded networks. In: IDIN 2009, June 2009, pp. 599–605 (2009)
20. Sen, R., Roman, G.-C., Gill, C.D.: Cian: A workflow engine for manets. In: Lea, D., Zavattaro, G. (eds.) COORDINATION 2008. LNCS, vol. 5052, pp. 280–295. Springer, Heidelberg (2008)
21. Singh, A., Ramakrishnan, C.R., Smolka, S.A.: A process calculus for mobile ad hoc networks. In: Lea, D., Zavattaro, G. (eds.) COORDINATION 2008. LNCS, vol. 5052, pp. 296–314. Springer, Heidelberg (2008)
22. Viroli, M., Casadei, M.: Biochemical tuple spaces for self-organising coordination. In: Field, J., Vasconcelos, V.T. (eds.) COORDINATION 2009. LNCS, vol. 5521, pp. 143–162. Springer, Heidelberg (2009)

Simulation and Analysis of Distributed Systems in KLAIM

Francesco Calzolai and Michele Loreti

Dipartimento di Sistemi e Informatica
Università di Firenze

Abstract. Network and distributed systems typically consists of a large number of actors that act and interact with each other in a highly dynamic environment. Due to the number of involved actors and their strong dependence on mobility and interaction, performance and dependability issues are of utmost importance for this class of systems. STOKLAIM is a stochastic extension of KLAIM specifically thought to facilitate the incorporation of random phenomena in models for network-aware computing. In this paper we show how STOKLAIM can be used to specify and verify quantitative properties of distributed systems. To support the analysis an automatic tool is introduced and used.

1 Introduction

Network and distributed systems typically consist of a large number of actors that act and interact with each other in a highly dynamic environment. Many programming and specification formalisms have been developed that can deal with issues such as (code and agent) mobility, remote execution, security, privacy and integrity. Important examples of such languages and frameworks are, among others, Obliq [6], Seal [7], ULM [5] and KLAIM (*Kernel Language for Agents Interaction and Mobility*) [8,4].

Performance and dependability issues are of utmost importance for "network-aware" computing, due to the number of involved actors and their strong dependence on mobility and interaction. Spontaneous computer crashes may easily lead to failure of remote execution or process movement, while spurious network failures may cause loss of code fragments or unpredictable delays.

Correctness in network and distributed systems, as well as their safety guarantees, is not a rigid notion "*either it is correct or not*" but has a less absolute nature: "in 99.7% of the cases, safety can be ensured"'.

To facilitate the incorporation of random phenomena in models for network-aware computing a stochastic extension of KLAIM [8,4], named STOKLAIM, has been proposed in [9]. KLAIM is an experimental language for distributed systems that is aimed at modelling and programming mobile code applications, i.e., applications for which exploiting code mobility is the prime distinctive feature. In STOKLAIM, every action has a random duration governed by a negative exponential distribution.

D. Clarke and G. Agha (Eds.): COORDINATION 2010, LNCS 6116, pp. 122–136, 2010.

In [10], MoSL (*Mobile Stochastic Logic*), a logic that allows one to refer to the spatial structure of the network for the specification of properties for StoKlaim models as been proposed. MoSL is a stochastic logic (inspired by CSL [2,3]) that, together with qualitative properties, permits specifying time-bounded probabilistic reachability properties, such as "the likelihood to reach a goal state within t time units while visiting only legal states is at least 0.92". MoSL is also equipped with operators that permit describing properties resulting from resource production and consumption. In particular, state properties incorporate features for resource management and context verification. Context verification allows the verification of assumptions on resources and processes in a system at the logical level, i.e. without having to change the model to investigate the effect of each assumption on the system behaviour.

In this paper we show how StoKlaim can be used for specifying and verifying quantitative properties of distributed systems. In the paper we use StoKlaim to model three classical leader election algorithm. To support the analysis of StoKlaim systems we use SAM (Stochastic Analyser for Mobility). This is a *command-line* tool that provide functionalities for executing, simulating and model-checking specifications.

Structure of the paper. In Section 2 we recall the modelling language StoKlaim, while in Section 3 we briefly describe *MoSL* and its intuitive semantics. In Section 4 we describe SAM and its main functionalities. This tool is used for analysing three leader election protocols. This analyses are described in Section 5. Section 6 concludes the paper.

2 Klaim

Klaim [4] is a formalism introduced for specifying concurrent and distributed systems. It has been designed to provide programmers with primitives for handling physical distribution, scoping and mobility of processes. Klaim is based on process algebras but makes use of Linda-like asynchronous communication and models distribution via multiple shared tuple spaces [13]. Tuple spaces and processes are distributed over different localities and the classical Linda operations are indexed with the location of the tuple space they operate on.

The Linda communication model was originally proposed for parallel programming on isolated machines. The model permits *time uncoupling* (data life time is independent of the life time of the producer process), *destination uncoupling* (the producer of a datum does not need to know the future use or the final destination of that datum) and *space uncoupling* (communicating processes need to know a single interface, i.e. the operations over the tuple space).

A Klaim system, called a *net*, is a set of *nodes*, each of which is identified by a *physical locality*. *Physical Localities* can be seen as the addresses of network nodes. Every node has a computational component (a set of processes running in parallel), an *allocation environment* and a data component (a tuple space). Processes interact with each other either locally or remotely by posting and retrieving tuples to and from a tuple space. Processes can refer nodes by using either physical localities or *logical localities.* While physical localities have a global meaning, logical localities have a local meaning and their interpretation depends on the node where processes run. Indeed, each node is equipped with an allocation environment mapping logical localities to physical localities. When a process uses a logical locality, the allocation environment is used to resolve this name into a physical address.

Processes interact with each other by means of messages, named *tuples*, inserted into located tuple spaces. Tuples are retrieved from tuple spaces via *pattern matching* using *templates.* Processes can also be spawned to be evaluated remotely.

2.1 StoKlaim: Stochastic Klaim

In order to deal with performance and dependability issues Klaim has been extended by adding distribution rates to its actions [9]. In the proposed extension, actions are assumed to have a random duration governed by a negative exponential distribution. System specifying by means of the stochastic extension of Klaim can be formally analysed by using the logic and the model checking technique presented in [10].

Syntactic categories. We distinguish the following basic syntactic categories.

- Val, ranged over by $v, v', v_1, \ldots$, is a set of (basic data) *values*;
- LLoc, ranged over by $l, l', l_1, \ldots$, is a set of *logical localities*, also called *localities*; we assume the locality self $\in$ LLoc;
- PLoc, ranged over by $s, s', s_1, \ldots$, is a set of *physical localities*, also called *sites*;
- Val-var, ranged over by $x, x', x_1, \ldots$, is a a set of *value variables*;
- Loc-var, ranged over by $u, u', u_1, \ldots$, is set of *locality variables*;
- Proc-var, ranged over by $X, X', X_1, \ldots$, be a set of *process variables.*

All the above sets are countable and are mutually disjoint. Let ℓ, ℓ', ℓ_1 range over Loc $=$ LLoc $\cup$ PLoc $\cup$ Loc-var. We will also use $e, e', e_1, \ldots$ to denote value expressions. The precise syntax of expressions e is not specified since it is irrelevant for the purpose of the present paper. We assume that expressions contain, at least, basic values Val and variables Val-var.

We adopt the $(\tilde{\cdot})$-notation for sequences; e.g., $\tilde{l} = l_1, l_2, \ldots, l_n$ denotes a sequence over Loc and $\tilde{x} = x_1, x_2, \ldots, x_m$ is a sequence over Val-var. For sequence $\tilde{s} = s_1, \ldots, s_n$, let $\{\tilde{s}\}$ denote the set of elements in $\tilde{s}$, i.e., $\{\tilde{s}\} = \{s_1, \ldots, s_n\}$. One-element sequences and singleton sets are denoted as the element they contain, i.e., $\{s\}$ is denoted as s and $\tilde{s} = s'$ as s'. The empty sequence is denoted by ϵ.

Syntax. Syntax of StoKlaim nets is reported in Table 1. Specifications in StoKlaim consist of nets and processes. The most elementary net is the null

Table 1. STOKLAIM syntax

$$
\begin{aligned}
N &::= \mathbf{0} \mid l :: E \mid N \parallel N \\
E &::= P \mid \langle \tilde{d} \rangle \\
d &::= P \mid l \mid e \\
P &::= \mathbf{nil} \mid (A, \lambda).P \mid P + P \mid P \mid P \mid X \\
A &::= \mathbf{out}(\tilde{d})@\ell \mid \mathbf{in}(\tilde{t})@\ell \mid \mathbf{read}(\tilde{t})@\ell \mid \mathbf{eval}(P)@\ell \mid \mathbf{newloc}(!x) \\
t &::= d \mid ?X \mid ?x \mid ?u
\end{aligned}
$$

net, denoted **0**. A net consisting of a single node with *locality* l is denoted $l :: E$ where E is a *node element*. In general, nets consist of several nodes composed in parallel.

Node elements are either processes executing at a node ($l :: P$) or data represented as a *tuple* $\langle \tilde{d} \rangle$ that is stored at a node $((l :: \langle \tilde{d} \rangle))$,

Processes are built up from the terminated process **nil**, a set of randomly delayed actions, and standard process algebraic constructors such as prefix, choice, parallel composition and process instantiation with optional parameters.

The process $(A, \lambda).P$ executes action A with a random duration that is distributed exponentially with rate $\lambda \in \mathbb{R}^+$.

A process can write tuple $\tilde{d}$ in repository ℓ by the action $\mathbf{out}(\tilde{d})@\ell$. With an input action $\mathbf{in}(t)@\ell$ a process can withdraw a tuple matching pattern $\tilde{t}$ from ℓ.

A pattern is a sequence of *template fields.* These can be either actual fields or a *formal fields*, i.e. a variables prefixed with an question mark to indicate binding of such a variable. Matching predicate *match* is formally defined in Table 2. This leads to a substitution Θ associating values to the corresponding variables, where $\Theta_1 \lhd \Theta_2$ denotes the usual composition of substitutions Θ_1 and Θ_2.

Action $\mathbf{read}(\tilde{t})@\ell$ is similar to $\mathbf{in}(\tilde{t})@\ell$ except that retrieved tuple is not deleted from the tuple spaces at ℓ. The action $\mathbf{eval}(P)@\ell$ spawns process P at site ℓ.

Action $\mathbf{newloc}(?u)$ creates a new node. This action will have also the effect of creating a fresh new address, say l, that identifies the new created nodes. The allocation environment associated to l is obtained by extending the allocation environment ρ of the node where the action is executed, so to bind locality self to l.

Table 2. Pattern-matching of tuples against templates

$$
match(l, l) =_{\text{def}} [\,] \qquad match(v, v) =_{\text{def}} [\,]
$$

$$
match(?u, l) =_{\text{def}} [l/u] \qquad match(?x, v) =_{\text{def}} [v/x] \qquad match(?X, P) =_{\text{def}} [P/X]
$$

$$
\frac{match(t_1, d_1) = \Theta_1 \quad \ldots \quad match(t_n, d_n) = \Theta_n}{match((t_1, \ldots, t_n), (d_1, \ldots, d_n)) =_{\text{def}} \Theta_1 \lhd \ldots \lhd \Theta_n}
$$

Specifications. A StoKlaim specification $\mathcal{S}$ is a triple $\mathcal{E}, \Delta \vdash N$ where:

- $\mathcal{E}$ is a function associating to each site in the net N an *allocation environment*;
- Δ is the set of process definitions ($X \triangleq P$);
- N is a net describing both the structure and the behaviour of a system.

Allocation environments are used to associate *logical localities* to *physical localities*. Formally, an allocation environment ρ is a (total) function from Loc to PLoc.

We say that a StoKlaim *specification* $\mathcal{E}, \Delta \vdash N$ is *well-formed* if and only if it is type-correct and:

- for each $s \in \mathsf{PLoc}$, if $\mathcal{E}(s) = \rho$ then:
  - $\forall s' \in \mathsf{PLoc}$: $\rho(s') = s'$;
  - $\rho(\mathsf{self}) = s$
- for each $X \triangleq P \in \Delta$, process variable X occurs *guarded*, i.e. prefixed by an action, in P or as the argument of an **eval** action;
- processes use only localities that really exist.

In the remainder of this paper we assume specifications to be *well-formed.* Moreover, we will also omit $\mathcal{E}$ and Δ from the specification when their definition is clear from the context. Finally we let Spec denotes the set of StoKlaim specifications.

Operational semantics. Stochastic behaviour of StoKlaim specifications is defined by means of an *action-labelled* CTMCs (AMCs). These are Continuous Time Markov Chains where transitions are equipped with a label:

Definition 1. *An* action-labelled *CTMC (AMC)* $\mathbb{A}$ *is a triple* $(S, ACT, \mapsto)$ *where* S *is a set of states,* ACT *is a set of actions, and* $\mapsto$ *is the transition function, which is a total function from* $S \times ACT \times S$ *to the set of non-negative real numbers* $\mathbb{R}_{\geq 0}$.

Semantics of StoKlaim specifications is described as an AMC $\mathcal{R}_{SK} = (\mathsf{Spec}, \Lambda, \mapsto)$. Where Spec is the set of StoKlaim specifications, while Λ is the set of transition labels $\mathcal{A}$ defined according to the grammar below:

$$\mathcal{A} ::= s_1 : \mathbf{n}(s) \mid s_1 : \mathbf{o}(\tilde{d}, s_2) \mid s_1 : \mathbf{i}(\tilde{d})s_2 \mid s_1 : \mathbf{r}(\tilde{d}, s_2) \mid s_1 : \mathbf{e}(P, s_2)$$

Each label identifies the site where the action is performed, the argument of the action and the site where the action takes effect.For instance, $i_1 : \mathbf{o}(v, i_2)$ represents the uploading of value v from site i_1 to site i_2. Interested reader can refer to [10] for a complete description of StoKlaim semantics.

3 MoSL: Mobile Stochastic Logic

Performance and dependability properties of StoKlaim systems can be specified by means MoSL [10] (Mobile Stochastic Logic). Key features of this logic are:

- it is a *temporal logic* that permits describing the dynamic evolution of the system;
- it is both *action*- and *state*-based;
- it is a *real-time* logic that permits the use of real-time bounds in the logical characterisation of the behaviours of interest;
- it is a *probabilistic logic* that permits expressing not only functional properties, but also properties related to performance and dependability aspects; and, finally
- it is a *spatial logic* that references the spatial structure of the network for the specification.

In this section we briefly recall syntax (Table 3) and the intuitive semantics of *MoSL*.

As in the branching-time temporal logic CTL, also in MoSL two classes of formulae are considered: *state* formulae $\Phi, \Phi', \Phi_1, \ldots$ and *path* formulae $\varphi, \varphi', \varphi_1, \ldots$.

There are three categories of state formulae. The first category includes formulae in propositional logic, where the atomic propositions are tt and the basic state formulae. The second category includes statements about the likelihood of paths satisfying a property. Finally there are the so-called long-run properties.

Basic state formulae are built using a variant of *MoMo* [11] *consumption* ($\rightarrow$) and *production* ($\leftarrow$) operators. Production and consumption operators permit formalising properties concerning the availability of resources (i.e. located tuples and processes) and system's reactions to placement of new resources in a state. For instance, a consumption formula $Q@\imath \rightarrow \Phi$ holds for a network whenever in the network there exists a process Q running at a node, of site $\imath$, and the "remaining" network, namely Q's context, satisfies Φ.

Path formulae basic rely on the CTL *until* operator $\Phi \;\, \mathcal{U} \, \Psi$. In order to be able to refer also to actions executed along a path, a variant of the *until* operator as originally proposed in action-based CTL [12] is used. To that end, the until-operator is parameterised with two *action specifiers*.

Here, $\top$ stands for "any set" and can be used when no requirement on actions is imposed. A set of action specifiers is satisfied by an action if the latter satisfies at least one of the elements of the set. Action specifiers (ξ) are a kind of templates for actions. The action specifier $s_1 : \mathbf{O}(\tilde{d}, s_2)$, is satisfied only by

Table 3. Syntax of MoSL formulae

$$
\begin{array}{lll}
\Phi & ::= \mathtt{tt} \quad | \quad \aleph \quad | \quad \neg\Phi \quad | \quad \Phi \vee \Phi \quad | \quad \mathcal{P}_{\bowtie p}(\varphi) \quad | \quad \mathcal{S}_{\bowtie p}(\Phi) \\
\varphi & ::= \Phi \;{}_{\Lambda}\mathcal{U}_{\Omega}^{<t}\; \Psi \mid \Phi \;{}_{\Delta}\mathcal{U}^{<t}\; \Psi \\
\aleph & ::= PTF@\imath \rightarrow \Phi \mid \langle\tilde{F}\rangle@\imath \rightarrow \Phi \mid Q(\tilde{Q}', \tilde{\ell}, \tilde{e})@\imath \leftarrow \Phi \mid \langle\tilde{f}\rangle@\imath \leftarrow \Phi \\
PTF & ::= Q(\tilde{Q}', \tilde{\ell}, \tilde{e}) \mid !X \\
\Delta & ::= \top \mid \{\} \mid \{\xi_1, \ldots, \xi_n\} \\
\xi & ::= g : \mathbf{N}(g) \mid g : \mathbf{O}(\tilde{F}, g) \mid g : \mathbf{I}(\tilde{F}, g) \mid g : \mathbf{R}(\tilde{F}, g) \mid g : \mathbf{E}(PTF, g)
\end{array}
$$

action $(s_1 : \mathbf{o}(\tilde{d}, s_2))$. Action specifiers may contain binders that bind their variables to corresponding values in actions in the path; e.g., the action specifier $?u_1 : \mathbf{o}(\tilde{t}, !u_2)$ is satisfied by any action, executed at some site, which uploads a tuple matching $\tilde{t}$ to some site. Action specifiers and their matching to actions generate substitutions that bind variables in subformulae. The meaning of the other action specifiers is now self-explanatory.

A path satisfies $\Phi \ {}_{\Delta}\mathcal{U}_{\Omega} \ \Psi$ whenever eventually a state satisfying Ψ—in the sequel, a Ψ-state—is reached via a Φ-path—i.e. a path composed only of Φ-states—*and*, in addition, while evolving between Φ states, actions are performed satisfying Δ and the Ψ-state is entered via an action satisfying Ω. Finally, we add a time constraint on path formulae. This is done by adding time parameter t—in much the same way as in timed CTL [1]—which is either a real number or may be infinite. In addition to the requirements described just above, it is now imposed that a Ψ-state should be reached within t time units. If $t = \infty$, this time constraint is vacuously true, and the until from action-based CTL is obtained. Similarly, a path satisfies $\Phi \ {}_{\Delta}\mathcal{U}^{<t} \ \Psi$ if the initial state satisfies Ψ (at time 0) or eventually a Ψ state will be reached in the path, by time t via a Φ-path, and, in addition, while evolving between Φ-states, actions are performed satisfying Δ.

4 SAM

In this section we present SAM (Stochastic Analyser for Mobility) [22]. This is a *command-line* tool, developed in OCAML, that supports the stochastic analysis of STOKLAIM specifications. SAM can be used for:

- executing interactively specifications;
- simulating stochastic behaviours;
- model checking MoSL formulae.

Running a specification. SAM provides an environment for interactive execution of STOKLAIM specification. When a specification is executed, a user can select interactively possible computations.

Simulating a specification. To analyse behaviour of distributed systems specified in STOKLAIM, SAM provides a simulator. This module randomly generates possible computations. At each step of the simulation the next state is determined by using the Gillespie Algorithm [14]. A simulation continues until in the considered computation either a *time limit* or a deadlock configuration is reached.

Fixed a *sampling time*, each computation is described in term of the number of resources (located tuple) available in the system during the computation. At the end of a simulation, the average amount of resources available in the system at specified time intervals is provided.

To identify the values to collect in a simulation a sequence of elements (named *experiments*) of the form:

label : $\langle \tilde{d} \rangle @lp$

is provided. An experiments associate a label (label in the example above) to a locate tuple ($\langle \tilde{d} \rangle @lp$) where lp can be either a site or a wildcard (*). In the former case, the number of tuples in the considered localities are counted. In the latter, the tuples in all the localities are summed.

For instance what follows are two experiments that can be used for computing the number of tuple ⟨"FOLLOWER"⟩ and ⟨"LEADER"⟩ available in a net:

follower: ⟨"FOLLOWER"⟩@$*$
leader: ⟨"LEADER"⟩@$*$

Model checking SAM permits verifying whether a given STOKLAIM specification satisfies or not a MoSL formula. This module, which implements the model checking algorithm proposed in [10], use an existing state-based stochastic model-checker, the Markov Reward Model Checker (MRMC) [19], and wrapping it in the MoSL model-checking algorithm. After loading a STOKLAIM specification and a MoSL formula, it verifies, by means of one or more calls to MRMC, the satisfaction of the formula by the specification.

Unfortunately, even simple STOKLAIM specification can generate a very large number of states. For this reason, the *numerical* model checking cannot always be applied. To overcome the state explosion problem, a *statistical model-checker* has been also implemented in SAM. The statistical approach has been successfully used in existing model checkers [15,21,24,25].

While in a numerical model checker the exact probability to satisfy a path-formula is computed up to a precision ϵ, in a *statistical model-checker* the probability associated to a path-formula is determined after a set of independent observations. This algorithm is parametrised with respect to a given *tolerance* ε and *error probability* p. The algorithm guarantees that the difference between the computed values and the exact ones are greater than ε with a probability that is less than p.

5 Leader Election in STOKLAIM

In this Section we use STOKLAIM for specifying a system where n distributed sites (nodes) have to elect a leader (a uniquely designed process): we will consider three well known leader election protocols [23,17]: *All The Way, As far as it can* and *Asynchronous leader election.* The first two protocols are modelled by relying on agents and code mobility, while the third is modelled by relying on message passing.

In all the considered algorithms, it is assumed that the nodes are always arranged in a ring: in this particular network topology every node is connected to two other nodes (called *prev* and *next*). This is a common assumption for leader election algorithms [23].

In StoKlaim the system consists of n nodes each of which hosts the execution of an agent or a process. We assume these nodes are identified by sites ($s_0,\ldots,$ s_{n-1}). The index associated to a site identifies the position of the node in the ring: the process located at s_i precedes (follows) the one located at $s_{i+1 \bmod n}$ ($s_{i-1 \bmod n}$) in the ring. We also assume that the allocation environment ρ_i of sites s_i, beside the standard mapping $\mathsf{self} \mapsto s_i$, maps logical locality next to $s_{i+1 \bmod n}$ and logical locality pred to $s_{i-1 \bmod n}$. In the performance analysis we will consider four ring sizes: 25, 50, 75 and 100. Notice that, for these configurations, standard model checking techniques are note easily applicable. Indeed, if n is the number of nodes in the ring, the first two algorithms generate models with more than $n!$ states while the models generated from the third algorithm are composed of more than 2^n states.

In the considered models we assume that local communications are performed with rate 15.0 while remote communications have rate 1.0.

In the analysis we will use simulations and (statistical) model checking. Simulations will be performed by considering 300 iterations and will be used to determine how, in the average, process change their state. Statistical model checking will be used to compute the probability, when t varies from 0 to 600, of:

$$\mathsf{tt}\ {}_{\top}\mathcal{U}^{<t} \bigvee_i \langle \text{``}\mathsf{LEADER}\text{''} \rangle @ s_i \rightarrow \mathsf{tt}$$

This formula identifies the paths that leads one of the site to become a leader within time t.

5.1 All the Way

In this algorithm every participants is univocally identified by an *id* selected randomly. For this reason, at the beginning each process retrieve a value (the *localID*) from a specific site (*rg*) that acts as random generator. The leader will be the node with the minimum *id*.

When a process has determined its *id*, an agent is sent to the next node in the ring. This agent carries a node *id* and the minimum seen so far (*min*). Agent travels *all the way* along the ring in order to find the minimum value in the net. When an agent arrives in a node, it reads the site's *id* and updates the minimum accordingly. As soon as an agent returns to the originating node, it is able to determine the node's roles: *leader* if its *id* is the smallest in the ring, *follower* otherwise.

What follows is the agent devoted to find the minimum *id* on the ring and that decides if its starting node can be the leader[1]:

[1] SAM uses a richer syntax for specifying processes. This contains standard command like selection and iterations and typed variables.

$agent[int\ id,\ int\ min] \triangleq$
(**read**("ID", ?lId)@self, $local$).
if ($id = lId$) **then**
if ($id = min$) **then**
(**out**("LEADER")@self, $local$)
else
(**out**("FOLLOWER")@self, $local$)
else
if ($min < lId$) **then**
(**eval**($agent(id,\ min)$)@next, $remote$)
else
(**eval**($agent(id,\ lId)$)@next, $remote$)

The result of the simulation of the system is reported in Figures 1(a) and 1(b): on the left-hand side it is shown the average number of leaders, while on the right-hand side it is shown the average number of followers. From these pictures it is clear that, in the average, all the nodes (both *leader* and *followers*) terminate the algorithm approximately at the same time. This means that a *follower* continues to play an active role in the system till the end of the computation.

5.2 As Far as It Can

The algorithm considered in the previous section is not very efficient. Indeed, every agent keeps travelling even if its *id* is not the smaller. An improvement of the *All the way* algorithm is the *As far as it can*. In this algorithm an agent moves to the next node if and only if its *id* is smaller than the local identifier. An agent travels along the ring "as far as it can", until it stops in a site with a smaller (or equals) *id*. Only the agent with the smaller *id* is able to return to its starting site, all the others will be eventually stopped. After the survivor agent travelling all the ring, it sets the starting node as *leader* and then creates the agent notify that revisits all the other nodes setting them as *follower*.

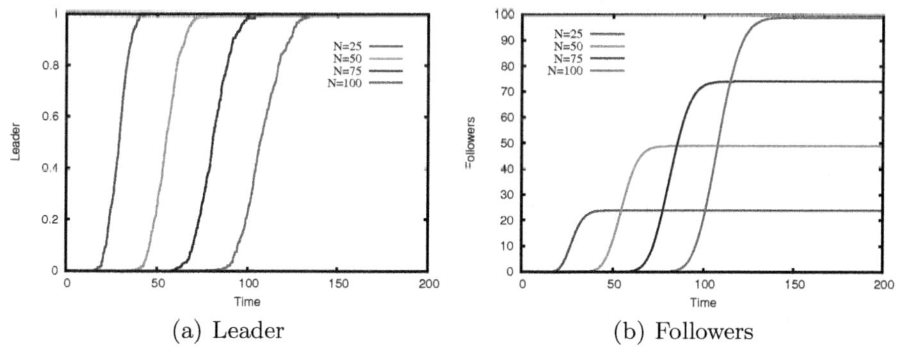

(a) Leader (b) Followers

Fig. 1. *AllTheWay* simulation

The following is the agent used in the StoKlaim specification to visit the ring:

$agent[int\ id,\ int\ min] \triangleq$
  $(\mathbf{read}(\text{"ID"},\ ?lId)@\mathsf{self}, local).$
  $\mathbf{if}\ (id = lId)\ \mathbf{then}$
    $(\mathbf{out}(\text{"LEADER"})@\mathsf{self}, local).$
    $(\mathbf{eval}(notify(id))@\mathsf{next}, remote)$
  $\mathbf{else}$
    $\mathbf{if}\ (min < lId)\ \mathbf{then}$
      $(\mathbf{eval}(agent(id,\ min))@\mathsf{next}, remote)$

$notify[int\ id] \triangleq$
  $(\mathbf{read}(\text{"ID"},\ ?lId)@\mathsf{self}, local).$
  $\mathbf{if}\ (id! = lId)\ \mathbf{then}$
    $(\mathbf{out}(\text{"FOLLOWER"})@\mathsf{self}, local).$
    $(\mathbf{eval}(notify(id))@\mathsf{next}, remote)$

Simulation results, reported in Figure 2, shows that, differently from *All the way*, the leader is selected rapidly.

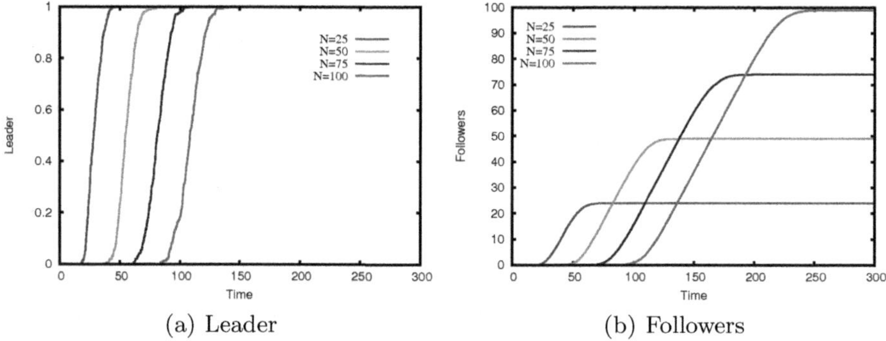

(a) Leader (b) Followers

Fig. 2. *AsFarAsItCan* simulation

5.3 Asynchronous Leader Election

The algorithm considered in the previous sections identify the leader as the node with the minimum *id*. In this section we consider a *randomised* protocol that is an adaptation of the *asynchronous leader election protocol* proposed in [17].

Processes in the system can be either *active* or *inactive*. Until a process becomes inactive, it performs the following steps:

1. Chooses 0 or 1 each with a given probability, and sends the choice to the next process.
2. If the process chose 0 and the active process preceding it in the ring chose 1 it becomes inactive and only continues to relay received messages.
3. If it is still active, it sends a counter around the ring to check whether it is the only active process. In that case it becomes the leader, otherwise another round of the algorithm is repeated.

The model for an *active* process is shown below. Notice that process *testLeader* is the process used for verifying if the current node is a leader. An *active* process is modelled in StoKlaim as follows:

```
active[int id] ≜
  (out(0)@next, remote).
    (in(?val)@self, local).
    if (val = 1) then
      (out("FOLLOWER")@self, local).
      inactive()
    else
      testLeader(id)
  +(out(1)@next, remote).
    (in(?val)@self, local).
    testLeader(id)

testLeader[int id] ≜
  (out("CHECK", id)@next, remote).
  (in("CHECK", ?c :)@self, local).
  if (c = id) then
    (out("LEADER")@self, local)
  else
    active(id)
```

The simulation of considered system (Figure 3) shows that, differently from the specifications considered in previous sections, a large number of nodes become *inactive* before the leader is selected. Unfortunately, the time needed to determine the leader increases significantly.

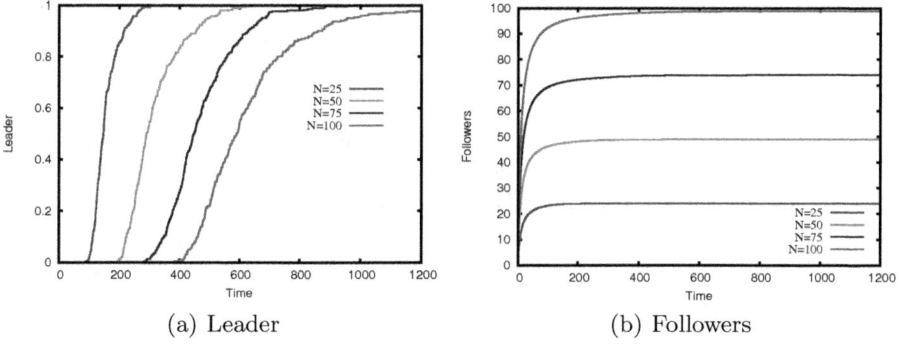

(a) Leader (b) Followers

Fig. 3. *Asynchronous* simulation

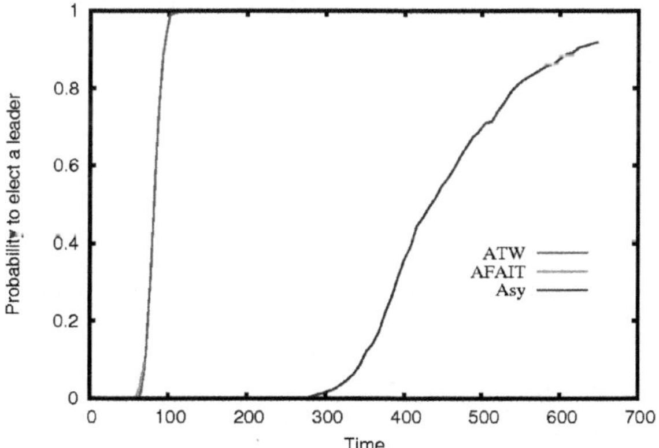

Fig. 4. Comparison between the three algorithm

5.4 Final Considerations

We now use statistical model checking to contrast the three considered algorithms. In particular we study how the probability to select a leader within t time units varies in the three algorithms. In Figure 4 are reported the model checking results for a configuration with $n = 75$ nodes in the ring. The results respect the one obtained with the simulation. *All the way* algorithm and *As far as it can*, in the average, are faster then the *Asynchronous leader election*.

Notice that to compute the probability of the considered formulae, due to the size of considered system, the use of numerical model checking is not practicable. On the contrary, statistical model checker allow us to compute an approximation of the requested probability.

6 Conclusions and Future Works

In this paper we have shown how StoKlaim can be used for specifying and verifying quantitative aspects of distributed systems. In the paper the analysis of three well known leader election algorithms are considered. The proposed analysis have been performed by relying on SAM: Stochastic Analyser for Mobility. This is a *command-line* tool that provide functionalities for executing, simulating and model-checking specifications.

Several software tools have been developed for supporting verification (via model checking) of quantitative aspects of concurrent systems. We just mention PRISM [20], ETMCC [16] and *MRMC* [18]. However, many of these frameworks either do not use a process algebra to support system specification (like, for instance, MRMC and ETMCC), or the considered process algebra does not provide linguistic primitives for describing distribution and mobility. On the contrary, the use of StoKlaim, where *localities* and *process mobility* are first class citizens, simplifies the specification and the analysis of distributed systems.

As a future work we plan to study the possibility to extend the model checker in order to take into account rewards. Notice that the algorithms considered in Section 5 are analysed by considering the time needed to select a leader. By introducing rewards in the logic, other interesting aspects, like for instance the average number of messages exchanged by the different algorithms, can be taken into account.

References

1. Alur, R., Dill, D.: A theory of timed automata. Theoret. Comput. Sci. 126, 183–235 (1994)
2. Aziz, A., Sanwal, K., Singhal, V., Brayton, R.: Model checking Continuous Time Markov Chains. Transations on Computational Logic 1(1), 162–170 (2000)
3. Baier, C., Katoen, J.-P., Hermanns, H.: Approximate Symbolic Model Checking of Continuous-Time Markov Chains. In: Baeten, J.C.M., Mauw, S. (eds.) CONCUR 1999. LNCS, vol. 1664, pp. 146–162. Springer, Heidelberg (1999)

4. Bettini, L., Bono, V., De Nicola, R., Ferrari, G., Gorla, D., Loreti, M., Moggi, E., Pugliese, R., Tuosto, E., Venneri, B.: The Klaim Project: Theory and Practice. In: Priami, C. (ed.) GC 2003. LNCS, vol. 2874, pp. 88–150. Springer, Heidelberg (2003)
5. Boudol, G.: ULM: a core programming model for global computing (extended abstract). In: Schmidt, D. (ed.) ESOP 2004. LNCS, vol. 2986, pp. 234–248. Springer, Heidelberg (2004)
6. Cardelli, L.: A Language with Distributed Scope. In: 22nd Annual ACM Symposium on Principles of Programming Languages, pp. 286–297. ACM, New York (1995)
7. Castagna, G., Vitek, J.: Seal: A framework for Secure Mobile Computations. In: Bal, H.E., Cardelli, L., Belkhouche, B. (eds.) ICCL-WS 1998. LNCS, vol. 1686, pp. 47–77. Springer, Heidelberg (1999)
8. De Nicola, R., Ferrari, G., Pugliese, R.: KLAIM: A Kernel Language for Agents Interaction and Mobility. IEEE Transactions on Software Engineering 24(5), 315–329 (1998)
9. De Nicola, R., Katoen, J.-P., Latella, D., Loreti, M., Massink, M.: KLAIM and its stochastic semantics. Technical report, Dipartimento di Sistemi e Informatica, Università di Firenze (2006), `http://rap.dsi.unifi.it/~loreti/papers/TR062006.pdf`
10. De Nicola, R., Katoen, J.-P., Latella, D., Loreti, M., Massink, M.: Model checking mobile stochastic logic. Theoretical Computer Science 382(1), 42–70 (2007)
11. De Nicola, R., Loreti, M.: Multiple-Labelled Transition Systems for nominal calculi and their logics. Mathematical Structures in Computer Science 18(1), 107–143 (2008)
12. De Nicola, R., Vaandrager, F.: Action versus state based logics for transition systems. In: Guessarian, I. (ed.) LITP 1990. LNCS, vol. 469, pp. 407–419. Springer, Heidelberg (1990)
13. Gelernter, D.: Generative Communication in Linda 7(1), 80–112 (1985)
14. Gillespie, D.T.: Exact stochastic simulation of coupled chemical reactions. The Journal of Physical Chemistry 81(25), 2340–2361 (1977)
15. Younes, G.N.H., Kwiatkowska, M., Parker, D.: Numerical vs. statistical probabilistic model checking. International Journal on Software Tools for Technology Transfer 8(3), 216–228 (2006)
16. Hermanns, H., Katoen, J.-P., Meyer-Kayser, J., Siegle, M.: A Tool for Model-Checking Markov Chains. International Journal on Software Tools for Technology Transfer 4(2), 153–172 (2003)
17. Itai, A., Rodeh, M.: Symmetry breaking in distributed networks. Information and Computation 88(1) (1990)
18. Katoen, J.-P., Khattri, M., Zapreev, I.: A Markov reward model checker. In: Second International Conference on the Quantitative Evaluation of Systems (QEST 2005), pp. 243–244. IEEE Computer Society, Los Alamitos (2005)
19. Katoen, J.-P., Khattri, M., Zapreev, I.S.: A Markov reward model checker. In: Quantitative Evaluation of Systems (QEST), pp. 243–244. IEEE CS Press, Los Alamitos (2005)
20. Kwiatkowska, M., Norman, G., Parker, D.: Probabilistic Symbolic Model Checking using PRISM: A Hybrid Approach. International Journal on Software Tools for Technology Transfer 6(2), 128–142 (2004)
21. Quaglia, P., Schivo, S.: Approximate model checking of stochastic cows. In: Proc. of TGC 2010 (to appear 2010)

22. Sam: Stochastic analyser for mobility, `http://rap.dsi.unifi.it/SAM/`
23. Santoro, N.: Design and Analysis of Distributed Algorithms. Wiley, Chichester (2006)
24. Sen, K., Viswanathan, M., Agha, G.: Statistical model checking of black-box probabilistic systems. In: Alur, R., Peled, D.A. (eds.) CAV 2004. LNCS, vol. 3114, pp. 202–215. Springer, Heidelberg (2004)
25. Sen, K., Viswanathan, M., Agha, G.: On statistical model checking of stochastic systems. In: Etessami, K., Rajamani, S.K. (eds.) CAV 2005. LNCS, vol. 3576, pp. 266–280. Springer, Heidelberg (2005)

Modelling Railway Interlocking Tables Using Coloured Petri Nets*

Somsak Vanit-Anunchai

School of Telecommunication Engineering
Institute of Engineering, Suranaree University of Technology
Muang, Nakhon Ratchasima 30000, Thailand
somsav@sut.ac.th

Abstract. Interlocking tables are the functional specification defining the routes, on which the passage of the train is allowed. Associated with the route, the states and actions of all related signalling equipment are also specified. This paper formally models the interlocking tables using Coloured Petri Nets (CPN). The CPN model comprises two parts: *Signaling Layout* and *Interlocking Control*. The *Signaling Layout* part is used to simulate the passage of the train. It stores geographic information of the signalling layout in *tokens*. The *Interlocking Control* part models actions of the controller according to the functions specified in the interlocking tables. The arc inscriptions in the model represent the content of the interlocking tables. Following our modelling approach we can reuse the same CPN net structure to model any new or modified interlocking system regardless of its size. Experimental results are presented to provide increased confidence in the model correctness.

Keywords: Control Tables, Railway Signalling Systems, State space analysis, XML, XSLT.

1 Introduction

Background. Currently the State Railway of Thailand (SRT) has been undertaking several railway signalling projects involving either improvement of the existing signalling systems or expansion of the existing railway lines. During the whole process of designing, installing and testing the signalling system, "Interlocking Tables" or "Control Tables" play a vital role. The control table is a tabular representation specifying how the trains move together with the required states and actions of all related equipment. This important document also acts as an agreement between the railway administrators and the contractors. Many signalling contractors have software tools for editing, generating and verifying the control tables. Usually the control table generated by a software tool is bound up with a specific railway company. But SRT has its own operating regulations, requirements and signalling principles that control tables need to comply with. Thus after the control tables are designed and checked by the contractors, they

* Supported by National Research Council of Thailand Grant no. PorKor/2551-153.

D. Clarke and G. Agha (Eds.): COORDINATION 2010, LNCS 6116, pp. 137–151, 2010.

need to be rechecked by SRT's signal engineers. Now SRT signal engineers manually inspect the submitted control tables without any software tools. Thus the checking process is very slow, labour intensive and prone to errors. In order to assist their inspection, detect and rectify errors rapidly, we propose to formally model and analyze the control tables using Coloured Petri Nets (CPNs) [9]. Because SRT's railway signalling project involves hundreds of interlocking systems, we wish to seek out an approach to rapidly build and analyse the CPN model of the control tables especially for a very large interlocking system.

Related Work. In [5], Fokkink and Hollingshead divide the railway signalling system into three layers: infrastructure, interlocking and logistics layers. The infrastructure layer involves objects or equipment used in the yard. The work in this category, for instance [2, 10], ties closely with manufacturer's products. The logistics layer involves human operation and train scheduling which aims at efficiency and absence of deadlocks. It involves the operation of the whole railway network (e.g., [6, 8, 11]) thus the state space explosion problem is often encountered. The interlocking layer provides the interface between logistics and infrastructure layers. It prevents accidents caused by human errors or equipment failure. The work in this category models the interlocking tables and verifies them against the signalling principles. For example [5, 14] use theorem provers and [15] uses a model checker to verify interlocking tables.

Hansen [7] presents a VDM model of a railway interlocking system, and validates it through simulation using Meta Language (ML). The work of [7] focuses on the principles and concepts of Danish systems rather than a generic interlocking system. In [7], it is also pointed out that interlocking systems from other countries may be different from the interlocking described in that paper. Winter et al. [13] propose to create two formal models during the design process. One is the formal model of signalling principles called the principle model. The other is the formal model of the functional specification for a specific track-layout called the interlocking model. The control tables are translated into an interlocking model and then checked against the principle model. In [13] CSP (Communicating Sequential Processes) is used as a modelling language but in [15] it is observed that the CSP models of the interlocking system and the signalling principle are difficult to understand and validate. Thus [15] uses ASM (Abstract State Machine) notation to model the semantics of control tables. The ASM model is then automatically transformed to NuSMV code [3] while the safety properties are modeled in CTL (Computational Tree Logic).

Petri Nets, including CPNs, have been used extensively to model railway systems. Most researchers focus on train scheduling and performance measures. Without modelling signalling equipment, [11] uses Interval Timed Coloured Petri Nets (ITCPN) to model train movement through railway stations and analyses throughput and waiting times of trains using the Modified Transition System Reduction Technique (MTSRT). Similar to [11], Hagalisletto et al. [6] use CPNs to model Oslo subway and analyse the train schedule but their refined model includes signalling equipment such as track circuits and points. Durmus and

Soylemez [4] use an extension of Petri Nets, Automation Petri Nets (APN), to design a simple railway yard. The APN model is then translated into a ladder diagram and Code generated for a programable logic controller. Even though [11, 6, 4] and our work use Petri Nets, our application is different from them. [11, 6] are in the logistics layer which aims to analyse the train scheduling. [4] is in the infrastructure layer which involves code generation. Our work is in the interlocking layer which is similar to [1]. Basten [1] simulates and analyses a railway interlocking specification using ExSpect which is a software tool based on high level Petri Nets. However formal verification of railway interlockings is not possible because the interlockings are too complex for the technology at that time.

Choosing Petri Nets. Designing and testing a large railway signalling systems is a complicated tasks involving a lot of details. Our counterpart, SRT signal engineers, suggest to build, maintain and modify the formal models of railway signalling themselves. According to our experience most of the formal techniques previously discussed are too difficult for the signal engineers to comprehend. On the contrary, Coloured Petri Nets (CPNs) provide a graphical notation with hierarchical structuring facilities and the inclusion of a rich set of data types providing a high level of user friendliness. CPNs are also well suited to formalising interlocking tables. In this paper we investigate the feasibility of using CPN Tools by signal engineers.

Contribution. In [12] we modelled and analysed a single track railway station using CPNs. This paper extends that work to consider a more complex double track station. The contribution of this paper is three fold. Firstly, in [12] we developed a static model where the CPN structure reflected the signaling layout of the railway station. In this paper we encode the signalling layout into *tokens*, and automatically generate these *tokens* from the drawing file[1]. This allows our CPN model to easily handle signalling layouts of other stations. Secondly, we propose to standardize the format of control tables using XML and use XSLT to transform the *content* of the control table to ML functions called from the CPN model. By generating the ML functions, we can reuse the CPN net structure for different interlocking tables. As a result, once signal engineers have an understanding of the CPN net structure and methodology, they can apply it to arbitrary railway stations and interlocking systems. Finally, we perform formal analysis, which has so far revealed several errors in the submitted interlocking table from the contractor.

The rest of this paper is organised as follows. Section 2 briefly explains the concept of railway signalling system and control tables. Section 3 defines the scope of work by discussing the assumptions, the modelling approach and the model structure. The CPN model of Panthong control table is explained in Section 4. Section 5 describes our analysis techniques and results. Conclusions and future work are presented in Section 6.

[1] Proprietary software is used to edit the drawing.

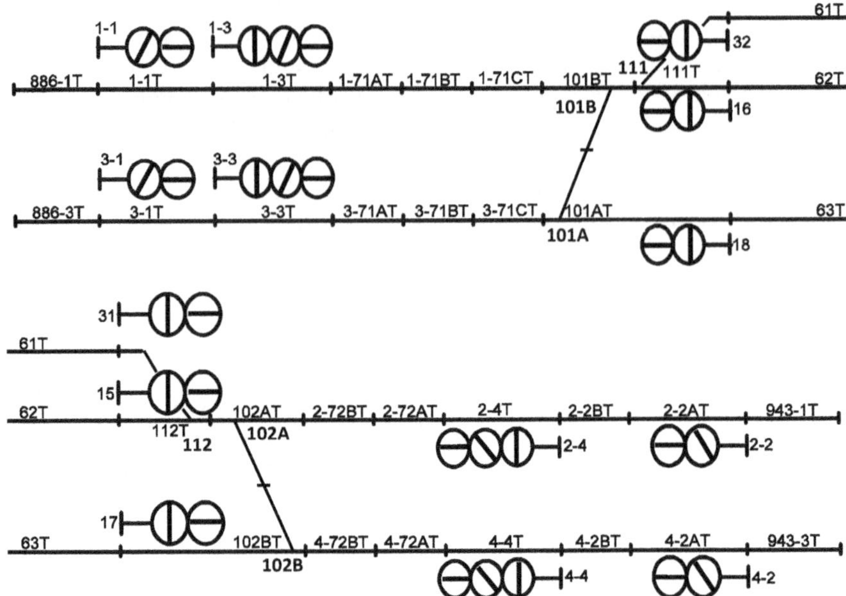

Fig. 1. Signalling layout of the Panthong Station (double track)

2 Railway Signalling Systems and Control Tables

2.1 Signalling Systems

In general the railway lines are divided into *sections*. To avoid collision, only one train is allowed in one *section* at a time. The train can enter or leave a *section* when the driver receives authorization from a signal man via a signal indicator. Before the signal man issues the authorization, he needs to ensure that no object blocks the passage of the train. The *section* between two railway stations, which involves two signal men, is called "*block section*". To prevent human error, which often leads to collisions, the strict operation on a *block section* is controlled by equipment called "Block Instruments". Figure 1 shows the signalling layout of a double track station named "Panthong". The signalling layout comprises a collection of railway tracks and signalling equipment such as track circuits, points and signals. (e.g., signal no.1-3 and signal no.2-4). Each piece of signalling equipment has an identification number and holds a certain state as follows.

Track Circuits. A track circuit is an electrical device used to detect the presence of a train. A track circuit (e.g., 61T, 1-3T) is either *clear* indicating no train on the track or *occupied* indicating the possible presence of a train[2].

[2] When the track circuit fails, its state is occupied even if there is no train.

Warner signals. A warner signal (e.g., 1-1, 2-2, 3-1,4-2) has two aspects: *yellow* or *green*. It informs drivers about the status of the next signal.

Home signals. A home signal (e.g., 1-3, 2-4, 3-3, 4-4) has three aspects: *red*, *yellow* or *green*. It displays *red* when the train is forbidden to enter the *station area*. It displays *yellow* giving the driver the authority to move the train into the *station area* and prepare to stop at the next signal. It displays *green* giving the driver the authority to move the train passing the *station* and enter the next *block section*.

Starter signals. A starter (e.g., 15, 16, 17, 18, 31, 32) has two aspects: *red* or *green*. It displays *red* when forbidding the train to enter the *block section*. It displays *green* when giving the driver the authority to move the train into the *block section*.

Point. A point (e.g., 101A, 101B, 111, 112, 102A, 102B) or railway switch or turnout is a mechanical installation used to guide a train from one track to another. A point usually has a straight through track called "main-line" and a diverging track called loop line. A point is right-hand when a moving train from a joint track diverges to the right of the straight track. Similarly a left-hand point has the diverging track on the opposite side of a right-hand point. When a point diverges the train, it is in reverse position. When a point lets the train move straight through, it is in normal position.

2.2 Control Tables

A collection of track circuits along the reserved *section* is called a "*route*". An entry signal shall be clear to let the train enter the route. Although the request to clear the entry signal is issued by the signal man, the route entry permission is decided by the interlocking system using safety rules and control methods specified in the agreed control tables. Tables 1 and 2 are the (partial) control tables for Panthong station, of which the signalling layout is shown in Fig. 1. Data in the first column, "From", is the route identifications which are labeled by the entry signal: 1-3(1); 1-3(2); 3-3(1); 3-3(2); 3-3(3); 2-4(1); 2-4(2); 4-4(1); 4-4(2); 4-4(3); 15(1); 15(2); 16(1); 16(2); 31(1);31(2); 32(1);32(2); 17 and 18. Due to space limitation we show only 2 routes in Tables 1 and 2. Each row in the tables represents the requirement how to set and release each route. For example, route 1-3(2) comprises the track circuits 1-3T, 1-71AT, 1-71BT,1-71CT,101BT, 111T, 62T, 112T and requires that the points 101, 111 and 112 are in normal position. Routes 1-3(1) and 1-3(2) specify that behind signal 1-3 two routes are possible. Similar rule applies to routes 3-3; 2-4; and 4-4. The column "Requires Route Normal" shows conflict routes. A route cannot be set if any conflict routes have been set and not yet released. For route 1-3(2) the conflict routes are 1-3(1), 16(1), 16(2), 32(1), 32(2), 3-3(1), 3-3(2), 2-4(1), 2-4(2), 4-4(1) and 4-4(2). The exit (starter) signal of this route is 15, and if home signal 1-3 shows green, then starter signal 15 shows green.

Table 1. A control table for Panthong station (part 1:Route locking)

<table>
<tr><th colspan="2" rowspan="2">ROUTE</th><th colspan="3">INTERLOCKING</th><th colspan="3">CONTROLS</th></tr>
<tr><th>REQUIRES</th><th colspan="2">SET & LOCKS POINTS</th><th rowspan="2">ASPECT</th><th rowspan="2">SIGNAL AHEAD</th><th rowspan="2">REQUIRES TC CLEAR</th></tr>
<tr><th>FROM</th><th>TO</th><th>ROUTE NORMAL</th><th>NORMAL</th><th>REVERSE</th></tr>
<tr><td>1-3(1)</td><td>31</td><td>16(1), 16(2), 32(1), 32(2), 3-3(1), 3-3(2), 1-3(2), 2-4(1), 2-4(2)</td><td>101</td><td>111, 112</td><td>Y</td><td>31 AT R#</td><td>1-3T, 1-71AT, 1-71BT, 1-71CT, 101BT, 111T, 61T, 112T</td></tr>
<tr><td>1-3(2)</td><td>15</td><td>16(1), 16(2), 32(1), 32(2), 3-3(1), 3-3(2), 1-3(1), 2-4(1), 2-4(2) , 4-4(1) , 4-4(2)</td><td>101,111, 112</td><td></td><td>Y
G</td><td>15 AT R#
15 AT G#</td><td>1-3T, 1-71CT, 1-71BT, 1-71AT, 101BT, 111T, 62T, 112T</td></tr>
</table>

Table 2. A control table for Panthong station (part 2:Approach locking)

<table>
<tr><th colspan="2" rowspan="3">ROUTE</th><th colspan="7">CONTROL</th></tr>
<tr><th colspan="2" rowspan="2">APPROACH LOCKED
WHEN SIGNAL CLEARED AND</th><th colspan="4">ROUTE RELEASED BY</th><th>Notes</th></tr>
<tr><th>TC</th><th>TC OCC</th><th rowspan="2">TC OCC</th><th rowspan="2">OR
EMERCENCY RELEASE AFTER</th><th rowspan="2">AND / OR
REMARKS</th></tr>
<tr><th>From</th><th>TO</th><th>TC OCC</th><th>OR
TIME</th><th>CLEAR</th><th>& CLEAR</th></tr>
<tr><td>1-3(1)</td><td>31</td><td>1-1T</td><td>120 sec</td><td>1-3T,1-71AT , 1-71BT, 1-71CT, 101BT</td><td>111T</td><td>61T</td><td>240 sec</td><td>DOWN BLOCK 1 NOT SET</td></tr>
<tr><td>1-3(2)</td><td>15</td><td>1-1T</td><td>120 sec</td><td>1-3T,1-71AT , 1-71BT, 1-71CT, 101BT</td><td>111T</td><td>62T</td><td>240 sec</td><td>DOWN BLOCK 1 NOT SET</td></tr>
</table>

Different Interlocking systems from different manufacturers may have different control methods. However there are four basic control methods, explained below, which are widely accepted and used among railway companies.

Route locking. Route setting involves a collection of adjacent track circuits, points and signals. A route can be set and reserved for a passage of a train along this route. To assure the safety, firstly, the interlocking system verifies that the route does not conflict with other routes previously set. Secondly, the points along the route are locked in the correct positions. If the related points are not in the correct positions, the controller will attempt to set and lock them in the correct positions. Thirdly, the track circuits along the required route are all clear or unoccupied so that nothing obstructs the passage of the train. Then the entry signal can be cleared (showing yellow or green).

Approach locking. After a route is set; the point is locked; and the entry signal is cleared, if the track circuit in front of (approaching) the entry signal is occupied, then the signal man cannot cancel the route and the entry signal by the normal procedure. Approach locking prevents the train driver from the sudden change of signal aspect from green or yellow to red. Column 3 in Table 2,

"APPROACH LOCKED WHEN SIGNAL CLEARED & TC OCC", presents locking when a route is set and the approach track circuit is occupied. For example, route 1-3(2) will be approach locked if the route is set and track 1-1T is occupied.

Route released. After the passage of the train, the reserved route is released automatically. Column "Route Released by" in Table 2 presents route released mechanism for the signalling layout in Fig. 1. Route 1-3(2) will be released when the track circuits 1-3T, 1-71AT, 1-71BT, 1-71CT, 101BT are clear; the track circuit 111T is occupied and then clear; and the track circuit 62T is occupied.

Flank protection. The equipment within the surrounding area of the reserved route that may cause an accident shall be protected even if no train is expected to pass such a signal or such points. For example points should be in such positions that they do not give immediate access to the route: for example route 1-3(2), the track circuit 61T, which is not in the route 1-3(2), shall be unoccupied; if it is occupied, the object on the track circuit 61T should stand still. This condition is implied when the track 61T is occupied for longer than 1 minute.

3 CPN Model of the Panthong's Control Table - Overview

Coloured Petri Nets (CPNs) [9] are a graphical modelling language for design, verification and analysis of distributed, concurrent and complex systems. CPNs include hierarchical constructs that allow modular specifications to be created. CPN Tools [9] is a software tool used to create, maintain, simulate and analyse CPNs. We use CPN Tools to create and analyse our railway signaling model using state space analysis.

3.1 Modelling Scope and Assumptions

To reduce the complexity of the model as well as avoid the state explosion problem when analysing railway networks [15,6], we need to make the following assumptions regarding train movement and signalling operations:

1. We assume that a train has no length and it occupies one track at a time. The train moves in only one direction. Train shunting is not considered.
2. We assume the trains are running at the same speed.
3. Our model does not include the auxiliary signals such as Call-on, Shunting and Junction indicators.
4. Our model does not include timers. However we use time stamps when modelling the trains moving along the track. This implies that the train must not move through a track circuit so fast that the interlocking cannot detect the presence of the train.
5. Our model does not consider equipment failure.
6. Our model does not include level crossings.

7. Our model includes high level abstraction of block systems but we do not model their operations in detail.
8. Our model does not include flank protections.
9. The train drivers strictly obey the signals.

3.2 Modelling Approach and Model Structure

Signalling layout and control tables are two important documents that are used as references during design and installation of any railway signalling systems. Corresponding to these two documents, in [12] we divided the CPN model into two parts: *Signalling Layout* and *Interlocking Control*.

Signalling Layout. We proposed in [12] to use CPN diagram to mimic the signalling layout so that the train movement can be simulated. Basically our CPN model simulates three kinds of train movements: Train movement between two consecutive track circuits; Trains passing a signal; and Trains passing a point. Despite the fact that the top level CPN model of the signalling layout is easy to read and understand, we encountered two problems while modeled a large station. Firstly, it took about 2-3 days to edit the new CPN model of the signalling layout of a large station. Secondly, where points and signals are located nearby each other, the second level CPN diagrams modelling these equipments are too complex. To solve these two problems, this paper proposes to represent the signalling layout by *tokens* with a complex data structure. Because the geographic information is encoded in the *tokens*, the CPN diagram is not changed when signaling layout is modified or rebuilt. To prevent human error we used C++ to generate a text file containing a list of the *tokens* directly from a drawing file of the signalling layout.

Interlocking Control. The *Interlocking Control* part models point setting, route locking, signal clearing and route release functions as specified in the control table and described in Section 2.2. Unlike [14] that does not include the functionality of approach locking (to avoid the state explosion problem), our CPN model does include the approach locking function. Even though the control table of each railway station has different contents, the functions—router locking, approach locking, route release, and flank protection—are essentially the same. To create a generic interlocking model, we extract the content of the control table and code them into ML functions which are used in arc inscriptions. To model control tables of other railway stations we simply change the content of the ML functions while using the same CPN models of the *Interlocking Control* part.

Next we create these ML functions automatically as illustrated in Fig. 2. In previous projects contractors submitted the control table files in Microsoft-EXCEL format to SRT; we encourage SRT to maintain the control table in XML format instead. As shown in Fig. 2 the control table in Microsoft-EXCEL is transformed to XML. Then it is transformed to ML functions using Extensible Stylesheet Language Transformations (XSLT). All operations are done using Microsoft-Excel and Microsoft-Word version 7.

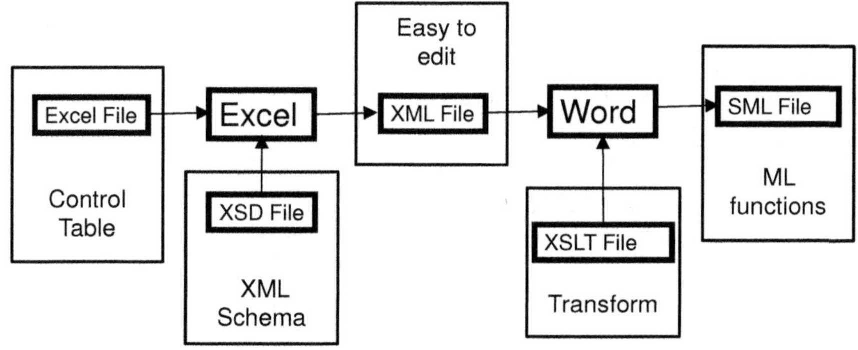

Fig. 2. Transformation of the control table to ML functions using XSLT

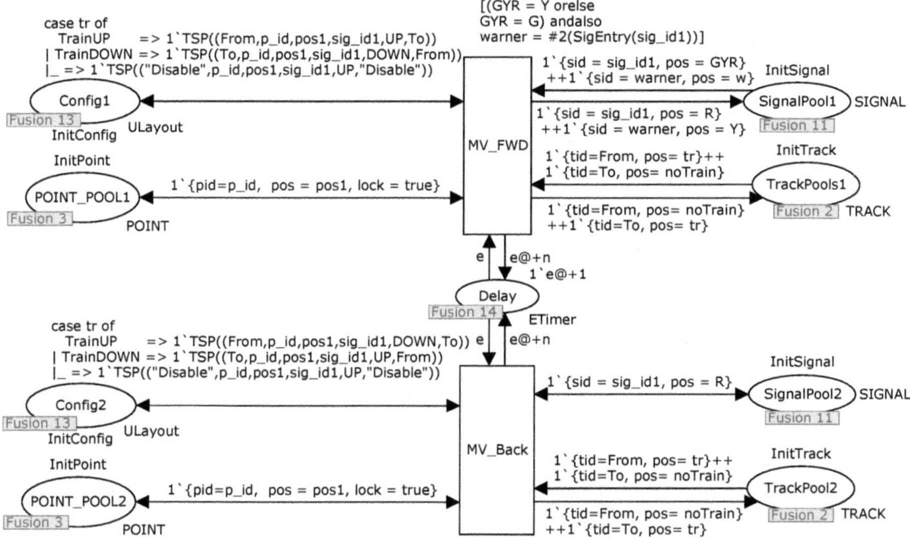

Fig. 3. CPN model: MoveXSignalPoint page

4 The CPN Model of a Signalling System

As discussed in Section 3, our CPN model comprises two parts: the *Signalling Layout* and the *Interlocking Control*. Due to space limitation we explain only the CPN model of *Signalling Layout*. The CPN model of *Signalling Layout* actually models the train movement comprising 6 transitions; and 5 fusion places. Due to space limitation we choose to explain only two transitions shown in Fig. 3. Fusion places `Config1` and `Config2`, typed by `ULayout`, store geographic information of signalling layout in their tokens. Each token basically contains identification numbers of two adjacent track circuits.

Listing 1.1. Declarations

```
1  colset E = with e;
2  colset ETimer = E timed;
3  colset NR = with Normal | Reverse;
4  colset TC_ID = STRING;
5  colset P_ID = STRING;
6  colset SIG_ID = STRING;
7  colset ConfigT2T = product TC_ID*TC_ID;
8  colset ConfigTPT = product TC_ID*P_ID*NR*TC_ID;
9  colset ConfigTST = product TC_ID*SIG_ID*UPDOWN*TC_ID;
10 colset ConfigTSP = product TC_ID*P_ID*NR*SIG_ID
11                            *UPDOWN*TC_ID;
12 colset ULayout = union T2T:ConfigT2T + TST:ConfigTST
13                        +TPT:ConfigTPT + TSP:ConfigTSP;
14 var pos1:NR;
```

Listing 1.2. Declarations

```
1  colset TD = with noTrain | TrainUP | TrainDOWN;
2  var tr:TD;
3  colset TRACK = record tid:STRING * pos:TD;
4  colset SIGNAL = record sid:STRING * pos:SIG;
5  var p_id,tc_id1,tc_id2,sig_id1,sig_id2:STRING;
6  colset ROUTE = STRING;
7  colset ROUTExSIG_ID = product ROUTE * STRING;
8  colset POINT = record pid:STRING * pos:NR * lock:BOOL;
9  var point:POINT;
10 colset BLOCK_POS = with COMING | NORMAL | GOING;
11 var CNG:BLOCK_POS;
12 colset BLOCK = record bid:STRING * pos:BLOCK_POS;
13 var x:BOOL;
```

We classify the tokens into four categories, as follows:

1) Typed by ConfigT2T (line 8 of listing 1.1) : one track circuit connects to the adjacent one;

2) Typed by ConfigTPT (line 9): a track circuit (either the main line or the loop line) connects to the point track. The position of the point is required to identify which track circuit is connected to the point track;

3) Typed by ConfigTST (line 10): a signal is located between two adjacent tracks;

4) Typed by ConfigTSP (line 11): a signal is located between a track circuit (either the main line or the loop line) and a point track.

Thus ULayout (line 13 of listing 1.1) is defined as the union of the above four colour sets. Actually Fig. 3 is the CPN diagram modelling the fourth category of the train movement. Transition MV_FWD models when the train moves facing the signal (e.g., 32) toward the point track (e.g., 111T). Transition MV_Back models when the train moves from the point track (e.g., 111T) facing the back of the signal (e.g., 32).

The train movement requires three pieces of information about the state of equipment, namely, the presence of the trains, the signal cleared, and the point locked in a correct position. Three fusion places are used to store these states of equipment: TrackPool (typed by TRACK - line 4 of listing 1.2); SignalPool (typed by SIGNAL - line 5); PointPool (typed by POINT - line 9). TRACK is defined as a record of track identification and train description. `SIGNAL` is defined as a record of signal identification and its aspect (green, yellow or red). `POINT` is defined as record of point identification, its position (Normal or Reverse) and locking status.

5 Analysis

5.1 Desired Property

A basic safety property that railway signalling shall provide is to prevent train collision. In Fig. 3 moving a train requires a token with `noTrain` in the designated track circuit. Each track circuit can contain only one train. Our modelling decision causes two effects. First, two trains in the same track circuit are not allowed. Second, trains cannot move pass each other. We conclude that two trains have a chance of collision if they are on two consecutive track circuits.

To get more confidence about the correctness of our CPN model and the control table, the CPN model is analysed using state space method in CPN Tools. The investigation of the generated state spaces is conducted on a AMD9650 computer with 2.30 GHz and 3.5 GB of RAM. After generating each state space, we use ML query functions searching the entire state space for the markings that have trains in two consecutive track circuits.

5.2 Initial Configurations

Despite the fact that we can analyze various scenarios by changing the initial markings, due to space limitation, we select to discuss only four cases with the initial configurations shown in Table 3. The initial configurations are:

Case A is when four trains are coming from the north and south directions and three trains are on the platform tracks. We set the route request commands for all routes. This is the deadlock case because no train can enter or leave the platform tracks.

Case B is when four trains are coming from the north and south directions and two trains are leaving the platform tracks. We set the route request commands for all routes. Case B-1 and B-2 are similar to Case B but the number of route request commands are fewer in order to reduce the state space sizes.

Table 3. Initial configurations of track circuits and route request commands

Case	886-1T	886-2T	61T	62T	63T	943-1T	943-3T	Route Request Commands
A	TrainUP	TrainUP	TrainUP	TrainDOWN	TrainUP	TrainDOWN	TrainDOWN	All Routes
B	TrainUP	TrainUP	noTrain	TrainDOWN	TrainUP	TrainDOWN	TrainDOWN	All Routes
B-1	TrainUP	TrainUP	noTrain	TrainUP	TrainUP	TrainDOWN	TrainDOWN	All Incoming Routes and 15(1),15(2),31(1),31(2),17
B-2	TrainUP	TrainUP	noTrain	TrainDOWN	TrainDOWN	TrainDOWN	TrainDOWN	All Incoming Routes and 16(1),16(2),32(1),32(2),18

Table 4. Summary of state space results

Case	Nodes	Arcs	Time hh:mm:ss	Terminal Markings
A	36	84	00:01:01	1
B	261,522	1,189,280	11:28:44	57
B-1	9,059	30,954	01:18:24	9
B-2	8,981	27,831	01:17:23	9

Table 5. Terminal Markings of Case B-1.

Route Used 1-3(1)	BlockDown1 GOING	886-1T noTrain	1-1T noTrain	61T TrainUP	62T TrainUP	2-2BT TrainDOWN	943-1T noTrain	BlockUP2 COMING
	BlockDown3 COMING	886-3T noTrain	3-1T TrainUP		63T TrainUP	4-2BT TrainDOWN	943-3T noTrain	BlockUP4 COMING
Route Used 3-3(1)	BlockDown1 COMING	886-1T noTrain	1-1T TrainUP	61T TrainUP	62T TrainUP	2-2BT TrainDOWN	943-1T noTrain	BlockUP2 COMING
	BlockDown3 GOING	886-3T noTrain	3-1T noTrain		63T TrainUP	4-2BT TrainDOWN	943-3T noTrain	BlockUP4 COMING
Route Used 2-4(1)	BlockDown1 COMING	886-1T noTrain	1-1T TrainUP	61T TrainDOWN	62T TrainUP	2-2BT noTrain	943-1T noTrain	BlockUP2 GOING
31(1)G	BlockDown3 COMING	886-3T noTrain	3-1T TrainUP		63T TrainUP	4-2BT TrainDOWN	943-3T noTrain	BlockUP4 COMING
Route Used 4-4(1)	BlockDown1 COMING	886-1T noTrain	1-1T TrainUP	61T TrainDOWN	62T TrainUP	2-2BT TrainDOWN	943-1T noTrain	BlockUP2 COMING
31(2)G	BlockDown3 COMING	886-3T noTrain	3-1T TrainUP		63T TrainUP	4-2BT noTrain	943-3T noTrain	BlockUP4 GOING
Route Used 2-4(1)	BlockDown1 GOING	886-1T noTrain	1-1T noTrain	61T TrainDOWN	62T TrainUP	2-2BT noTrain	943-1T TrainUP	BlockUP2 GOING
15(1) 1-3(2)	BlockDown2 COMING	886-3T noTrain	3-1T TrainUP		63T TrainUP	4-2BT TrainDOWN	943-3T noTrain	BlockUP4 COMING
Route Used 2-4(1)	BlockDown1 COMING	886-1T noTrain	1-1T TrainUP	61T TrainDOWN	62T TrainUP	2-2BT noTrain	943-1T TrainUP	BlockUP2 GOING
15(1) 3-3(2)	BlockDown3 GOING	886-3T noTrain	3-1T noTrain		63T TrainUP	4-2BT TrainDOWN	943-3T noTrain	BlockUP4 COMING
Route Used 4-4(1)	BlockDown1 GOING	886-1T noTrain	1-1T noTrain	61T TrainDOWN	62T TrainUP	2-2BT TrainDOWN	943-1T noTrain	BlockUP2 COMING
15(2) 1-3(2)	BlockDown3 COMING	886-3T noTrain	3-1T TrainUP		63T TrainUP	4-2BT noTrain	943-3T TrainUP	BlockUP4 GOING
Route Used 4-4(1)	BlockDown1 COMING	886-1T noTrain	1-1T TrainUP	61T TrainDOWN	62T TrainUP	2-2BT TrainDOWN	943-1T noTrain	BlockUP2 COMING
15(2) 3-3(2)	BlockDown3 GOING	886-3T noTrain	3-1T noTrain		63T TrainUP	4-2BT noTrain	943-3T TrainUP	BlockUP4 GOING
Route Used 4-4(1)	BlockDown1 COMING	886-1T noTrain	1-1T TrainUP	61T TrainDOWN	62T TrainUP	2-2BT TrainDOWN	943-1T noTrain	BlockUP2 COMING
17 3-3(3)	BlockDown3 GOING	886-3T noTrain	3-1T noTrain		63T TrainUP	4-2BT noTrain	943-3T TrainUP	BlockUP4 GOING

In all initial markings, other track circuits are unoccupied; all points are in `Normal` position and unlocked. All signals are in normal states. Blocks in every directions are initially in the `Incoming` state. One block request command for each outgoing direction is set for the departure train. The block request command cannot be executed unless the block state returns to `Normal`.

5.3 Analysis Results

Tables 4 shows the analysis results: state space sizes; execute time; and the number of terminal markings. Actually we choose to focus on these cases because the number of terminal markings is so few that can be inspected manually. In particular while we were inspecting the terminal markings of case B-1 and B-2, we found several errors in the control table designed by the contractor. These errors were rectified and reported to the contractor. After the errors were rectified, we exhaustively searched the entire state spaces for the train collision condition as discussed in Section 5.1. So far we have not found the train collision in any cases.

A terminal marking in Case A is occurred when the route request commands cannot be executed because required track circuits are not clear. Incoming trains are moved and stopped in the front of the home signals. For Case B even though we are able to manually investigate all 57 terminal markings, we cannot show them here. Due to space limitation we can only show the detail of nine terminal markings of case B-1 (Table 5) and explain only two terminal markings as follows.

a) In the third markings in Table 5, when the first route request command 2-4(1) is set, the train moves from 943-1T to 61T. BlockUP2 is returned to `Normal` and then set to `GOING`. The second request command 31(1) is set for the train on 61T going toward north but the train on 61T (`TrainDOWN`) plans to go toward south instead.

b) In the last markings in Table 5, when the first route request command 4-4(1) is set, the train moves from 943-3T to 61T. BlockUP4 is returned to `Normal` and then set to `GOING`. The second train moves from 63T to 943-3T via route 17 and the third train moves from 886-3T to 63T via route 3-3(3). BlockDOWN3 is returned to `Normal` and then set to `GOING`.

6 Conclusions

This paper has outlined an approach for developing a CPN model of SRT's railway signalling system. The CPN model comprises two parts: *Signalling Layout* and *Interlocking*. Geographic information how each piece of equipment connects to each other is stored in the *tokens*. Thus the CPN net structure of the *Signalling Layout* part does not depend on the signalling plan. Similarly the *Interlocking* part does not depend on the signalling plan as well. It has the contents of the control tables encoded in the ML functions. Thus we can use the same net structure to model any interlocking systems regardless of the size of the interlocking. We also discuss the analysis results to demonstrate the applicability of our approach. Despite prior expectations, several errors in the control tables were discovered during analysis.

There are two lines of future work we would like to pursue. Firstly, we had encountered the state space explosion problem while we were attempting to verify the interlocking table of a large station. Thus we wish to seek out a systematic approach to tackle this problem. Secondly, we would like to relax the modelling assumptions and refine the model.

Acknowledgments. The author is thankful to the anonymous reviewers and also to MohammadReza Mousavi and Steve Gordon. Their constructive feedback has helped the author improve the quality of this paper.

References

1. Basten, T., Bol, R., Voorhoeve, M.: Simulating and Analyzing Railway Interlockings in ExSpec. IEEE Parallel and Distributed Technology, Systems and Applications 3(3), 50–62 (1995)
2. Chevilat, C., Carrington, D., Strooper, P., Süß, J.G., Wildman, L.: Model-Based Generation of Interlocking Controller Software from Control Tables. In: Schieferdecker, I., Hartman, A. (eds.) ECMDA-FA 2008. LNCS, vol. 5095, pp. 349–360. Springer, Heidelberg (2008)
3. Cimatti, A., Clarke, E.E., Giunchiglia, F., Roveri, M.: NuSMV: A new symbolic model verifier. In: Halbwachs, N., Peled, D.A. (eds.) CAV 1999. LNCS, vol. 1633, pp. 495–499. Springer, Heidelberg (1999)
4. Durmus, M.S., Soylemez, M.T.: Railway Signalization and Interlocking Design via Automation Petri Nets. In: Proceedings of the 7th Asian Control Conference, Hong Kong, August 27-29, 2009, pp. 1558–1563 (2009)
5. Fokkink, W.J., Hollingshead, P.R.: Verification of Interlockings: from Control Tables to Ladder Logic Diagrams. In: Proceedings of the 3rd Workshop on Formal Methods for Industrial Critical Systems (FMICS 1998), Amsterdam, May 1998, pp. 171–185. Stichting Mathematisch Centrum (1998)
6. Hagalisletto, A.M., Bjørk, J., Yu, I.C., Enger, P.: Constructing and Refining Large-Scale Railway Models Represented by Petri Nets. IEEE Transactions on Systems, Man, and Cybernetics, Part C 37(4), 444–460 (2007)
7. Hansen, K.M.: Formalizing Railway Interlocking Systems. In: Nordic Seminar on Dependable Computing Systems, Department of Computer Science, Technical University of Denmark, pp. 83–94 (1994)
8. Janczura, C.W.: Modelling and Analysis of Railway Network Control Logic using Coloured Petri Nets. PhD thesis, School of Mathematics and Institute for Telecommunications Research, University of South Australia, Adelaide, Australia (August 1998)
9. Jensen, K., Kristensen, L.M., Wells, L.: Coloured Petri Nets and CPN Tools for Modelling and Validation of Concurrent Systems. International Journal on Software Tools for Technology Transfer 9(3-4), 213–254 (2007)
10. Svendsen, A., Olsen, G.K., Endresen, J., Moen, T., Carlson, E., Alme, K., Haugen, Ø.: The Future of Train Signaling. In: Czarnecki, K., Ober, I., Bruel, J.-M., Uhl, A., Völter, M. (eds.) MODELS 2008. LNCS, vol. 5301, pp. 128–142. Springer, Heidelberg (2008)
11. van der Aalst, W.M.P., Odijk, M.A.: Analysis of Railway Stations by Means of Interval Timed Coloured Petri Nets. Real-Time Systems 9(3), 1–23 (1995)
12. Vanit-Anunchai, S.: Verification of Railway Interlocking Tables using Coloured Petri Nets. In: The Tenth Workshop and Tutorial on Practical Use of Coloured Petri Nets and the CPN Tools, DAIMI PB 590, Department of Computer Science, University of Aarhus, October 19-21, pp. 139–158 (2009)

13. Winter, K.: Model Checking Railway Interlocking Systems. In: Oudshoorn, M. (ed.) Proceeding of the 25th Australasian Computer Science Conference (ACSC 2002), Melbourne, Australia, vol. 4, pp. 303–310. Australian Computer Society (2002)
14. Winter, K., Johnston, W., Robinson, P., Strooper, P., van den Berg, L.: Tool Support for Checking Railway Interlocking Designs. In: Cant, T. (ed.) Proceeding of the 10th Australian Workshop on Safety Related Programmable Systems (SCS 2005), Sydney, Australia, vol. 55, pp. 101–107. Australian Computer Society (2005)
15. Winter, K., Robinson, N.: Modelling Large Railway Interlockings and Model Checking Small Ones. In: Oudshoorn, M. (ed.) Proceeding of the 26th Australasian Cumputer Science Conference (ACSC 2003), Adelaide, Australia, vol. 16, pp. 309–316. Australian Computer Society (2003)

Efficient Session Type Guided Distributed Interaction

K.C. Sivaramakrishnan, Karthik Nagaraj, Lukasz Ziarek, and Patrick Eugster

Purdue University, West Lafayette IN, USA
{chandras,knagara,lziarek,peugster}@cs.purdue.edu

Abstract. Recently, there has been much interest in multi-party session types (MPSTs) as a means of rigorously specifying protocols for interaction among multiple distributed participants. By capturing distributed interaction as series of typed interactions, MPSTs allow for the static verification of compliance of corresponding distributed object programs. We observe that explicit control flow information manifested by MPST opens intriguing avenues also for performance enhancements. In this paper, we present a session type assisted performance enhancement framework for distributed object interaction in Java. Experimental evaluation within our distributed runtime infrastructure illustrates the costs and benefits of our composable enhancement strategies.

1 Introduction

Interaction between software components is one of the fundamental concerns of software development, and yet precisely describing the interactions between components remains a difficult endeavor. Real-world distributed systems involve multiple remote components, independently communicating messages and coordinating activities among one another. Web services, e-commerce applications, and protocols like SMTP, POP3, are just some examples for structured protocols involving multiple interacting peers. Such interactions are usually implemented using message transfer over reliable socket communication. Unfortunately, such low level communication neither offers type safety on messages nor the ability to specify and statically type check communication protocols, making development of distributed software difficult.

Session types have been proposed as a way to precisely capture *complex* interactions between peers [14]. They describe interaction protocols by specifying the type of messages exchanged between the participants. Implicit control flow information such as branching and loops can also be enumerated. Session types were originally envisioned for languages closely based on process calculi, and initially used for specifying bi-party interaction. They have since been extended to *multi-party session types* (MPSTs) [10]. Explicit control flow information manifest in MPSTs, opens intriguing avenues for global performance enhancement of distributed multi-party interaction. In this paper, we present a session type assisted protocol enhancement framework for optimizing distributed object interaction in Java. To illustrate our approach, consider the example in Fig. 1,

D. Clarke and G. Agha (Eds.): COORDINATION 2010, LNCS 6116, pp. 152–167, 2010.

```
void inviteCoworkers() {
  Event evt = me.createEvent("Party", date);
  Employer myEmp = me.getEmployer();
  Location myLoc = me.getLocation();
  for (Member mbr : me.getFriends()) {
    if (myEmp.equals(mbr.getEmployer()) &&
        myLoc.equals(mbr.getLocation()))
        mailSvr.sendMail(mbr.getEmailAddress(), evt);
  }
}
```

Fig. 1. Client implementation to invite co-workers to a party

which describes a simple protocol implemented in Java RMI, to invite co-workers obtained from a social networking database to a party.

Abstractly, the client iterates through a list of friends sending an email invitation to those who are employed by the same employer and work at the same location. In this example, me, mbr and mailSvr are remote objects, therefore, all of the method invocations on these objects are done remotely requiring a network round trip. In a high latency network the client, unfortunately, would spend most of its time stalled on responses from the server. In this manner, excessive remote method invocations quickly lead to serious scalability and performance concerns.

A standard technique to overcome the network delays is to structure code based on *data transfer objects* (DTOs) or *remote facade* patterns [6]. Such patterns advocate that new remote interfaces be defined in the Member class specifically to invite co-workers to an event. Although such a specialized definition can reduce the number of remote method invocations (RMI), it is neither composable nor extensible, as new features would require further specialization. To make matters worse, specialization is not even possible if an RMI call depends on local operations. Previous work has looked at alleviating some of these costs through various techniques, but are limited to bi-party interaction, semantically restricted to part of the protocol [12], or require code to be written in a style amenable to enhancement [13].

Guided by the MPST information, we introduce *combined* type and compiler driven performance enhancements. Our approach extends the previously described bi-party enhancements to multiple participants, and, more importantly, seamlessly composes enhancements techniques.

Fig. 2 illustrates the abstract description of the invitation protocol for the example described in Fig. 1. The programmer defines a new global session type [10] through the use of a **protocol** block. This block explicitly defines the participants of the protocol, the types of messages exchanged between the participants, and the order in which the messages are exchanged. Messages are sent asynchronously between the participants. We use, client: **begin** to express that the client initiates the protocol. Each message in the protocol has a syntax A->B: <T>, defining that the participant A sends to participant B a message whose type is T. For each friend

```
1  protocol invitation {
2    participants client, infoSvr, mailSvr;
3    client: begin;
4    infoSvr->client: <Employer>;
5    infoSvr->client: <Location>;
6    infoSvr:
7      [infoSvr->client: <Member>;
8       infoSvr->client: <Employer>;
9       infoSvr->client: <Location>;
10      infoSvr->client: <EmailID>;
11      client:
12       {INVITE: client->mailSvr: <EmailID, Event>,
13        NOOP: }
14     ]*
15 }
```

Fig. 2. Global session type of invitation example

on the friends list, the infoSvr sends the member information to the client. This is represented by a recursive type, `infoSvr:[...]*` (see lines 6 to 14). `infoSvr` is the loop guard in the recursive type since it decides whether the next iteration of the loop is executed. Based on the location and employer, the client chooses to send an email invitation (see lines 11 to 13). Notice that the protocol is abstract in both the event and who is invited. The actual implementation of the protocol is specified by the client. The participants can be statically verified for conformance.

It is evident from the session type of the invitation protocol that the first two messages from the `infoSvr`: `Employer` and `Location`, can be batched together as a single message. Similarly, the first four messages in the recursive type are batched together. However, is it possible to batch multiple iterations of the recursive type together? This is less clear. First, we must assert that the `INVITE` message sent by the client to the `mailSvr` does *not* influence the next iteration of the `infoSvr`. Since MPSTs explicitly defines all remote interactions, we can statically assert that there is no causal dependence between message sent to `mailSvr` and subsequent iteration decisions of `infoSvr`. With this knowledge, the code can be rewritten such that all of the friend's information is sent to the client in one batch. The client sends the `mailSvr` a batch of email addresses of friends who are to be invited to the party. Thus the entire protocol is performed in two batched network calls, while still adhering to the protocol specification.

In this paper, we also study the interaction, composability, and performance of enhancement strategies for interacting distributed objects. To our knowledge this is the first work that utilizes session types for global enhancement of interaction. In summary, the main contributions of the paper include:

– A Java extension that integrates MPSTs (Sec. 2).
– A detailed study of performance enhancements in the presence of a global interaction protocol (Sec. 3).
– An empirical analysis of optimization strategies in a prototype framework (Sec. 4).

2 Programming with Session Types

Global session types [10] in a multi-party session provide a universal view of the protocol involving all of the participants. For every properly defined session type, there exists a local view of the global session type, called the *local session type*. A projection from a global session type to such a local session type is well-defined. Local session types for the invitation protocol projected from the global session types in Fig. 2 are shown below. The local types are, indeed, very similar to global types except that only those actions which influence the participant appear in the participant's local session type. Message sends and receives are explicit in the local session type as is the order in which they are performed.

In our system, the programmer defines the global session types, and the coresponding local session types are automatically generated. The programmer implements each participant code such that they conform to their corresponding local types.

```
protocol invitation@infoSvr {
 client: ?begin;
 client: !<Employer>;
 client: !<Location>;
 ![client: !<Member>;
   client: !<Employer>;
   client: !<Location>;
   client: !<EmailAddr>]* }

protocol invitation@mailSvr {
 client: ?begin;
 infoSvr:
 ?[client:
  ?{INVITE: client: ?<EmailAddr,
                      Event>,
    NOOP: }]* }
```

```
protocol invitation@client {
 !begin;
 infoSvr: ?<Employer>;
 infoSvr: ?<Location>;
 infoSvr:
 ?[infoSvr: ?<Member>;
   infoSvr: ?<Employer>;
   infoSvr: ?<Location>;
   !{INVITE: mailSvr:!<EmailAddr,
                       Event>,
     NOOP: }]* }
```

Fig. 3. Local session types for client, infoSvr and mailSvr

The local type for the `infoSvr` is given in **`protocol`** `invitation@infoSvr`. `client:?begin` indicates that this protocol is initiated by the client. Message sends are represented by `A: !<T>`, defining that the local participant sends to participant `A` a message of type `T`. Conversely, `B: ?<T>` shows that the local participant waits to receive a message of type `T` from participant `B`. The syntax `![...]*` represents that this participant controls the loop iteration while all the participants with `A: ?[...]*` execute the next iteration of the loop only if `A` chooses to execute the next iteration. Similarly, syntax `!{L1:T1,...}` states that this participant chooses one of the set of labels `{L1,...}` to execute and other participants with `A: ?{L1:T1',...}` also execute the same label.

The **`protocol`** keyword is used to define the global session type, which is registered with the *session registry* (similar to an RMI registry). After the protocol has been registered, a host can register as a participant by creating a *session socket*. A session socket allows a host to act as a participant and communicate with other participants as dictated by the protocol. Communications on the session socket are type checked using the corresponding local type to ensure that the participant adheres to the protocol. The programmer can create a new protocol instance using the `instantiate` command, with a string representing the instance name. This name must be unique for each instance of the protocol in a session registry. Thus multiple instances of the same protocol can execute concurrently.

```
SessionRegistry.instantiate(invitation, "i");
```

The session registry prepares session sockets for each participant. A host wishing to participate in the invitation protocol as a client would request the session registry as shown below. Here we create a new session socket `ss` reflecting the type `invitation@client` for the invitation protocol for the instance `i`:

```
SessionSocket ss=SessionRegistry.lookup(invitation,"i","client");
```

Once a session socket has been created, the programmer uses a *session API* to implement the actual communication and control structures. We adopt a Java syntax for session API similar to what has been described in SessionJava [11]. Fig 4 shows the mapping between protocol description syntax and session API. We extend the `send` and `receive` syntax to explicitly denote the participant who performs the matching communication. Previous work on multi-party session types explicitly creates channels for communication between the peers [10]. We assume that each participant has a unique channel to every other participant. We also assume that the participants are single-threaded. This ensures that all communication over channels is linear.

`!`**`begin`**	`ss.begin()`	//initiates protocol
`A: ?`**`begin`**	`ss.awaitBegin()`	//waits for protocol begin
`A: !<T>`	`ss.send(A, obj)`	//obj is of type T
`A: ?<T>`	`ss.receive(A)`	//received obj is of type T
`!{L:T, ...}`	`ss.outbranch(L){}`	//body of case L of type T
`A: ?{L:T, ...}`	`ss.inbranch(L){}`	//body of case L of type T
`![T]*`	`ss.outwhile(bool_expr){}`	//body of outwhile of type T
`A: ?[T]*`	`ss.inwhile(A){}`	//body of inwhile of type T

Fig. 4. Protocol description syntax and their mapping to session API

Using the session API described above, the client described in Fig. 1 would be expressed as outlined in Fig. 5. As per the protocol description, only one participant initiates the protocol by invoking `begin`, while all other participants wait for this notification by invoking `awaitBegin`. In this example, the client initiates the protocol while the `infoSvr` and `mailSvr` wait for the request from the client. The `inwhile` loop runs an iteration if the corresponding `outwhile` loop at the `infoSvr` is chosen to run an iteration. The label choice made at

```
void inviteCoworkers() {
  SessionSocket ss =
    SessionRegistry.lookup("invitation", "client");
  ss.begin();
  Employer myEmp = ss.receive("infoSvr");
  Location myLoc = ss.receive("infoSvr");
  Event evt = me.createEvent("Movie", date);
  ss.inwhile("server") {
    Member m = ss.receive("infoSvr");
    if (myEmp.equals(ss.receive("infoSvr")) &&
        myLoc.equals(ss.receive("infoSvr"))) {
        EmailID eid = ss.receive("infoSvr");
        ss.outbranch(INVITE) {
          ss.send("mailSvr", eid); ss.send("mailSvr", evt);}}
    else {ss.outbranch(PASS) {}}
}}
```

Fig. 5. Client implementation of invitation protocol using session API

the `outbranch` is communicated to the peers who wait on the corresponding `inbranch`. The peers then execute the code under the chosen label.

In order to type check the participants for protocol conformance, we assume that the protocol description is available at every participant during compilation. Exceptions might be raised while instantiating protocols from the registry if the instance name is not unique or if a program tries to create multiple session sockets for the same participant. Exceptions are also raised if any of the participants of the protocol fail. A node failure results in the termination of the protocol, though we could envision a system where a participant replica could be assigned the task of continuing the protocol.

3 Performance Enhancement Strategies

We classify the enhancements into two categories based on the information required to perform them – (1) type driven enhancements and (2) compiler driven enhancement (see Fig. 6). Type driven enhancements are performed by the *type inspector*, based *only* on the information provided by the session types. Our compiler performs static analysis on the remote interaction code *in combination with* session types. Such enhancements are classified as compiler driven enhancements.

3.1 Type Driven Enhancements

Batching sends. Multiple consecutive sends to the *same* participant are batched together, provided there are no intervening receives by the sender. For example, in the session type shown in Fig. 2, the two sends at the beginning are batched together by the type inspector. These batched sends are represented in the optimized session type as:

```
server->client: <Employer, Location>
```

When the runtime system encounters the first message send of type `Employer`, instead of eagerly pushing the message out, it waits for the second message of type `Location`. A batch is created with both of these messages and sent to the server. The runtime at the server decouples the messages and passes them individually to the program. Batching, therefore, remains transparent to the program. The type inspector also batches sends in a recursive type if the participant acting as the loop guard does not perform any receives in the body of the loop.

```
server: [server->client1: <String>;
         client1->client2: <int>]*
```

is optimized to

```
server->client1: <String>*
client1->client2: <int>*
```

where all of the messages from `server` to `client1` and from `client1` to `client2` are sent in individual batches. Notice that the optimized session type does not have a loop. The sends occurring in a loop pattern are often resolved during batch data update, when objects belonging to a collection are updated. If the loop guard performs a receive in the body of the loop, sends in the loop cannot be batched since the decision to run the next iteration of the loop might depend on the value of the message received. Consider

```
client: [server->client: <bool>]*
```

where a possible `client` implementation could be

```
ss.outwhile(ss.receive("server"));
```

Here, sends should not be batched as every receive depends on the previously received value.

Choice lifting. Choice lifting is an enhancement by which label selection in a choice is made as early as possible so that more opportunities for enhancements are exposed. Consider the following snippet of protocol description:

```
B->A: <bool>;
A: [A->B: <int>; A: {L1: A->B: <String>, L2: A->B: <bool>}]*
```

The number of messages sent in the above protocol is $1 + 2 * num\_iterations$. Participant `A` is the guard in both the recursive type and the choice. Since the boolean conditional at the choice can only depend on the last received message at `A` (which is the receive of a **bool** at line 1), the choice can be lifted as far as the most recent message reception. The choice can be lifted out of the recursive type since the label choice at `A` is made independent of the looping decision made at `B`. The result of the enhancement is

```
B->A:<bool>;
A: {L1: A: [A->B: <int, String>]*, L2: A: [A->B: <int, bool>]*}
```

We can further optimize the above type by batching the loop sends as described earlier. The optimized session type is given below. Notice that the optimized session type needs to perform just 2 message sends; a **bool** from B to A and a batch from A to B.

```
B->A:<bool>;
A: {L1: A->B: <int,String>*, L2: A->B: <int,bool>*}
```

3.2 Compiler Driven Enhancements

Data flow analysis. In client/server systems, often we encounter a pattern where a client requests items in a collection and based on some property of the item, chooses to perform an action on a subset of the items in the collection. This is analogous to the UPDATE statement of SQL where the WHERE clause describes the subset to be updated. The example described in Fig. 2 falls into this category where, based on the employer and location of the member, the client chooses to invite the member to the party. The following snippet shows the optimized local type at the server.

```
1  protocol invitation@server {
2    client: ?begin;
3    client: !<Employer, Location>;
4    ![client: !<Member, Employer, Location>;
5      client: ?{INVITE: client: ?<Event>,
6                PASS: }]*
7  }
```

The server is the loop guard in this example, deciding whether to execute the next iteration of the loop. At every iteration, the server might receive a value of type Event from the client (line 5). Session types do not tell us whether such a received value influences the boolean conditional at the loop entry or the sends in the loop. Session types gives us the control flow information, but no data flow information. Hence, we implement a flow sensitive data flow analysis in the compiler which determines whether the loop conditional or the sends are dependent on any of the receives in the loop body. This analysis is similar to the one described in remote batch invocation [12]. Session type information allows us to precisely determine the scope of the analysis. In the above example, the data flow analysis shows that neither the loop conditional nor the sends are dependent on the receives. Hence, we can optimize the session type as below, in which all of the sends are batched, followed by a second batch with all receives.

```
protocol invitation@server {
  client: ?begin;
  client: !<Employer, Location>;
  client: !<Member, Employer, Location>*;
  client: ?{INVITE: client: ?<Event>, PASS: }*;
}
```

Exporting continuations. Let us reexamine the example in Fig. 1. The client just examines the location and employer of the member profiles — all of which are located on the server — to decide on invitations. Importantly, our flow sensitive data flow analysis shows that none of the client operations depend on the local state of the client, except for the date and the type of event, which is created before any of the remote operations. In such a scenario, we execute entire client code on the server. However, this enhancement requires the corresponding fragment of the client's code to be available at the server. Such exportable pieces of code are called *first-class continuations*. Java does not offer language support for capturing, passing, or utilizing such continuations.

Luckily, full-fledged continuations are not necessary. Instead, we leverage compiler support to statically move the continuation code to the destination. We assume that during compilation process, the whole program code is available. Thus, when our compiler determines that the invitation protocol at the client could be executed in its entirety at the server, it compiles the server with the readily available client code. Since our enhancements are performed statically, we are able to compile the remote code into the local code.

By exporting code to where the data is instead of the other way around, we can make immense savings on the data transferred over the network. This is especially beneficial for clients connected to a slow network. However, continuation exporting is impossible if the code to be exported depends on local state. Consider an extension to the invitation example of Fig. 1, where along with checking if a member works for the same employer and location of the person hosting the party, we also require user confirmation before sending out each invitation. The user intervention required at each loop iteration makes continuation exporting impossible. But batching as discussed earlier still applies since the computation is performed at the client. Continuation exporting can also hamper performance, since the computation is offloaded to a remote node. For a compute-intensive task, offloading all the computation might overload the server and thus bring down the overall performance. Our experimental results show that continuation exporting benefits thin clients and fat servers (see Sec. 4.2).

Chaining. Chaining is a technique to reduce the number of cross site RMIs. Chaining can significantly reduce end-to-end latency in a setting where the participants are Geo-distributed [13]. Consider a user shopping for music online over a 3G network. The user requests an album and buys songs with ratings higher than 8 from that album. The user then transfers the songs to his iMac. Assume that the desktop machine is connected to the Internet. The following snippet shows the pseudo code for the phone written in an RMI style.

```
void onlineShopping() {
  Album a = Vendor.album ("Electric␣Ladyland");
  for (SongInfo si : a) {
    if (si.rating() > 8) {
      Song s = si.buy();
      iMac.put(s);
}}}
```

The corresponding session type for this protocol is given below.

```
protocol onlineShopping {
  participants vendor, phone, iMac;
  phone: begin;
  phone->vendor: <String>;
  vendor->phone: <Album>;
  vendor:
  [vendor->phone: <SongInfo>;
   vendor->phone: <int>;
   phone: {BUY: vendor->phone: <Song>;
                phone->iMac: <Song>;
           PASS: }]*
}
```

Our type inspector performs batching sends enhancement on the loop with vendor as the loop guard, thereby sending all the SongInfo in a batch to the phone. Based on the rating, the phone downloads the song and puts it on an iMac desktop machine. Observe that songs are transferred to the iMac through the phone connected to a high latency, low bandwidth network. Chaining allows the songs to be directly transferred to iMac. Let us observe the local type of onlineShopping protocol at the phone. The following code snippet shows the local type under BUY label of the choice.

```
!{BUY: vendor: ?<Song>; iMac: !<Song>, PASS: }
```

The type inspector observes that the phone performs a reception of a message of type Song from the vendor before the sending of a Song. When such a potential forwarding pattern is encountered, the compiler is informed to inspect the intermediate code block to find if the intermediate computation depends on local state. If the intermediate computation is stateless, we export the continuation to the original sender, so that the data can directly be forwarded to the destination. In this case, the phone chooses to forward the song based on the rating received from the server. Hence, we export this continuation from phone to vendor, which makes the forwarding decisions and forwards the song to the desktop machine in one batch. Notice that instead of two transfers of the songs on a slow 3G network, we transfer the songs once over high-speed Internet.

One of the key advantages of our system is the ability to seamlessly combine various enhancement strategies. Notice that, the example just described effectively combines batching sends (to send songs in one batch), chaining (to skip the phone in the transfer) and continuation exporting (the logic to only choose the song with rating of at least 8).

3.3 System Design

Our system architecture is depicted in Fig. 6 – the compiler is a combination of a type inspector and Java compiler, whereas the runtime is a veneer on top of JVM. The compiler is utilized to analyze the program, discover enhancement potential,

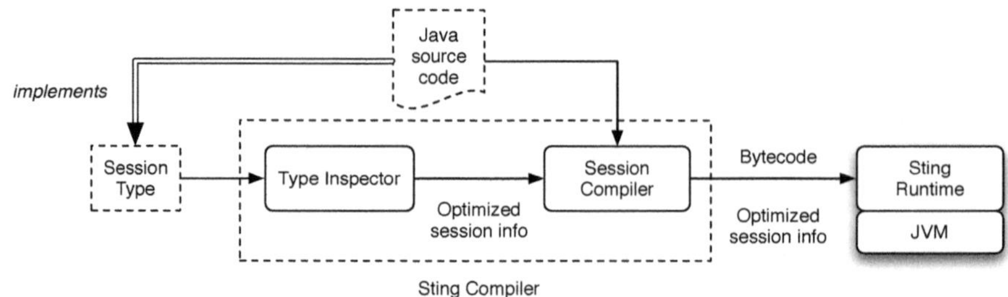

Fig. 6. System design with enhancement strategies

pre-generate code for enhancements, and provide an object model amenable to marshaling and serialization. Thus, the compiler generates specialized code based on our optimizations and decisions to utilize the optimizations are made at runtime.

4 Evaluation

We evaluate the performance gains of our optimizations from experiments that characterize typical scenarios in distributed systems. The experiments were conducted on Emulab [16] which emulates network bandwidth and latency. We used a two node setup for the batching experiments with 1Mbps link bandwidth and RTT values of 40, 80 and 150ms, inspired from ping latencies seen on the Internet. For the chaining experiments, we used 3 nodes, one of which was assigned to be the client machine with low bandwidth and high latency to the servers. The servers have Gigabit links with LAN latency interconnects. Sun Java 1.6 was used for running all our client and server Java programs. The Emulab machines were 850MHz Pentium 3 with 512MB RAM.

4.1 Batching

We study the benefits of batching sends and receives through an experiment conducted using a client-server scenario with 2 nodes. We define an operation where the client sends a cryptographic signature to the server, which verifies the signature using the public key and returns a boolean indicating success, following the session type:

```
client:
  [client->server: <Signature>;
   server->client: <boolean>]*
```

This is implemented both using a basic send and receive, and in our framework. We vary the signature size, the number of successive calls (which can be batched) and network RTT and measure the time required to complete the entire operation. As expected, the results showed that batching improves performance linearly with batch size. Batching performed better with increasing latency as the number of network round trips were reduced.

4.2 Exporting Continuation

We define two remote operations `fetchStockPrice` and `tradeStock`, which are used to fetch the current price of a *stock*, and trade a given amount of stock with the broker respectively. The client first obtains the price of the stock, performs algorithmic trading computations on the prices and intimates the broker with the decision to buy or sell. This essentially depicts a situation where we have two remote interactions surrounding a fairly compute intensive local computation (trading). This structure of communication is commonly found in many distributed systems applications. For our experiments, we compare the basic approach with exporting continuation of trading. We export the trade computation to the remote server and batch the whole block as a single remote invocation. We ran these experiments using a server program executing on a 3GHz dual-core machine with 4GB RAM. The clients were executed on different machines with identical configuration.

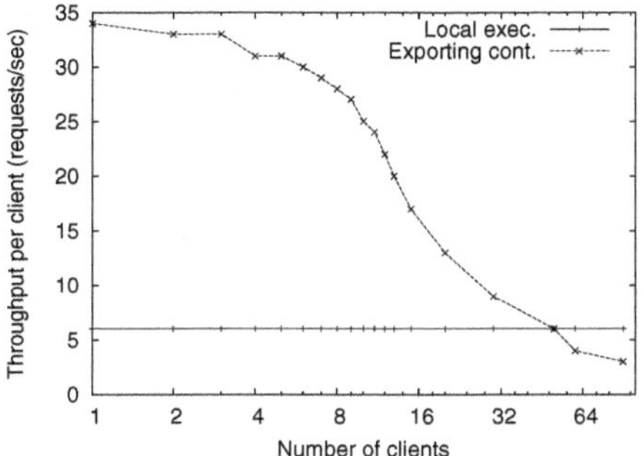

Fig. 7. Client request throughput

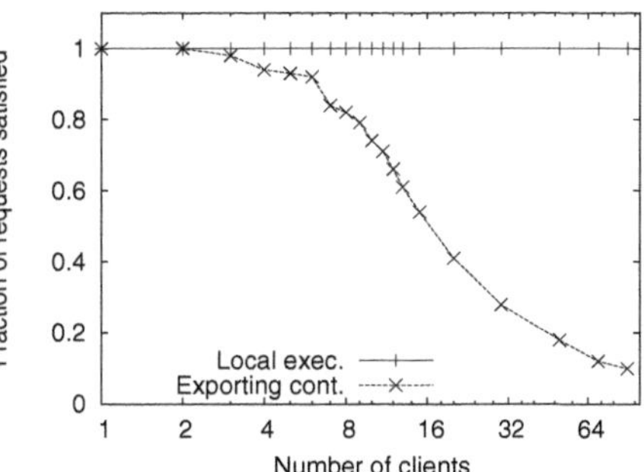

Fig. 8. Server request throughput

Client throughput. Fig. 7 shows the throughput of requests serviced per client as we increase the number of concurrent clients. The client requests are throttled at 34 requests/second. For the basic local execution of the trade on the client, the throughput achieved is independent of the number of clients. This is shown as a horizontal line with at 6 requests/sec. In this case, the critical path of computation is executed locally at the client, and hence the throughput is upper bounded by the client resources. Exporting continuation is represented by the higher throughput curve which is about 6 times larger, attributed to a powerful server. This throughput gain is understood by the ratio of computational power of the server and the client. As we increase the number of simultaneous clients, however, we see that the throughput starts dropping exponentially after about 6 clients. Note that the abscissa is in logarithmic scale.

Server throughput. Fig. 8 shows the fraction of requests satisfied. Local execution achieves a ratio of 1 shown by the straight line, because the server is under-utilized by just the remote interaction and is hence able to serve all requests received. With exported continuations, the request processing rate starts at 1 when the server is loaded on a small number of clients. As the number of clients increases, the server resources saturate and the requests are not handled at the same rate as they are received and the processing rate drops exponentially. It is important to note that the server is still able to provide higher throughput than the clients themselves, which is evident from the client throughput graph.

Server CPU utilization. Fig. 9 shows the CPU usage at the server during this experiment. About 6 parallel client requests and associated computation saturates one of the cores at 50% utilization. The remote operation is not inherently parallel and does not scale linearly on the two cores. The performance benefits beyond this point are much smaller. When the number of clients is about 50, the server CPU completely saturates and the per-client throughput equals that achieved by client's computational resources. At this point, it ceases to be worthwhile to export computation to the overloaded server for performance. This region can be estimated by comparing the performance difference between the client and the server.

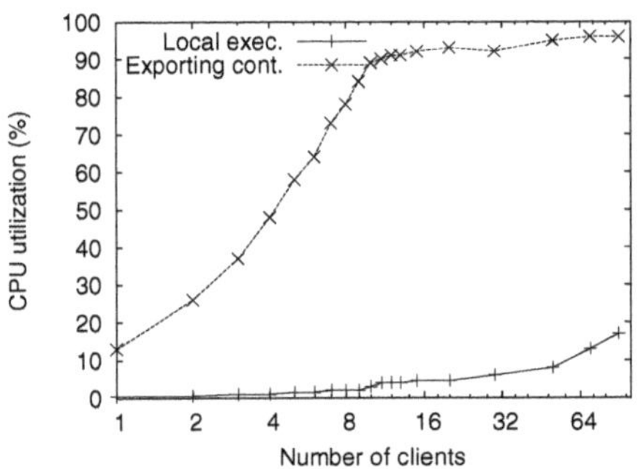

Fig. 9. Server CPU utilization

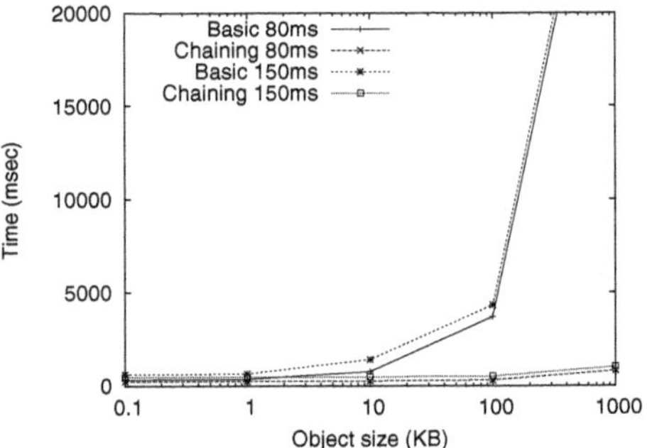

Fig. 10. Time for basic vs. chaining

Batching reduces the number of separate remote communication to one and is therefore affected only by a single RTT. Increasing the RTT would reduce the throughput of both approaches as a result of increased client latency. However, by exporting the continuation, increase in client latency is lesser and so is the decrease in throughput. As shown before, the single batched call would score ahead in large RTT settings with both network and computation benefits.

4.3 Chaining

We implemented the example of purchasing songs from the phone discussed in Sec. 3.2, where chaining is exploited to reduce communication involving the slow phone. Fig. 10 shows the comparing chained and non-chained versions. We set the network up such that the phone has a 1Mbps high latency link to the server and the PC, and the server is connected to the PC on a 100Mbps link with 2ms latency. We vary the size of the object being chained from 0.1KB to 1MB and experiment with RTT values of 80 and 150ms. The upper two curves in the graph show the basic approach used to transfer the object through the phone. In this case, the speed of transfer is limited by the link capacity of the phone's 3G network and hence we see an exponential increase in time as the size increases. However, chaining the calls has a drastic improvement in time by using the high bandwidth link to transfer the song.

5 Related Work

Session types [14] allow precise specification of typed distributed interaction. Early session types described interaction between two parties, which has then been extended to multi-party interaction by Honda et al. [10] and Bonelli et al. [3]. Honda et al. conduct a linearity analysis and prove progress of MPSTs. Linearity analysis in our system is simplified by the fact that each participant has a unique statically defined channel to every other participant, and channels are not first-class citizens. The work of Bejleri and Yoshida [2] extends that of Honda et al. [10] for synchronous communication specification among multiple interacting peers. We choose asynchronous over synchronous communication as the resulting looser coupling facilitates more aggressive optimizations.

Session types have have been applied to functional(e.g. [7])), component-based systems (e.g. [15]), object-oriented (e.g. [11]), and operating system services (e.g. [5]). Asynchronous session types for have been studied for Java [4]. Bi-party session types have been implemented in Java [11]. Our protocol description syntax is inspired from the syntax described in that work. Our framework supports multi-party protocol specification and interaction. We have also implemented a session registry to facilitate initiation of multi-party sessions. Gay et al. [8] describe how to marry session types with classes, allowing for participants to be implemented in a modular fashion. This work could be used to extend our framework.

Yeung and Kelly [17] propose runtime batching on Java RMI by performing static analysis on bytecode to determine batches. In these systems, ordering of remote and local operations influences the effectiveness of batching. Any operation performed on the result of remote method calls forces the method call to be flushed. *Remote batch invocation* (RBI) [12] performs batching on a block of code marked by the programmer. RBI reorders operations such that all remote operations are performed after the local operations and the code is exported to the server. RBI would not be able to batch a loop which requires user input on every iteration. RBI is also limited to batching specialized control structures and cannot handle arbitrary computation. Our system allows global optimization decisions to be made, and can batch across *multiple* participants.

First-class continuations [1] are a general idea to allow arbitrary computation to be captured and sent as arguments to other functions. In a distributed setting, exporting continuations are advantageous where the cost of moving data is much larger than the cost of moving computation to the data. *RPC chains* [13] reduce cross site remote procedure call overheads by exporting the callback functions to the remote host. This system requires that the user writes code in a non-intuitive *continuation passing* (CP) style [1]. Also, the callback functions cannot manipulate local state. Our system chains arbitrary code segments written in imperative style. Though we require all code to be available during compilation, our system can support separate compilation of participants, if the code were provided in CP style.

6 Conclusions

This paper is to the best of our knowledge the first to attempt to exploit session types for performance enhancements. We have shown that *combining* session types with information gathered from static analysis can yield performance improvement for distributed object interactions. We demonstrated the benefits of our approach; in particular, we have shown that our continuation exportation scheme benefits applications with thin clients and fat servers.

Acknowledgements. We are very grateful to A. Ibrahim, Y. Jiao, E. Tilevich, and W. Cook for sharing insights and the source code for RBI [12] with us.

References

1. Appel, A.W.: Compiling with Continuations. Cambridge University Press, Cambridge (2007)
2. Bejleri, A., Yoshida, N.: Synchronous Multiparty Session Types. Electron. Notes Theor. Comput. Sci. 241, 3–33 (2009)
3. Bonelli, E., Compagnoni, A.: Multisession Session Types for a Distributed Calculus. In: Barthe, G., Fournet, C. (eds.) TGC 2007 and FODO 2008. LNCS, vol. 4912, pp. 38–57. Springer, Heidelberg (2008)
4. Dezani-ciancaglini, M., Yoshida, N.: Asynchronous Session Types and Progress for Object-oriented Languages. In: Bonsangue, M.M., Johnsen, E.B. (eds.) FMOODS 2007. LNCS, vol. 4468, pp. 1–31. Springer, Heidelberg (2007)
5. Fähndrich, M., Aiken, M., Hawblitzel, C., Hodson, O., Hunt, G., Larus, J.R., Levi, S.: Language Support for Fast and Reliable Message-based Communication in Singularity OS. In: EuroSys 2006, pp. 177–190 (2006)
6. Fowler, M.: Patterns of Enterprise Application Architecture. Addison-Wesley, Reading (2002)
7. Gay, S., Vasconcelos, V., Ravara, A.: Session Types for Inter-process Communication. Tech. rep., University of Glasgow (2003)
8. Gay, S., Vasconcelos, V., Ravara, A., Gesbert, N., Caldeira, A.: Modular Session Types for Distributed Object-oriented Programming. In: POPL 2010 (2010)
9. Honda, K., Vasconcelos, V.T., Kubo, M.: Language Primitives and Type Discipline for Structured Communication-Based Programming. In: Hankin, C. (ed.) ESOP 1998. LNCS, vol. 1381, pp. 122–138. Springer, Heidelberg (1998)
10. Honda, K., Yoshida, N., Carbone, M.: Multiparty Asynchronous Session Types. In: POPL 2008, pp. 273–284 (2008)
11. Hu, R., Yoshida, N., Honda, K.: Session-Based Distributed Programming in Java. In: Vitek, J. (ed.) ECOOP 2008. LNCS, vol. 5142, pp. 516–541. Springer, Heidelberg (2008)

12. Ibrahim, A., Jiao, Y., Tilevich, E., Cook, W.R.: Remote Batch Invocation for Compositional Object Services. In: Drossopoulou, S. (ed.) ECOOP 2009. LNCS, vol. 5653, pp. 595–617. Springer, Heidelberg (2009)
13. Song, Y.J., Aguilera, M.K., Kotla, R., Malkhi, D.: Rpc Chains: Efficient Client-Server Communication in Geodistributed Systems. In: NSDI 2009, pp. 17–30 (2009)
14. Takeuchi, K., Honda, K., Kubo, M.: An Interaction-based Language and its Typing System. In: Halatsis, C., Philokyprou, G., Maritsas, D., Theodoridis, S. (eds.) PARLE 1994. LNCS, vol. 817, pp. 398–413. Springer, Heidelberg (1994)
15. Vallecillo, A., Vasconcelos, V.T., Ravara, A.: Typing the behavior of Software Components using Session Types. Fundam. Inf. 73(4), 583–598 (2006)
16. White, B., Lepreau, J., Stoller, L., Ricci, R., Guruprasad, S., Newbold, M., Hibler, M., Barb, C., Joglekar, A.: An Integrated Experimental Environment for Distributed Systems and Networks. In: NSDI 2002, pp. 255–270 (2002)
17. Yeung, K.C., Kelly, P.H.J.: Optimising Java RMI Programs by Communication Restructuring. In: Endler, M., Schmidt, D.C. (eds.) Middleware 2003. LNCS, vol. 2672, pp. 324–343. Springer, Heidelberg (2003)

Scalable Efficient Composite Event Detection*

K.R. Jayaram and Patrick Eugster

Department of Computer Science, Purdue University
{jayaram,peugster}@cs.purdue.edu

Abstract. Composite event detection (CED) is the task of identifying combinations of events which are meaningful with respect to program-defined patterns. Recent research in event-based programming has focused on language design (in different paradigms), leading to a wealth of prototype programming models and languages. However, implementing CED in an efficient and scalable manner remains an under-addressed problem. In fact, the lack of scalable algorithms is the main roadblock to incorporating support for more expressive event patterns into prominent event-based programming languages. This lack of scalable algorithms is a particularly acute problem in event stream processing, where event patterns can additionally be specified over time windows. In this paper we describe GenTrie, a deterministic trie-based algorithm for CED. We describe how complex event patterns are split, how each sub-pattern maps to a node in the trie, and demonstrate through empirical evaluation that GenTrie has higher throughput than current implementations of related languages.

1 Introduction

An event-based system consists of a set of software components that interact by notifying each other of events, where an event is any happening of interest – typically a change in the state of a component. Mouse clicks, keyboard events, timers, OS interrupts, sensor readings, stock quotes, and news articles are all examples of events. Events have data attributes attached to them. A stock quote, for instance has the name of the corporation and the price of the stock as attributes.

Event-based programming aims to eliminate coupling as much as possible in a software system, thereby reducing its overall complexity and making it easier to understand, debug, test, and maintain. Event-based programming underpins a wide variety of software – operating systems, graphical interfaces, news dissemination, algorithmic stock/commodity trading, network management and intrusion detection.

Simple event handling of *singleton* events is supported in most mainstream programming languages through libraries – examples are Java's JFC/Swing, RTSJ's AsyncEvents and C's POSIX condition variables. The event handler, also called a *reaction*, is executed when a corresponding event occurs, and is often

* This work is supported by NSF grants 0644013 and 0834619.

D. Clarke and G. Agha (Eds.): COORDINATION 2010, LNCS 6116, pp. 168–182, 2010.

a method, executed asynchronously to the caller. Reacting to simple events, though common, is not sufficient to support a growing class of event-based applications which are centered around *patterns* of events, called *composite* (or *complex*) events. Composite events are defined by quantification over combinations of events exhibiting some desired relationships.

The efficacy of an event-based programming language is governed by (R1) its expressivity, i.e., the ability of the language to precisely capture the complex event patterns of interest and, (R2) the ability of the runtime to match events to patterns in a timely and efficient manner. As expected, R1 and R2 are related, and many language designers choose to restrict patterns to things that can be efficiently implemented with standard data structures and custom off the shelf components. The lack of efficient algorithms for *composite event detection* (CED) turns out to be a main reason why many programming languages like Polyphonic C# [1] or JoinJava [5] only support limited CED through simple event *joins* without predicates on event attributes. Detecting such unpredicated joins is possible in $O(1)$ [1].

The lack of efficient algorithms for event correlation is especially acute in distributed event *stream* processing, where events of different types arrive at different independent rates. If an event pattern p involves predicates on two types of events e_1 and e_2, with e_1 occurring more frequently than e_2, events of type e_1 may satisfy some of the predicates of p, thus *partially* matching p. In this example, an event-processing algorithm must store partially matched events and decide if and when events of any type expire, i.e., how long events of type e_1 should be stored waiting for event e_2 to occur. Research in event-based programming has focussed on programming language design, semantics of event joins and concurrency issues in dispatching reactions, but there is little research on scalable and efficient algorithms for actual event matching.

Fueled by these observations, this paper makes the following contributions:

1. An abstract model and a formal definition of CED.
2. An original *trie*-based algorithm for CED called GenTrie.
3. An empirical evaluation of GenTrie, compared to existing solutions.

While 1. allows us to compare the expressiveness of existing event-based programming languages and systems, our objective is not to determine whether any one is better than the others. Other distinctions may also exist (e.g. support for distribution, persistence, synchronous events) in the semantics. Concisely defining the problem of CED allows us to present our algorithm in an abstract manner, so that it can be used or adapted by any compiler designer for any existing or future language.

Roadmap. Section 2 introduces our model of CED and uses it to summarize related systems and languages for event-based programming. Section 3 presents GenTrie. Section 4 evaluates GenTrie on several benchmark programs introduced by others as well as through stress-testing to illustrate its scalability. Section 5 discusses options. Section 6 draws final conclusions.

2 Problem Description and State of the Art

2.1 Events, Patterns and Reactions

An event, sometimes explicitly referred to as a *simple* event to disambiguate it from more general *composite* (or *complex*) events, is a change in the state of a system component. Events have (type) names and data attributes. As an example, StockQuote(organization: "IBM", price: 56.78, opening: 57.90) represents a stock quote event. Events can be typed like methods, which can be exploited by representing event types and events by event method headers and event method invocations respectively. The signature of StockQuote events for instance can be represented as StockQuote(String organization, **float** price, **float** opening). A composite event is any *pattern* of simple events, i.e., it is a set of events satisfying a specific *predicate*. Examples are: (1) the average of 100 consecutive temperature readings from a sensor, (2) a drop in the price of a stock by more than 30% after a negative analyst rating, (3) the price of a stock exceeds its 52-week moving average, and (4) the debut of a new Volkswagen car with 5 positive reviews.

A *reaction* is a program fragment (usually a method body), executed by a software component upon receipt of a simple or composite event. In the case of a composite event, all simple events that are part of it are said to *share* the reaction (method body).

We use e and its indexed variants to range over event names, which are uniquely associated with types as well as events. The meaning of e will be clear from the context. For example $e(T_1\ a_1, T_2\ a_2)$ refers to an event type, and $e(T_1 : v_1, T_2 : v_2)$ refers to an event. a and T refer to data attributes and their types respectively. We use v to range over values, which for the sake of brevity, are assumed to be strings, integers, or floats. In event type $e_i(T_{i,1}\ a_{i,1}, ..., T_{i,r}\ a_{i,r})$, $a_{i,j}$ is a data attribute of type $T_{i,j}$. We also assume for simplicity in the following that any event has at least one attribute.

2.2 Formal Definition of Composite Events

As mentioned, an event pattern describes a composite event as a set of events with a predicate they must satisfy. The BNF syntax of an event pattern $\mathcal{P}$ is:

attributes	t ::= $T\ \ a \mid t,\ T\ \ a$
join	j ::= $e(t)[v] \mid j, e(t)[v]$
condition	b ::= $true \mid e[\mathrm{i}].a\ op\ v \mid e[\mathrm{i}].a\ op\ e[\mathrm{i}].a$
predicate	p ::= $\forall \mathrm{i} \in [v, v]\ p \mid p\ \&\&\ p \mid p\ \|\|\ p \mid (p) \mid !p \mid b$
boolean operator	op ::= $> \mid < \mid >= \mid <= \mid == \mid !=$
pattern	$\mathcal{P}$ ::= j **if** p

The general form of an *m-way* event pattern $\mathcal{P}$, i.e., with m event types, where e_i contains r_i attributes is thus:

$$\mathcal{P} = e_1(T_{1,1}\ a_{1,1}, ..., T_{1,r_1}\ a_{1,r_1})[k_1], ..., e_m(T_{m,1}\ a_{m,1}, ..., T_{m,r_m}\ a_{m,r_m})[k_m] \ \ \textbf{if}\ \ p$$

We refer to k_i as *window size* of event type e_i in $\mathcal{P}$. It refers to the number of events of type e_i that are part of the composite event $\mathcal{P}$. An event in the window can be referred to in the predicate by using indices $1, ..., k_i$.

A *unary* condition compares an event attribute to a value; a *binary* condition compares two event attributes. *Intra-event* conditions are either unary conditions or binary conditions comparing two attributes of the same event type. *Inter-event* conditions are binary conditions comparing attributes of two distinct event types. More generally, a predicate is *n-ary* if the largest set of event types related transitively by inter-event conditions is of size n. For a predicate consisting only of intra-event predicates, n is trivially 1. We focus in the following on *well-formed* patterns, such that event attributes are compared to values of same types, and $n \leq m$.

As a concrete example, the composite event "*the release of a new Volkswagen Jetta with 5 positive reviews*" can be formally specified as:

$$\mathcal{P}_{vw} = \left\{ \begin{array}{c} \mathsf{VWRelease(String\ model, String\ date)[1]}, \\ \mathsf{Review(String\ model, String\ textReview, float\ rating)[5]} \end{array} \right\} \ \textbf{if}$$

$$\left(\begin{array}{lll} \forall\ \mathsf{i} \in [1,5] & \mathsf{Review[i].rating} > 3.5 & \&\& \\ & \mathsf{VWRelease[1].model} == \mathsf{"Jetta"} & \&\& \\ \forall\ \mathsf{i} \in [1,5] & \mathsf{Review[i].model} == \mathsf{VWRelease[1].model} & \end{array} \right)$$

Given a set $\mathcal{E}$ of events of t types $e_1, ..., e_t$, and an m-way event pattern $\mathcal{P}$, *composite event detection* (CED) is defined as the problem of finding a set $\mathcal{E}' \subseteq \mathcal{E}$, such that p is satisfied. We discuss limitations of our syntax of composite subscriptions together with semantic choices in Section 5.

Note that the events in a window do *not* have to be *consecutive* or *subsequent* – i.e. event $e[i]$ and $e[i+1]$ do not have to be consecutive, and $e[i]$ does not have to occur before $e[i+1]$. This however does not mean that windows of consecutive or subsequent events cannot be specified using the above syntax. A window of consecutive Review events can be specified by assuming that each event has a sequence number seq as one of its attributes, and by adding the following condition to the predicate: $\forall\ \mathsf{i} \in [1,4]\ \mathsf{Review[i].seq} <= \mathsf{Review[i+1].seq}$. A similar condition can be used to specify subsequent events, assuming that the time of occurrence of the event time is one of its arguments:

$\forall\ \mathsf{i} \in [1,4]\ \mathsf{Review[i].time} <= \mathsf{Review[i+1].time}$.

2.3 Event Joins

Event joins (or just joins) are one of the most common forms of composite events supported in programming languages; they are characterized by predicates of the form *true* and window sizes of $k = 1$. Joins were popularized by languages based on the *join calculus* [18] which predominantly reify events through asynchronous methods. A join has a method body associated with it, which is executed in a separate thread when all the m events in the join occur. The detection of a join is $O(1)$ and reaction dispatch can be performed in $O(m)$, e.g., as described below:

1. A queue q_i is used to store all events of type e_i.
2. Associate a bit array B of size m with an m-way join, where bit B_i corresponds to e_i in the join.
3. Upon arrival of an event of type e_i, enqueue it in q_i, and if now $|q_i| = 1$, set B_i to 1.
4. Detecting a join involves checking whether each bit in the bit array is 1. This can be accomplished in $O(1)$ time through a logical OR operation, i.e., checking whether B OR 0x0 $= 2^m$.
5. When an event join is detected, dequeue each event e_i from queue q_i. If now $|q_i| = 0$, set B_i to 0. This can be done in $O(m)$. The dequeued events are then consumed by the reaction executed in a separate thread.

Note that sometimes one synchronous event is permitted per join, in which case the reaction can be piggy-backed on the thread corresponding to that event. The presence of synchronous events does not affect the complexity of detecting event joins. Similarly, certain languages support unicasting of events while others offer multicast or both. This does not affect the detection complexity either, though some redundancy might be avoidable if a set of receivers have the exact same patterns and all corresponding events are multicast.

2.4 State of the Art of CED

Patterns in CED can be considered along three dimensions according to which programming languages and systems for CED can be classified (see Figure 1):

1. The (maximum) window sizes k for streams of individual event types (k-size windows).
2. The (maximum) number m of correlated event types ($m-$way joins).
3. The (maximum) number of event types n involved in predicates ($n-$ary predicates).

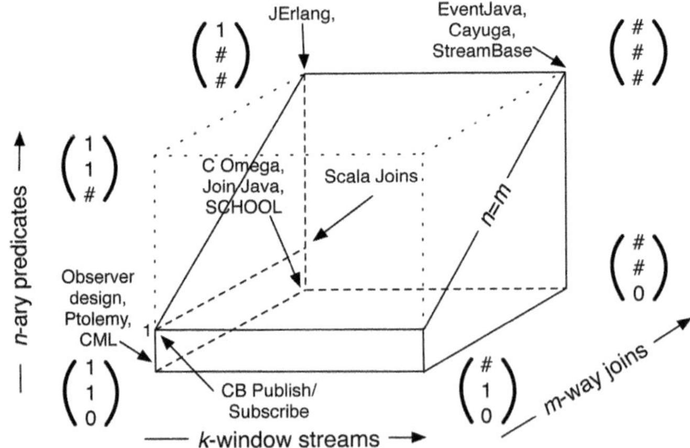

Fig. 1. Overview of features of event-based programming languages and systems. # represents the absence of a bound.

The first two dimensions can be viewed as representing time and space dimensions respectively and are clearly orthogonal. The third dimension, as mentioned, is not independent of the space dimension which leads to the division of the 3-dimensional space in Figure 1.[1] # stands for "unbounded".

Based on the admitted values for $\langle k, m, n \rangle$ we can coarsely classify languages and systems as follows (due to space limits the list is not exhaustive):

Simple event handlers $\langle 1, 1, 0 \rangle$**.** The observer design pattern and most library-based event handlers or simple languages like Ptolemy [8] support reactions to single event instances, without predicates. Languages which support only *staged* correlation where the consumption of a first event conditions the consumption of second one etc. also fall into this category (e.g. CML [7]).

Simple predicated event handlers $\langle 1, 1, 1 \rangle$**.** This includes content-based publish/subscribe multicast systems such as Siena [9] or languages inspired by the model (e.g., ECO [10], Java_{PS} [11]), as well as Actor-based languages or Actor libraries supporting predicates on individual messages (e.g., Erlang[2], Scala Actors [4], AmbientTalk [12]).

Join languages $\langle 1, \#, 0 \rangle$**.** This category corresponds to the join calculus family. Examples are given by JoinJava [5], SCHOOL [6], Russo's library for VisualBasic [17], or Polyphonic C# [1] – now Cω. The work of Sulzmann et al [13] is another citizen of this class.

Predicated join languages $\langle 1, \#, \# \rangle$**.** Second generation join languages (e.g., JErlang [16]) support n-ary predicates but no streams. Scala Joins [3] are special, isolated, case of predicated join language supporting only intra-event conditions ($\langle 1, \#, 1 \rangle$).

Generic correlation $\langle \#, \#, \# \rangle$**.** Database-derived systems such as Cayuga [14], Borealis [15] or the commercial StreamBase[3] support all features of CED. EventJava [2] mirrors these at the language level. Several content-based publish/subscribe systems have been extended for generic correlation, such as PADRES [19] which uses Jess [21].

3 GenTrie

In this section, we describe GenTrie, an algorithm that constructs an event-flow graph as a *generalized trie* to detect composite events.

3.1 Overview

Each node of the trie corresponds to a (intra- or inter-event) condition of a pattern. Figure 2 gives a high-level overview of GenTrie, whose stages are

[1] n could be defined as the total number of involved *events*, but we have not encountered any systems supporting streams *without* predicates (or without joins), thus n depends here only on m and not on k.

[2] http://www.erlang.org

[3] www.streambase.org

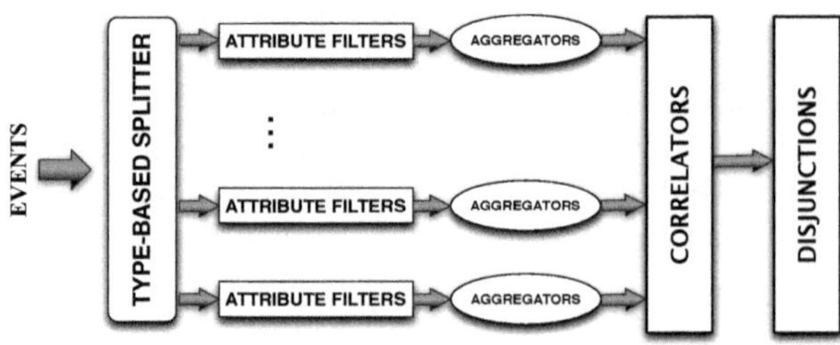

Fig. 2. An overview of GenTrie

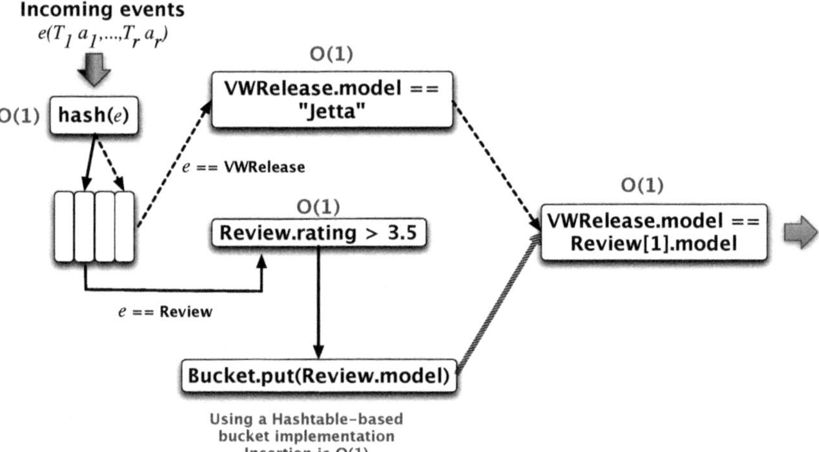

Fig. 3. GenTrie by example – "Release of a new Volkswagen Jetta with five positive reviews"

explained in this section through the "Volkswagen" Jetta example outlined in Section 2. Figure 3 illustrates the stages schematically. The five stages of GenTrie are:

1. *Type-based event filtering and splitting*: The input to this stage is a heterogenous input stream of simple events of different types, from which composite events have to be detected. In this stage, the input stream is split into several sub-streams for *individual event types.*
2. *Attribute filtering*: The input to this stage is a given stream of events of the same type. In this stage, each event is matched against all corresponding *intra-event conditions*, keeping track of the satisfied ones.
3. *Aggregation*: Some *inter-event conditions* aggregate *events of the same type* in corresponding windows. In this stage, events of the same type involved in such aggregations are grouped together.
4. *Correlation*: This stage combines event streams of different types and evaluates the remaining *inter-event conditions* on events, and groups of events of *different types.*

5. *Disjunctions*: For predicates involving disjunctions, this stage combines events that satisfy each of their components.

3.2 Predicate Simplification

Predicate simplification consists of removing quantification ($\forall$) and negation (!) and is done as a pre-stage preferably at compilation. Quantification can be simplified by the following equivalence rules:

$$\forall\, i \in [v_1, v_2]\ (p_1 \ \&\&\ p_2) \doteq \forall i \in [v_1, v_2]\ p_1 \ \&\&\ \forall\, i \in [v_1, v_2]\ p_2$$

$$\forall\, i \in [v_1, v_2]\ (p_1 \,||\, p_2) \doteq \begin{pmatrix} (\{^{v_1}/_{i}\}p_1 \,||\, \{^{v_1}/_{i}\}p_2)\ \&\& \\ \dots\ \&\& \\ (\{^{v_2}/_{i}\}p_1 \,||\, \{^{v_2}/_{i}\}p_2) \end{pmatrix}$$

$$\forall\, i \in [v_1, v_2]\ (e_1[i].a_1\ op\ e_2[i].a_2) \doteq \begin{pmatrix} e_1[v_1].a_1\ op\ e_2[v_1].a_2\ \&\& \\ \dots\ \&\& \\ e_1[v_2].a_1\ op\ e_2[v_2].a_2 \end{pmatrix}$$

$$\forall\, i \in [v_1, v_2]\ (e[i].a\ op\ v) \doteq \begin{pmatrix} e[v_1].a\ op\ v\ \&\& \\ \dots\ \&\& \\ e[v_2].a\ op\ v \end{pmatrix}$$

Negation can be removed easily using the following rules:

$$!(p_1 \ \&\&\ p_2) \doteq\ !p_1 \,||\, !p_2 \qquad !(p_1 \,||\, p_2) \doteq\ !p_1 \ \&\&\ !p_2$$
$$!!p \doteq p \qquad !(\forall i \in [v_1, v_2]\ p) \doteq \{^{v_1}/_{i}\}!p \,||\, \dots \,||\, \{^{v_2}/_{i}\}!p$$
$$!(e[i].a{<}e'[i].a') \doteq e[i].a{>=}e'[i].a' \qquad !(e[i].a{<=}e'[i].a') \doteq e[i].a{>}e'[i].a'$$
$$!(e[i].a{>}e'[i].a') \doteq e[i].a{<=}e'[i].a' \qquad !(e[i].a{>=}e'[i].a') \doteq e[i].a{<}e'[i].a'$$
$$!(e[i].a{==}e'[i].a') \doteq e[i].a{!=}e'[i].a' \qquad !(e[i].a{!=}e'[i].a') \doteq e[i].a{==}e'[i].a'$$

Now we only have conjunctions and disjunctions left in the predicate. Since we can do away with negation by changing individual conditions it is easy to see that any predicate can be be transformed into a disjunctive normal form (DNF), i.e., of the form $p_1 \,||\, \dots \,||\, p_n$ where each p_i is a conjunction of several conditions.

3.3 Type-Based Event Filtering and Splitting

The objective of this stage is to split a single input event stream into several streams, one corresponding to each type. This allows for the early application of intra-event conditions which involve attributes of a single event type. Filtering out events of no interest reduces the load on the correlation module. To efficiently implement this stage, a hash table is used. The key of the hash table is the event type, and the value consists of a filter node explained below. The hash of an event type (which is a String) can be performed in constant time [22]. This stage also adds a sequence number to each non-filtered event, to represent the order in which the algorithm received input events. In the example, this means separating out all events of types VWRelease and Review into separate sub-streams.

3.4 Attribute Filtering

A pattern may contain several intra-event conditions, each of which compares an attribute of an event type to a value or another attribute of the same event. If there are l_i intra-event conditions for event type e_i, a sequence of l_i filter nodes (in any order) is constructed, the output of each node being the input of the next. A pointer to the first attribute filter is stored in the hash table, as explained above. Each attribute filter processes an input event in constant time. Thus, if an event pattern $\mathcal{P}$ has m event types, and l_i intra-event conditions for event type e_i, the total number of attribute filters created are $\sum_{i=0}^{m} l_i$. Figure 3 illustrates how all intra-event conditions are linked to each other in the case of the running example.

3.5 Aggregation

In this stage, an aggregation node is created to process certain windows of events. Creating aggregation nodes is an optimization of GENTRIE. GENTRIE can detect composite events without aggregation nodes, but aggregation nodes simplify the detection of certain event windows. If an inter-event condition is of the form $\forall i \in [i_1, i_2] e[i].a \ op \ v$, or $\forall i \in [i_1, i_2] e[i].a \ op \ e'[1].a'$, where op is either $==$ or $!=$, then aggregation nodes are created. This is done by *bucketing* events, similar to the strategy used by a Bucket Sort or Bin Sort algorithm [22].

In the example, this step consists of collecting five Review events for each model. All Review events with the same model are put into the same bin. This is done by hashing Review.model, again in constant time. Once a bin gets five events, they are removed from the bin and sent to the correlation node.

3.6 Correlation

The predicate, being in DNF, is of the form $p_1 \,||\, ... \,||\, p_n$ where each p_i is a conjunction of several conditions. One correlation node is created for each condition in the p_i, which is of the form $e_1.a_1 \ op \ e_2.a_2$, with the output of one node being piped to the next. Then,

a. if op is $==$, a_2 of all incoming e_2 events are stored in a hash table. Then $e_2.a_2$ that equals $e_1.a_1$ can be found in constant time ($O(1)$) by hashing $e_1.a_1$.
b. if op is $<, <=, >, >=$, a_2 of all incoming e_2 events are stored in a B+ tree [22]. Insertion of a_2 into B+ tree containing n elements is $O(log_b n)$, where b is the *degree* or *fanout* of the B+ tree, i.e. each node in the B+ tree contains at least b children but no more than $2b$ children [22]. B+ trees store only keys in their internal nodes, and all data is stored in the leaves, which are linked to each other. It is well known that B+ trees are optimized for range queries [22]. If a B+ tree stores numerical values (either integers or floats), finding all values less than (greater than) c, for example, is $O(log_b n + k)$, where k is the number of values less than (greater than) c in the B+ tree. Hence, given an event of type e_1, finding all events of type e_2 that satisfy $e_1.a_1 \ op \ e_2.a_2$ is $O(log_b n + k)$.

c. if *op* is !=, a_2 of all incoming e_2 events are stored in a B+ tree [22]. The algorithm searches the B+ tree for $e_1.a_1$, and returns all the leaves of the B+ tree not equal to $e_1.a_1$ in $O(log_b n + k)$, where k is the number of values not equal to $e_1.a_1$ in the B+ tree.

In the example, since all groups of five Review events arriving at this node have the same Review.model, it is sufficient to check if the model attribute of one event matches that of VWRelease – again in constant time. Hence, using an aggregation node reduces the complexity of this correlation.

3.7 Disjunction

An event predicate being in DNF as described above, a sequence of correlation nodes are created for each inter-event condition of each predicate p_i. The output of the sequence, which is a set of events, is connected to a *union* node to handle disjunctions. The union node performs a set union on all its inputs. In other words, if a set of events $\mathcal{E}$ matches both p_i and p_j, then $\mathcal{E}$ is delivered by the algorithm only once. Set union is also implemented in linear time using the disjoint set data structure [22].

4 Evaluation

In this section we (1) show that GenTrie performs as well as existing solutions for languages with less expressiveness and that (2) such solutions can not compensate for our additional features without significant penalty; finally, we also (3) stress-test GenTrie to assess its scalability.

4.1 Santa Claus Problem

The *Santa Claus* problem was first proposed by Trono [23], and used by Benton [24] among others to test the expressiveness of concurrent programming languages. Santa Claus sleeps at the North pole until awakened by either all of the nine reindeer, or by a group of three out of ten elves. He performs one of two indivisible actions: [a] if awakened by the group of reindeer, Santa harnesses them to a sleigh, delivers toys, and finally unharnesses the reindeer who then go on holidays, and [b.] if awakened by a group of elves, Santa shows them into his office, consults with them on toy R&D, and finally shows them out so they can return to work constructing toys. A waiting group of reindeer must be served by Santa before a waiting group of elves. Since Santa's time is extremely valuable, marshaling the reindeer or elves into a group must not be done by Santa.

We implemented the Santa Claus problem analogously to the proposition by Benton [24]. The arrival of a reindeer or an elf is an event. Event patterns do not have any predicates. We generate "reindeer-arrival" and "elf-arrival" events randomly at different frequencies, and measure the number of synchronizations (either reindeer or elves) per second. Figure 4a compares the performance of GenTrie with that of Scala Joins and Cω. In Figure 4a, the abscissa plots the

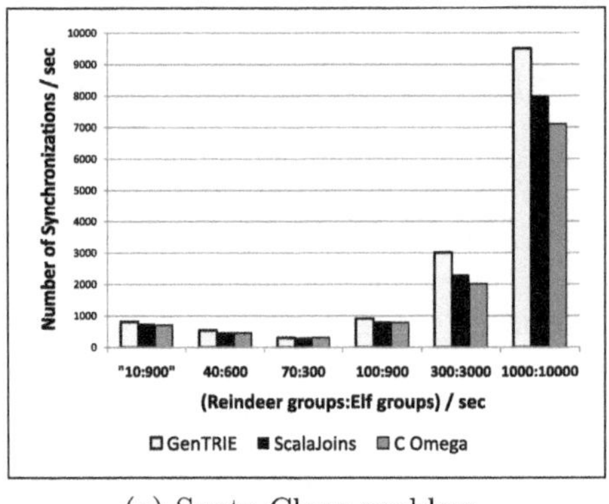

(a) Santa Claus problem

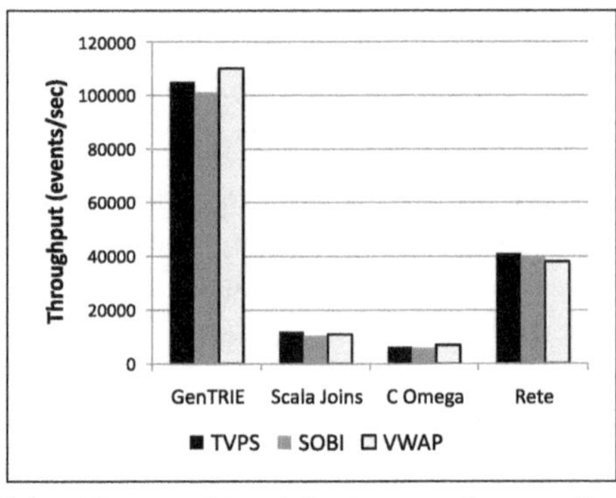

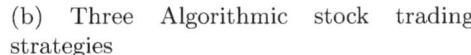

(b) Three Algorithmic stock trading strategies

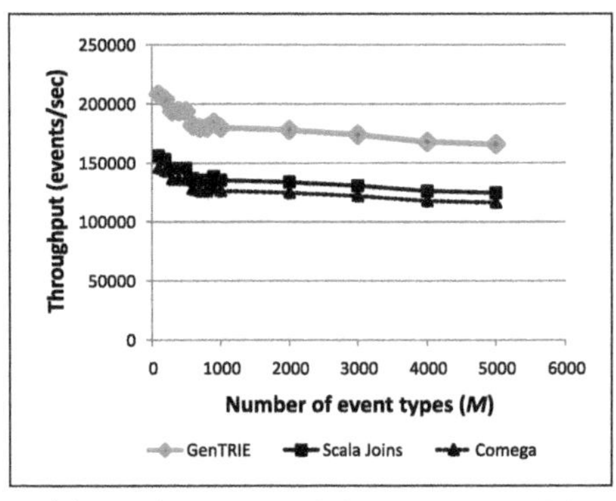

(c) Performance while increasing M

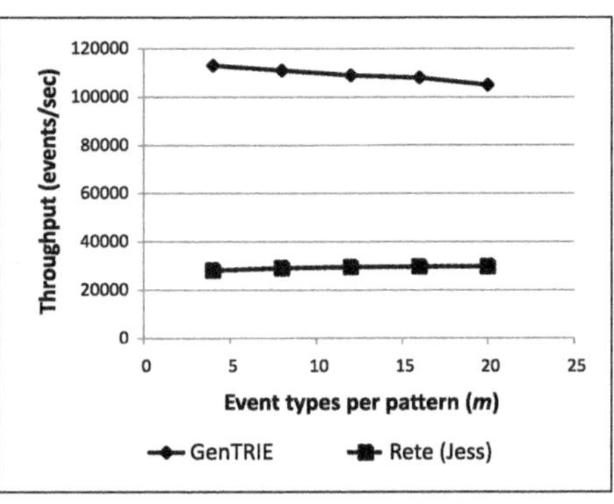

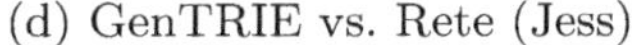

(d) GenTRIE vs. Rete (Jess)

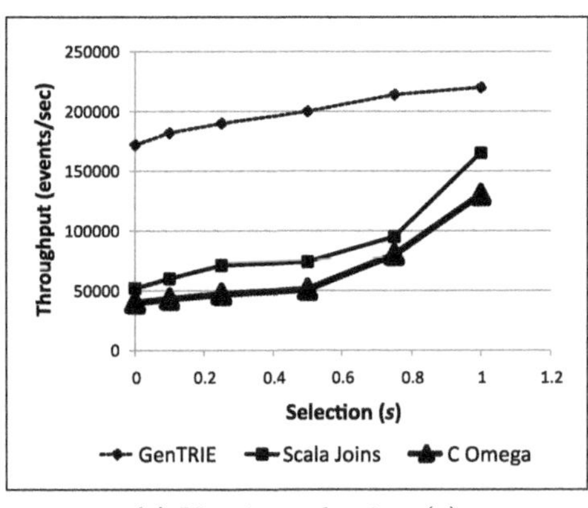

(e) Varying selection (s)

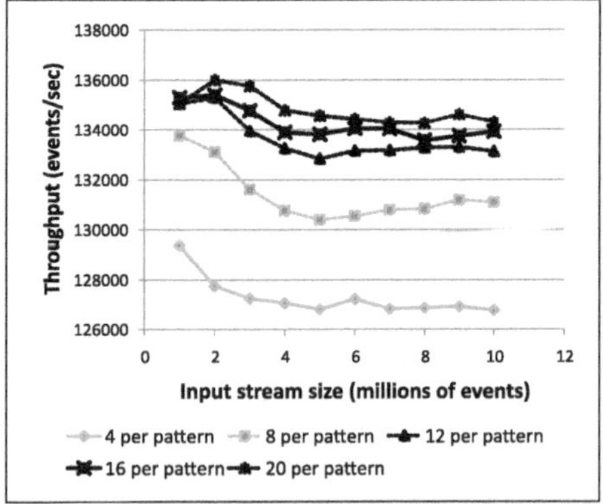

(f) Stability of GenTrie with varying m.

Fig. 4. Performance of GenTrie vs. Scala Joins, Jess and $C\omega$

ratio of the number of times per second all nine reindeer arrive to the number of times three out of ten elves arrive. Hence, if the ratio is 10:900, the ideal number of synchronizations per second is 910. As can be seen from Figure 4a, the performance of GenTrie is comparable to Scala Joins and Cω for simple event joins, though it is more complicated due to its support for (more expressive) predicates. As the number of synchronizations per second increases, GenTrie increasingly outperforms the other approaches.

4.2 Stock Monitoring

We take the stock monitoring component of an algorithmic trading application to evaluate the efficiency of GenTrie and to illustrate that manual implementations of streams and intra-event conditions are inefficient. The application used 200 stocks of 10 categories (finance, technology, minerals, power etc.), and three trading strategies, namely Target Volume Participation Strategy (TVPS) (cf. [25]), Static Order Book Imbalance (SOBI)[4], and Volume Weighted Average Price (VWAP)[5]. The application has 250 event types, 120 correlation patterns, and window sizes of 10. Figure 4b shows the event-processing throughput using each strategy. Figure 4b shows that the throughput of GenTrie is 2.5× that of the Jess [21] implementation of the well-known Rete [20] algorithm used by various systems for composite event detection including an earlier incarnation of our own EventJava [2] framework. GenTrie's throughput is also 10× that of Scala Joins and Cω. The general nature of Rete allowed us to implement the examples quite easily, while in Scala Joins and Cω we had to manually compensate in the application for the missing features, essentially leading to a staged event matching as for instance, CML. Note that the implemented semantics are equivalent, i.e., the same composite events are identified.

4.3 Scalability

While the need to use real applications for evaluation is obvious, individual applications can not fully *stress-test* GenTrie. Given the wide variance in system loads produced by different event-processing applications and by a same application over time, stress-testing plays an important role though in evaluating the scalability of event-processing algorithms. We thus algorithmically generate event types and event patterns, and randomly generate events to match these patterns. We strive to keep the generated event patterns as close as possible to real world patterns, by following benchmarks used by systems mirroring the features supported by EventJava (e.g., Cayuga [14]).

Parameters. Some of the parameters of GenTrie which govern its event-processing throughput are:

1. The number of event types involved in the application – M.
2. The number of event types per correlation pattern – m. Thus the number of correlation patterns is M/m.

[4] http://www.cis.upenn.edu/~mkearns/projects/sobi.html

[5] http://www.investopedia.com/terms/v/vwap.asp

3. The *selection* s of the predicates in the event pattern, i.e., the probability that an event matches the event pattern. A selection of 1 implies that no event is ever filtered out, whereas a selection of zero implies that all events are filtered away before any correlation. This can be achieved easily by generating events and predicates with unary conditions such that the events contain values that never match the conditions.

Results. Figure 4c compares the join processing throughput of GENTRIE against Scala Joins and Cω. Each join in this experiment contained $m = 4$ events and a *true* predicate. Figure 4c shows that GENTRIE's throughput is 25% higher than that of Scala Joins and 30% higher than Cω.

Figure 4d compares scalability of GENTRIE with respect to the number of event types per pattern m, in the presence of streams and predicates, to Rete. This experiment used $M = 5000$ event types, and streams windows of size $k = 5$. Predicates transitively linked all involved events of all types, exhibiting a combined selectivity of roughly 10%. The throughput of GENTRIE here is around 4× that of Rete; neither algorithm's performance varies significantly with an increasing m. This difference is representative of a large number of scenarios that we tested, but which can't be covered due to space restrictions.

Figure 4e shows the throughput of GENTRIE for a varying selection s, comparing also to Scala Joins and Cω. To make the comparison as fair as possible selection was achieved with unary conditions only (unary conditions are achieved via **if** statements inside reactions for Cω). For non-zero selection, the throughput of GENTRIE is approximately 3× that of Scala Joins and 4× that of Cω.

In addition to M, m and s, another important criterion is the *stability* of an algorithm's throughput over time. To evaluate this, we use a stream of 10 Mio events, and sample the throughput at intervals of 1 Mio events. Figure 4f shows that the throughput of GENTRIE remains fairly stable over time independently of m – variations in throughput are less than 2%. For an evaluation of the stability of Rete, refer [2].

5 Discussion

Multiple patterns and fairness. Like many other sources of semantic differences between languages and systems, we have not considered interaction across patterns. Languages based on the join calculus [18] typically allow several patterns/reactions to involve a same event type, and non-deterministically choose which reaction may consume a corresponding event. Such *exclusive* disjunctions (*X-OR* semantics) are rather easily implemented (pragmatically) in such languages devoid of predicates as events can be assigned to one pattern or another without further inspection, but the implementation intricacies may contribute to *fairness* issues [6] across patterns if a program relies on this non-determinism. In GENTRIE, we have chosen to support disjunction || in predicates as opposed to *forcing* programs to declare a separate pattern/reaction pair for each disjoined predicate on the same set of events (as is common in certain publish/subscribe systems [9]), as this may in some systems be interpreted as X-OR semantics and in others lead to non-exclusive disjunctions. X-OR semantics can be achieved in GENTRIE by duplicating events across queues corresponding to competing patterns, but keeping the copies linked to each other to ensure that matching and consumption of one instance leads to discarding all of them.

Garbage collection. In the presence of predicates, some events may a priori never be consumed. Program analysis together with annotations could be used in more strongly coupled systems to statically ensure that this does not occur. A pragmatic approach which is viable for many loosely coupled systems consists in defining garbage collection policies based on the application at hand, e.g., bounding queues (keeping *first received* or *most recent* events), assigning timestamps and timeouts. In the benchmarks which used predicates, once an event matches a pattern, older unmatched events of the same type are discarded. This is particularly relevant in the case of algorithmic trading, and can be used to make event matching *order-preserving* [2]. Discarding older unmatched events might prevent some matches after garbage collection, and should be used instead of other approaches like bounding queues only when warranted by the application that uses GENTRIE for event matching.

6 Conclusions and Future Work

We have presented a generic model of complex event detection (CED), and an efficient and scalable algorithm for CED implemented in EventJava [2]. We are currently in the process of extending the pattern grammar to become yet more expressive. Two thrusts focus on (1) *parametric* patterns which support variables besides values in unary boolean expressions ($e.a$ op x with x a program variable) and (2) supporting *combinators* on events. While (1) is already supported at local scope, we are interested in a distributed solution for EventJava and its decentralized runtime environment; this requires specific support to propagate variable changes across nodes in an efficient manner ensuring properties such as ordering of the appearance of these changes. For (2) we are in a first step interested in supporting operations on scalar event attributes (e.g. $e_1.a_1 + e_2.a_2 == e_3.a_3$) before investigating full support for methods as these may have side-effects.

References

1. Benton, N., Cardelli, L., Fournet, C.: Modern Concurrency Abstractions for C#. ACM TOPLAS 26(5), 769–804 (2004)
2. Eugster, P., Jayaram, K.R.: EventJava: An Extension of Java for Event Correlation. In: Drossopoulou, S. (ed.) ECOOP 2009. LNCS, vol. 5653, pp. 570–594. Springer, Heidelberg (2009)
3. Haller, P., Van Cutsem, T.: Implementing Joins using Extensible Pattern Matching. In: Lea, D., Zavattaro, G. (eds.) COORDINATION 2008. LNCS, vol. 5052, pp. 135–152. Springer, Heidelberg (2008)
4. Haller, P., Odersky, M.: Scala Actors: Unifying Thread-based and Event-based Programming. Theoretical Computer Science 410(2-3), 202–220

5. Von Itzstein, S.G., Kearney, D.A.: The Expression of Common Concurrency Patterns in Join Java. In: PDPTA 2004, pp. 1021–1025 (2004)
6. Petrounias, A., Eisenbach, S.: Fairness for Chorded Languages. In: Field, J., Vasconcelos, V.T. (eds.) COORDINATION 2009. LNCS, vol. 5521, pp. 86–105. Springer, Heidelberg (2009)
7. Reppy, J.H., Xiao, Y.: Specialization of CML Message-passing Primitives. In: POPL 2007, pp. 315–326 (2007)
8. Rajan, H., Leavens, G.T.: Ptolemy: A Language with Quantified, Typed Events. In: Vitek, J. (ed.) ECOOP 2008. LNCS, vol. 5142, pp. 155–179. Springer, Heidelberg (2008)
9. Carzaniga, A., Rutherford, M.J., Wolf, A.L.: Design and Evaluation of a Wide-area Event Notification Service. ACM TOCS 19(3), 332–383 (2001)
10. Haahr, M., Meier, R., Nixon, P., Cahill, V., Jul, E.: Filtering and Scalability in the ECO Distributed Event Model. In: PDSE 2000, pp. 83–92 (2000)
11. Eugster, P.: Type-based Publish/Subscribe: Concepts and Experiences. ACM TOPLAS 29(1) (2007)
12. Van Cutsem, T., Mostinckx, S., Gonzalez Boix, E., Dedecker, J., De Meuter, W.: AmbientTalk: Object-oriented Event-driven Programming in Mobile Ad hoc Networks. In: SCCC 2007 (2007)
13. Sulzmann, M., Lam, E.S.L., Van Weert, P.: Actors with Multi-headed Message Receive Patterns. In: Lea, D., Zavattaro, G. (eds.) COORDINATION 2008. LNCS, vol. 5052, pp. 315–330. Springer, Heidelberg (2008)
14. Demers, A.J., Gehrke, J., Hong, M., Riedewald, M., White, W.M.: Towards Expressive Publish/Subscribe Systems. In: Ioannidis, Y., Scholl, M.H., Schmidt, J.W., Matthes, F., Hatzopoulos, M., Böhm, K., Kemper, A., Grust, T., Böhm, C. (eds.) EDBT 2006. LNCS, vol. 3896, pp. 627–644. Springer, Heidelberg (2006)
15. Balazinska, M., Balakrishnan, H., Madden, S., Stonebraker, M.: Fault-tolerance in the Borealis Distributed Stream Processing System. In: SIGMOD 2005, pp. 13–24 (2005)
16. Plociniczak, H.: JErlang: Erlang with Joins, `http://www.doc.ic.ac.uk/teaching/distinguished-projects/2009/h.plociniczak.pdf`
17. Russo, C.V.: Join Patterns for Visual Basic. In: OOPSLA 2008, pp. 53–72 (2008)
18. Fournet, C., Gonthier, C.: The Reflexive Chemical Abstract Machine and the Join Calculus. In: POPL 1996, pp. 372–385 (1996)
19. Li, G., Jacobsen, H.A.: Composite Subscriptions in Content-Based Publish/Subscribe Systems. In: Alonso, G. (ed.) Middleware 2005. LNCS, vol. 3790, pp. 249–269. Springer, Heidelberg (2005)
20. Forgy, C.: Rete: a Fast Algorithm for the Many Patterns/Many Objects Match Problem. Artificial Intelligence 19(1), 17–37 (1982)
21. Friedman-Hill, E.: Jess (2008), `http://www.jessrules.com/jess/`
22. Cormen, T.H., Rivest, R.L., Leiserson, C., Stein, C.H.: Introduction to Algorithms. MIT Press, Cambridge (2009)
23. Trono, J.A.: A New Exercise in Concurrency. SIGCSE Bulletin 26(3), 8–10 (1994)
24. Benton, N.: Jingle Bells: Solving the Santa Claus Problem in Polyphonic C# (2003), `http://research.microsoft.com/en-us/um/people/nick/polyphony/santa.pdf`
25. Vhayu: Vhayu Velocity – Algorithmic Trading Case Study (2008), `http://www.vhayu.com/Content/CollateralItems/AlgoTradingCaseStudy.pdf`

Author Index

GPSR Compliance

The European Union's (EU) General Product Safety Regulation (GPSR) is a set of rules that requires consumer products to be safe and our obligations to ensure this.

If you have any concerns about our products, you can contact us on ProductSafety@springernature.com

In case Publisher is established outside the EU, the EU authorized representative is:

Springer Nature Customer Service Center GmbH
Europaplatz 3
69115 Heidelberg, Germany

Batch number: 09474016

Printed by Printforce, the Netherlands